D0934729

Praise for Dan Rattiner

"Dan's memoirs are like Dan's newspapers: charming, whimsical, fun, and filled with insightful knowledge of the East End conveyed with a twinkle in the eye."

—Walter Isaacson, author of *Steve Jobs*

"If there was an honorary mayor of the Hamptons it would have to be Dan Rattiner ... a raconteur with a wicked sense of humor and an eye for detail."

—*Long Island History Journal*

"If a guy says it happened in the Hamptons, and Dan Rattiner doesn't know about it, it didn't."

—Tom Wolfe

In the Hamptons 4Ever

In the Hamptons 4Ever

MOSTLY TRUE TALES FROM THE EAST END

DAN RATTINER

excelsior editions
State University of New York Press
Albany, New York

Cover art by Mickey Paraskevas

Published by
State University of New York Press, Albany

Copyright © 2015 by Dan Rattiner

All rights reserved

Printed in the United States of America

No part of this book may be used or reproduced in any manner whatsoever without written permission. No part of this book may be stored in a retrieval system or transmitted in any form or by any means including electronic, electrostatic, magnetic tape, mechanical, photocopying, recording, or otherwise without the prior permission in writing of the publisher.

For information, contact State University of New York Press, Albany, NY
www.sunypress.edu

Production by Diane Ganeles
Marketing by Fran Keneston

Excelsior Editions is an imprint of State University of New York Press

Library of Congress Cataloging-in-Publication Data

Rattiner, Dan.
  In the Hamptons 4ever: mostly true tales from the East End / Dan Rattiner ; foreword by Barbara L. Goldsmith. — Excelsior editions.
      pages cm
  Includes bibliographical references and index.
  ISBN 978-1-4384-5813-7 (hardcover : alk. paper)
  ISBN 978-1-4384-5815-1 (e-book)
  1. Hamptons (N.Y.)—History, Local.   2. Hamptons (N.Y.)—Social life and customs—Anecdotes.   3. Rattiner, Dan.   4. Millionaires—New York (State)—Hamptons—Social life and customs.   5. Celebrities—New York (State)—Hamptons—Social life and customs.   I. Title.   II. Title: Dan's papers.
  F127.S9R38 2015
  974.7'25—dc23   2014047229

10 9 8 7 6 5 4 3 2 1

*This book is dedicated to the seven children
and six grandchildren in my life,
Maya, Adam, David, Gabriel, Pam, Ben, Scoop,
Solange, Rhone, Eli, Arthur, Abraham and Owen.*

CONTENTS

FOREWORD

"He wears many hats," is an old adage, but Dan Rattiner literally and figuratively does just that. If you're on the lookout, you'll see his hatted head everywhere—at swanky galas, charity events, literary readings, polo matches, and parties, parties, parties. As far as I know, Dan's been wearing his signature hat forever.

We both came to the Hamptons about half a century ago, but back then it wasn't called "The Hamptons." East Hampton, where I lived, was just a lush and beachgrass hidden oasis away from the city. It had the most extraordinary clear light that attracted many artists (that and the affordable prices were winners for them). To many of us, Main Beach, fine and broad, drew us with its siren song. We'd sit there playing chess, largely with artists and writers, while our kids chased the waves. DeKooning promised me a painting if I'd spend the night with him, and when I turned him down he asked, "I can't drive, maybe sometimes you'd do *that* for me?" And I did, but never got a painting.

In the '60s and '70s, occasionally a hostess asked rather plaintively, "Can you wear a dress?" which meant not "festive dress" or "gala dress" or "formal dress" but "Please wear a dress because my grandmother is coming for dinner." There was one clothing store where you could buy the basics—jeans, t-shirts, and even underwear, which ironically you can't today. After I bought my house, it was still called by the locals for about fifteen years "Old Mrs. Hall's house." After that, people became convinced that I was here to stay.

With the road improvement (it used to take four hours on a good day) and airplanes and helicopters and vast wealth, this string of small towns became celebrity heaven. My late friend, the funny and brilliant screenwriter Peter Stone, said we should build a barrier across the Shinnecock Canal and if you said you had ever hired a caterer, or a DJ, or worn a gold chain, you would be turned back to Manhattan.

Dan's family were almost, but not quite, Bonackers, the early settlers of East Hampton and Springs, a term that derives from the Native American name for "root place," with names like Bennett, Conklin, Haven, King, Lester, Miller, and Strong. They owned the local potato farms and utilities and were superb fishermen. In this book, Dan writes all about the old times and then the gradual (or not so gradual) change to "The Hamptons." Dan's book, as does his newspaper, creates a chronicle of the women and men who have chosen to live in this magical place over these different decades, so one gets a very personal picture of how it was and is. Dan's seen it all and isn't keeping it under his very real hat. His crisp, clear, often poetic writing puts you in the moment to a mighty degree, and he writes excellent "you are there" dialogue as well.

Personally, one of my favorite chapters is the first, "Bob Steadman," set in 1960, a hilarious romp of a sailboat race engineered for eight- to ten-year-olds and usurped by Dan and his friend. Confronted by a dead wind, the friend jumps overboard into the waist high water and wades, pulling their sailboat over the finish line. At that point I wanted to yell, "Hooray," but Steadman screamed something much more colorful. I felt I was there and I could almost look at the little sailboats from that past era.

The chapter on Ira Rennert's home near the book's end, is also a favorite because it shows the trajectory from an innocent, unsophisticated place that still retained its enormous natural beauty to a place where almost everything else had changed. The fight over Rennert's $100 million complex turned the once-tranquil Sagaponack into a place of protest, political activism, and ethnic intolerance. The laughs were gone.

Once Dan interviewed me about my latest book, but it turned out that after a few glasses of wine, I interviewed him instead. He told me he's never felt he worked a day in his life and, as the lyric goes, "I did it my way." Somehow I forgot to ask him about the ubiquitous hat.

Barbara L. Goldsmith

Barbara L. Goldsmith is the author and historian of five award-winning *New York Times* best-selling books. She has written for the *New York Times*, *Vanity Fair*, and *The New Yorker*. Her most recent work, *Obsessive Genius: the Inner World of Marie Curie*, has been translated into 23 languages. Ms. Goldsmith has been elected to the American Academy of Arts and Sciences and was recently designated a "Living Landmark" by the New York Landmark Conservancy.

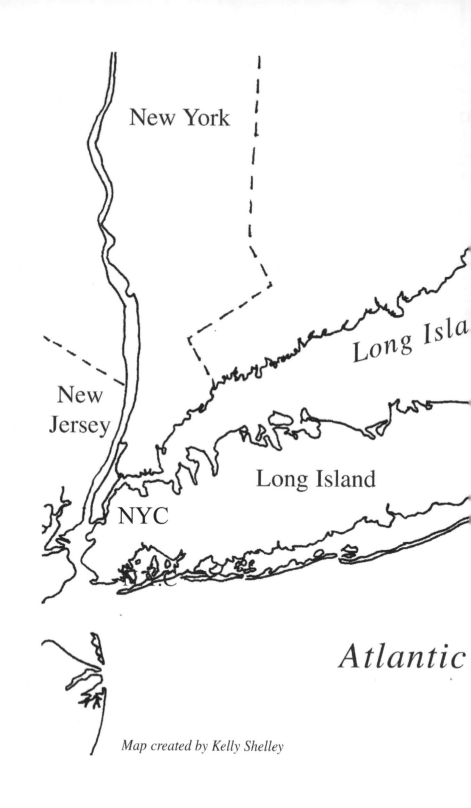

Map created by Kelly Shelley

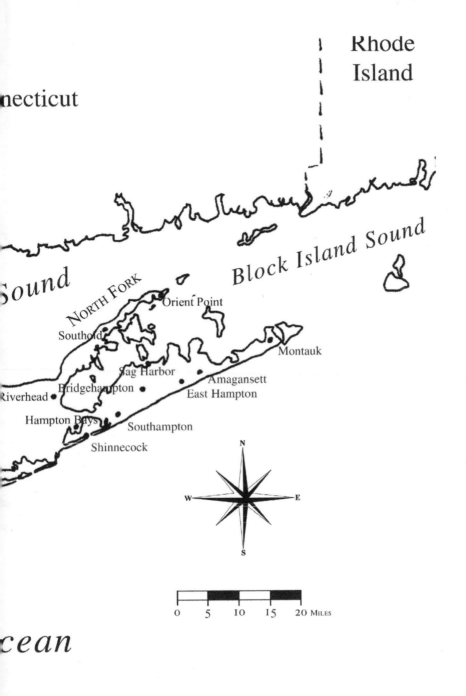

INTRODUCTION

This is the fourth volume of stories about interesting people I've encountered while running *Dan's Papers*, the free newspaper I founded as a teenager in the Hamptons in 1960. The title of all these books are variations of the phrase "In the Hamptons."

Fifty-five years ago, the Hamptons were a series of stunningly beautiful but sleepy old New England towns strung out into the ocean on a remote rural peninsula where people made their living farming and fishing. There were many bodies of water—lakes, ponds, harbors, bays and the Atlantic Ocean with its sixty miles of beaches. The landscape was fabulous, with cliffs, hillsides, long flat stretches of farmland, and wonderful vistas leading out over the land and the sea to the horizon. There were old English wood-shingled windmills. There were grand town greens and tall churches. The Hamptons still is a beautiful place, but it's mainly known today as the go-to summer place for anybody in America who is a billionaire or celebrity. So although the people I write about are the common thread of these books, the cast of characters changes. In the earlier chapters, you'll read about local railroad buff Ron Ziel and motel owner Sol Richer. But in later chapters, you'll read about the Ira Rennerts and Dr. Oz.

This volume, however, for the first time, also includes some of the hoaxes that have famously appeared in *Dan's Papers*. We still run them. I consider hoaxes to be a lively form of journalistic entertainment that wakes people up and gets them on their toes, particularly when they least expect it.

One of the first was "The MacKensie Seagull Whistle and Harness," a fake advertisement for a device that could get seagulls to tow your car off the beach from where you got it stuck.

That story resulted in hundreds of letters about this device, hundreds of orders, and hundreds of stories about the hoax in newspapers, TV news broadcasts, and magazines. *TIME Magazine* devoted a half page to it. The Associated Press distributed their version nationwide.

The most recent hoax is also in this book. "Lions in the Hamptons," was to appear in the newspaper on December 27, 2013. But because it takes several days to edit, headline, typeset, print, and deliver a newspaper, I'd written it a week earlier. However, the staff saw it when it arrived a week early, they loved it, and immediately posted it on our Website. By the time the paper came out, the dust was already clearing from the coverage of it around the country, not only on radio and TV and in other print media, but also in over a million blogs, tweets, and likes online.

I can't even predict where you would buy this book. On a tablet? In a brick-and-mortar bookstore. I hope you enjoy putting yourself *In the Hamptons 4Ever*.

Bob Steadman

~~~~~~

On a warm summer's morning in July of 1960, I saw a sign on the bulletin board inside the Montauk Post Office announcing the second annual Montauk Catboat Sailing Regatta for kids ages 8 to 12. It would take place in Lake Montauk at 1 p.m. on Saturday and was part of the kids' sailing program run by Bob Steadman, a former World War II Army officer living in town who had a sailing school in Montauk.

This was the first year I was running the newspaper, the first edition had come out in that town, and suddenly I was learning what all newspapermen learn, which is that the newspaper comes out every week—even if mine was just for the summer—and is constantly in need of fresh articles. Covering the sailing races, I could write about the winners and take pictures of all the determined little kids sailing around in Lake Montauk, the sails of their little boats bellowed out gracefully, looking for the finish line.

At nineteen, I was still living with my parents. My dad, four years earlier, had bought the pharmacy in Montauk and

had uprooted the family from where I grew up in Millburn, New Jersey. I missed my old high school classmates, and Millburn was just so far away. I'd call them, sometimes, and invite them out, but few came. That weekend, however, one of my best buddies, Howard Stone, was staying at the house. Howard could be my photographer.

And so, at 12:30 on Saturday, Howard and I, he with my camera and I with my pen and note pad, drove two miles down to Lake Montauk and the flotilla of small boats—six sail boats each about fourteen feet long, called "Penguins,"— that were tied up one next to the other at the dock there. This dock was part of a ten-acre waterfront property that had on it an abandoned building that had been at one time a bootlegger's gambling casino. Steadman was by the Penguins, and so were about fifteen kids, milling around the boats with their mothers and fathers. The Penguins were really little, all identical. They had a mast and a boom and a sail. Little boats for little kids.

I had met Steadman only once before, briefly, introduced to him by my dad. This had been the prior summer, when I worked in my dad's drugstore and he had come in one afternoon to buy something. Although in civilian clothes, he was nevertheless a ramrod straight military fellow. He had a full head of blond hair, walked with his jaw stuck out, talked in short machine-gun bursts, and he told my dad that, with the war over, he now worked during the school year at a high school up the island as a gym teacher. In the summer, he lived with his wife in Montauk and taught sailing.

Now, standing by the boats, Steadman took out a bullhorn.

"Okay, everybody, it's five minutes to race time. Go to your assigned boats. You have your boat numbers. Thank you, everybody."

The kids hopped to. The six boats were numbered. The kids found their assigned boats and stood on the dock by them, all eight-, nine-, and ten-year-olds, two kids to each boat. They looked at Mr. Steadman, who, pacing around in front of them, spoke on the bullhorn.

"The wind is brisk. No problem, though. Everybody please get in your boats now, careful, get in your designated positions. Okay. Now you will each sail down to the far end of the lake and turn around. You'll see the dock. That's the starting line. Sail in a group, cross the line together and, as you do, Timmy here will sound the horn. It's once around. You'll see the buoys I put out. They're all red. Eight of them. Just stay between the buoys and the shoreline, but not too close to the shore. The first one all the way around wins. Okay!"

Steadman was now looking at boat #4. There was nobody in boat #4.

"Where are the Akin twins?" he asked.

There was no answer.

"We'll wait a few minutes. Gotta have all the boats."

They waited a few minutes, but there were no Akin twins. Steadman now turned to me and Howard.

"You two. You guys with the camera. Get in that boat. Ever sail a boat?"

"I know how to handle a boat," I said.

"No matter. Just get in. We're gonna start this thing."

And so Howard and I hopped in. The boat shifted this way and that. But there were two plank benches. Howard sat on one and I sat on the other.

"Raise sails," Steadman shouted.

"I used to have a sailboat," I whispered to Howard.

"Just tell me what to do," Howard said.

"Just sit tight."

I reached past him to the boom and unhooked a rope from a cleat and began to pull the one sail, which had been all crumpled up on the boom, up the mast. Around me, there was the sound of ropes pulling up sails on each of the other five boats. Now there was the flapping sound of the white canvas up there, and in dark blue, little penguins near to the top. We were a jolly sight, I thought.

With the sails up, Steadman moved down the dock, quickly removing the lines from the cleats and throwing them into the boats. Then, one at a time, he shoved everybody off. Soon we were tacking this way and that, trying to turn around.

What great fun. The wind snapped our sail out, billowing it which, in turn, pushed our boat to the front. When we got to the turnaround at the far end of the lake, I let the sail go free, and as it luffed in the wind, we sat and waited.

"When everybody gets here, we'll lay back," I said to Howard who could hardly not have noticed we had beaten everybody to the starting line. "Most of these kids don't know what they are doing. When they all get here, we should move to the back and help the stragglers along."

"Okay," he said.

And so it began. Soon we had a fleet of ten little kids operating five little Penguins in front of us, zigging and zagging about, shouting to one another—"Hey, you're getting too close! I was here first!"—and we were herding them along like sheep. It was a gorgeous day. Our boat heeled over nicely against the wind. It slid gloriously across the surface of the lake going downwind.

I could easily gain on these kids in front if I wanted to, but I held back. And so it was after a while that the first of the boats crossed the starting line, and Timmy, on the shore next to Mr. Steadman, blew a loud blast on his air horn.

HHOOONNKK!

The parents cheered. We were underway.

For a considerable way on that first tack, Howard and I talked about some of our friends from Millburn High School in New Jersey and what had become of them. I had, after graduation, moved away with my mom, dad, and sister to Montauk, 130 miles away, so I had lost track. Howard filled me in. He had gone to Brandeis, and was studying the rabbinate. Mark Larner had gone to Lafayette. Most everyone had gone to college. We talked about the quality of the girls we'd chased the night before at Montauk's three nightspots—Surf and Sand, the Blue Marlin, and the Montauk Playhouse. And after a while, I told Howard about the boat I had owned the previous year.

"My parents got it for me for my birthday," I told him. "It was an old wooden boat, sixteen feet long, very wide and slow and heavy. It had one sail like this one, one mast and an iron centerboard you could pull up and down. In a brisk wind such as the one we are in now, the boat would get up to its full speed, maybe eight knots, which was really not very fast. But it felt faster because, when you got up to that speed, the iron centerboard would begin to sing—buzz, actually—from the water rushing by. It would be shaking in its slot, banging against it. And it would make the whole boat vibrate. You could feel it in your seat and hands. It was sort of a warning noise. Go any faster and the boat would fly apart. It was Breaking the Sound Barrier. Meanwhile, a whole lot of other boats would be scooting quietly by."

We laughed at this.

"Here was the most embarrassing thing I ever did in that boat. Once, I took my younger sister out onto the lake. She was about eleven at the time, but my mom said she was old enough for me to teach her how to sail. So, I'm telling her what to do, and the boom hits me a glancing blow on the head and knocks me right out of the boat and into the lake."

Howard was howling.

"I'm splashing around, spitting out water and everything, and Nancy is sitting there in the middle of the boat, and she looks down at me with this worried look and says, 'What am I supposed to do now?'"

"That's hilarious."

"But then in the fall, I went off to college. I'd left it tied to its buoy—you'd wade out to get to it—and I figured I'd bring it in over Thanksgiving. But then at school, third week I was there, my mother sent me a photograph. The hurricane had come through, and there is my boat on the narrow beach of the lake with a telephone pole crunched on top of her. End of boat."

At this point, we had rounded the first buoy heading north, hugging the shoreline. The kids in the Penguins in front of us were trying mightily, but they were continuing to squabble and shout and generally getting all mixed up. We passed a bunch of them—just couldn't help it. Now we were in third place.

You know, when you're in a boat race, even against a bunch of nine-year-olds, the competitive juices start getting up and you get to thinking.

"Only two in front of us now," Howard was saying. He was thinking the same thing.

Passing the second buoy, we passed the second-place boat, and as we rounded the third buoy, we passed the lead boat. As we did so, we high-fived each other. We were going to win.

Way up ahead, we could hear Steadman shouting orders over the bullhorn, but whatever it was, we couldn't make it out.

And then a strange thing happened. The wind, quite suddenly, died. It just stopped. We coasted to a halt. Behind us, the other boats came to a halt, too. We were all becalmed. Now, in that silence, we could hear Steadman loud and clear over the bullhorn.

"Let them by, you two! Men, pull in your lines, men, get them tight." They did that. It did them no good.

We both looked back. There was 30 yards of open water to boat #2 behind us, but it might as well have been ten miles. We weren't going anywhere. And neither were they. But this was also very tantalizing. We were now just 75 yards from the finish line. Behind us, two of the boats had sort of drifted into each other. The four boys in them were arguing and fighting anew. The booms were banging against one other.

"We'd let them by if we could," I shouted on ahead, but it seemed Steadman was unable to hear me. He continued with "let them by, let them by."

We all stayed like this for what seemed like the next half hour but was probably no more than ten minutes. The sun, which felt warm in the breeze, now felt hot. Off to one side, Steadman continued barking his orders. The boys were shouting and splashing—one had started to cry.

Finally, Howard Stone spoke.

"How deep is the water?" he asked.

"Probably no more than up to your waist," I said.

The bowline—the rope that ties to the front of the boat—was on the floor of the boat. Howard picked it up. "Want me to do this?" he asked.

I looked up at the sail. Not a puff.

"Go ahead," I said.

In one quick motion, fully clothed, Howard leaned back, threw a leg over the gunnel and made a gentle back flip into the water with a splash. Up ahead, Steadman was suddenly silent. Now Howard was up and splashing about. And then he found his footing.

"You're right," he said, standing up. This would be easy. Holding the rope, he waded to the front of the boat and began to pull us, mule fashion, toward the finish line. Penguin #4 lurched forward jerkily. We were on the move. Pulling away from the pack. Heading toward victory. And none of these other little kids behind us could do what Howard was doing. They were too short to stand up in the water.

Mr. Steadman, forgetting about the mothers and fathers standing near him, began to lose control.

"What the hell are you doing?" he screamed. "You can't do that!" He paused. "You! Get the fuck back into that boat. Now. Do you hear me? I said get the fuck back in."

Howard stopped pulling. The rope went slack. Penguin #4 began to glide to a halt.

"Keep going," I said, grimly.

He shrugged, and back he went to pulling.

"You assholes!" Steadman shouted. "You assholes are disqualified. Do you hear me? Disqualified. Wait till I get my hands on you assholes. Get over here!"

As he said that, we crossed the finish line. And, right on cue, Little Timmy, age nine, held his hand high in the air, pressed the button, and sounded the air horn.

HHOOONKKK!!

Sea Fair Week

~~~~~~

In June of 1961, my parents, who had driven from Montauk to Rochester, New York, to watch me graduate from the University of Rochester with a bachelor's degree in English, now drove me back home to Montauk in triumph. I would now start my second summer running my newspaper, the only newspaper for that town. After that I would be off to graduate school with a plan to continue on the following summer for the third year.

It was not possible for my parents to be more proud of me. I had, while an undergraduate, dreamt up the idea of running the newspaper, had hired a printer, written the articles, went around town soliciting advertising, printed it every other week, and had made enough money to pay not only for my senior year college tuition but also for all my expenses. At the end of that first summer running the paper, my dad took me to Plitt Ford in East Hampton and he bought me a Ford Fairlane convertible, secondhand to be sure, but very beautiful and fabulous nevertheless.

SOL RICHER WITH HIS WIFE AND DAUGHTER
(Courtesy the Richer Family)

Montauk, at the very tip of Long Island, was a brand new summer resort town in 1961, very unlike the old English towns in the Hamptons leading out to it. Forty modern new motels had been built in the prior ten years, twenty of them downtown by the ocean beach and the rest either out by the fishing docks or elsewhere on this twenty-mile long peninsula. The way things were going, Montauk would soon rival Cape Cod or the Catskills as the place to be when summer vacation came along.

I really didn't think of myself as some young hot-shot who could do no wrong when I came home for that second summer. I was still just a college kid. And all I wanted to do was publish the stories I wrote and the cartoons I drew so others could enjoy them. That in the process this could provide me enough money to see my way through college and grad school was secondary. That perception changed that June, however, when my dad asked me to stop by the store that afternoon so he could tell me something.

"I was at a Chamber of Commerce meeting yesterday," he said, "and your name came up. We'd decided to have a big week-long festival just before the end of the summer, to give the tourists something to remember us by. Make them want to come back next year. Sol Richer wanted me to ask you if you'd like to run it."

Sol Richer had built the newest motel on the strip, a hundred-room affair called the Atlantic Terrace.

"What's he got to do with the Chamber of Commerce?" I asked.

"He's the President of the Chamber of Commerce. And you may not know it, but he's a big fan of yours," my dad said. "After all you've done."

They wanted *me* to run this fall festival thing? "Of course I'll do it," I said.

"They'll give you all the help you need," dad said. He then reached out, smiled, and tousled my hair.

The following week I met with Sol in the oceanfront lounge of the Atlantic Terrace. Sol was about six foot two, barrel chested and curly haired. He was around forty years old at this time, and he not only was running this beautiful new motel, he had before that hired and supervised all the subcontractors in building it. My best memory of him was out there in the sunshine two years earlier, naked from the waist up, hauling lumber off the trucks so his workmen could carry it to where it had to go. He had the architect's plans. He was really enjoying being foreman in the construction of the place. And, of course, he built what he wanted. There was no town control, no town building approval needed, no zoning laws.

"We want you to put something together that would be like an Olympic Games," Sol told me. "You could have an event at the golf course, another at the tennis courts at the Montauk Manor, something out at the fishing docks, something at the Surf Club."

The Surf Club was a pink stucco building adjacent to the Atlantic Terrace. It is not there today. But then it was the centerpiece of the Montauk oceanfront, consisting of a giant swimming pool, cabanas, an outdoor restaurant area with umbrellas, and a beautiful boardwalk that went along the ocean in front of the cabanas for about 500 feet.

I envisioned a swimming race there, a diving competition and beauty contest. There could be a big banquet out there at the end, sort of a summing up and handing out of the trophies, with a dance band and, what, a dance contest?

The first edition of my newspaper, the *Montauk Pioneer* that second season, 5,000 copies, appeared the week before the Fourth of July. I had, as I had done the year before, distributed bundles of the newspaper to every place of business in town from the back seat of my old sedan, now from the back seat of my new convertible, with frequent stops at my parents' house on South Fairview Avenue to get more papers from the garage. There were fifty copies in a bundle. Some places got half a bundle, some got two bundles or twenty bundles. I recorded all the numbers I delivered to all the places in a composition book. There were about 150 stops. It took all day, and at the end of the day, all sweaty, I drove down to the beach, dashed across the sand past the sunbathers and jumped into the ocean for a swim. What fun delivery day was. And people loved the paper.

Oh, you're *back*! They shouted from the motel counters when I brought in a stack of the new edition. I watched them rush to pick up a copy. What had I done this time? I had written about rum running in Montauk. It made me so happy to see everyone enjoying what I wrote.

At the same time, early that summer, I proceeded to put everything together to make a big success out of "Sea Fair Week," as I had come to call it. Everyone was very cooperative. A restaurant donated a dance band for the last night. A marina would host a fishing tournament. Giordano's Lakeside Inn would have their band vocalist down at the Surf Club. The golf pro would supervise the golfing event at the Montauk Golf Course. Sometime in early June, I ordered the first-, second-, and third-place trophies from a company in Riverhead. When they came in early August, I had them all put onto a table in the lounge of the Atlantic Terrace, thirty of them ranging in size from one to three feet tall, and I had myself photographed smiling and standing next to Sol Richer on one side, and Chamber of Commerce Treasurer Nick Monte on the other, both men motel and hotel owners, the lad in the middle just three months out of college. We published it in the paper.

We also did other things to drum up business for Sea Fair Week. The Chamber, which paid for all this (and paid me a $100 fee to run this event), and took out ads in the *East Hampton Star* newspaper in the next town, took out ads in the New York *Daily News*, the New York *Mirror* and the New York *Journal-American*, all of which had resort hotel pages of stories and ads on Sundays. I also, on my third pass through town in late July, put up 150 posters about the events—on telephone poles, in stores on cigarette machines, or in motel lobbies, tacked to the front counters.

Two weeks before Sea Fair Week was to begin, I asked my parents if it would be okay if my best friend from college, George Lonkevich, came out during that last week in August.

"I was thinking I might need some help for Sea Fair Week," I said.

"It's okay with us," my dad said. We had a spare bedroom at the house.

I explained it all to George on the telephone. At school, he had heard me praise Montauk a lot and urge him to invite himself out sometime so he could see this wonderful place.

"I can't do Sea Fair Week all by myself," I said. "So we'd work doing these events. And then at night, we'd do the town. And I'll pay you half what they pay me."

"I can't wait," he said.

George drove out from his home in Morristown, New Jersey, on Saturday, August 26, the day before the first day of the eight days of Sea Fair Week. He was, and is, a handsome fellow of Russian heritage, happy go lucky and ready for any sort of fun. But he also was a serious student, majoring in computers leading to a degree from the Science Department. I had no idea about any of it. But we did hang out together most days, in the student lounge or, at night, out at clubs, one of which, the Bungalow, was a pretty disreputable beer parlor not far from campus in those years.

On that first Sunday at 1 p.m., we took the one trophy we would need that day and headed to the Montauk Airport—a little airstrip with a cabin for a terminal out at the end of East Lake Drive, its single runway built through wetlands parallel to the bay—for the first scheduled event of Sea Fair Week, a stunt-flying air show at two o'clock. Bob King, the airport manager, was out there, his hands on his hips when we arrived. There were half a dozen brightly colored stunt planes some friends of his had flown in. The pilots and navigators were all dressed in fireproof outfits. His wife was inside the little cabin, getting ready to announce things over the public address system they had. But there were almost no tourists. Maybe there were ten.

"It begins at two," Mrs. King said over the loud speaker.

We set the trophy out. It would be awarded to the best flier as selected by the tourists at the end of the show, by a show of hands.

"I'm sure there will be more people coming," I said.

Bob King looked at his watch.

The event went off without a hitch, a 45-minute show with fighter plane flyovers, the planes billowing smoke out the back, several doing rolls or loops, and with Mrs. King describing the action. Altogether there were forty people, each of whom had paid $1.50 to get in, or were supposed to have paid $1.50 to get in. Actually, none of them paid anything. Although we had a table where you could pay, nobody came over to it, and since the airport was not fenced, people just came and stood around wherever they wanted to.

At the end of the event, people clapped a few minutes and then wandered off. There had been no vote. I gave the trophy to Mr. King and asked him to thank everybody.

The next day, Monday at three, we held an event that was more of a success. Or so it seemed. It was at the Deep Hollow Ranch grounds and it consisted of the annual Deep Hollow Horse Show, which had been going on for years at that location in July, but for this summer, on the second day of Sea Fair Week. I had been to it the year before when about 150 people attended to watch the barrel races and roping events, and it seemed there were about the same number this year. When it was over, I gave the nine trophies to Shank Dickinson, the foreman of the ranch, who was running the event, to give out to his winners. Then we all went home.

Tuesday there was supposed to be a demonstration of the different golf clubs to use, and the trick shots you could do with them, on the driving range of the Montauk Downs Country Club by the club pro Pete Mazor. This was at 2 p.m. and would be followed by a distance driving contest, with the entrant who could hit the ball the farthest winning the big trophy and two runners-up winning the two smaller trophies.

But this was a serious embarrassment. Although it was a beautiful sunny day, absolutely nobody came to this event. We were able to round up a few people sitting in the clubhouse café having lunch for a bit, but that was it. Mazer gave his demonstration. Four people watched. Then those four people, golfers all, at our encouragement, arranged to hit golf balls as far as they could. Three of the four won trophies.

"What's the matter?" my father asked the two of us over dinner at home that night. "Cat got your tongues?"

"Nobody's coming to Sea Fair Week," I said.

"Well, it's just beginning," dad observed. "The best is yet to come."

"Everybody's down at the beach during the day," my mother said brightly. "You aren't going to get them off the beach."

I had an idea. "Maybe we could roust them from the beaches," I said. "Dad, could we borrow the jeep?"

"You going to drive it out on the beaches?"

"No, just through town and out to the beach ends. And I'm sure the Chamber has a loudspeaker system run on batteries. I've seen it used before. We could attach it to the roof."

All of us sitting there contemplated the Jeep. It was fifteen years old, had big tires, and had once been a maroon station wagon but had had to be redone because the body had entirely rusted out. A friend of my dad's, using a blowtorch, had taken all the doors and sides off it, replaced them with roll bars and canvas shades you could roll up, then painted everything an aquamarine green. Everybody knew this jeep. And we could easily mount speakers up on the roof. The roof, which had never rusted, was right up there.

The following morning, which was a Wednesday, George and I obtained the car battery and speaker system from the Chamber office, went to a hardware store and got clamps, and rigged up the speakers on the roof. Then, an hour and a half before the event—a bicycle race going round and round a carefully laid-out route through town from Terry's Bicycle Shop—we were out there with our loudspeaker on, rumbling along, up Emerson Street, down Essex Street, up Euclid Street and down Emory Street, shouting out for everybody to come.

"You know what you just said?" George asked me. He was driving. I was next to him, talking into the microphone.

"What?"

"You said 'Be sure to miss it if you can.' "

"I did not say that."

"Yes, you did. You said 'Be sure to miss it if you can.' And who thought up the names of these streets?" George asked. "Every one of them begins with an 'E.' "

"It was a developer in the 1920s named Carl Fisher. He built all the roads in the center of town. He named everything. And I have no idea why everything begins with an E."

"And what happened to Carl Fisher?"

"He failed."

Nobody seemed to be paying attention to us anyway, driving along in this queer jeep contraption with the loud speaker on the roof. They just marched along in their bathing suits and T-shirts, sunglasses and flip-flops, carrying their beach gear.

So twelve people showed up for the bicycle race. None had bicycles, so Terry grudgingly lent out all twelve of his bicycles and we fired a cap pistol and everybody was off, clutching the folded maps showing the route in their hands. We gave away the trophies.

It is very painful for me to tell you about the rest of the week. Thursday was the tennis matches at the Montauk Manor. The ball boys and the tennis pro, Bob Peterson, were there, and I think three other people. The idea was that it was to be a round-robin tournament, with the first person to win three matches getting the trophy. No matches were played. Everybody, even the ball boys, got the trophies.

Friday was a children's fishing-rod casting contest off the Montauk Commercial Dock. A second trophy at that event was supposed to be given to whoever caught the biggest fish. Nobody came. Saturday was the sailing contest. Nobody came.

At dinner that Saturday, my dad gave George and me a nice lecture about how we had stuck with it through thick and thin, mostly thin, about how we had set out to do this and we did this, and how he had spoken to Sol and he was very happy with everything, even if nobody came. It was great publicity for the town anyway, Dad said he said.

So off George and I went after dinner that Saturday night and sat in the dark at a table in the corner of the outdoor dining area at the Surf Club down on Edgemere Street where the climax of Sea Fair Week unfolded.

Actually, this was quite a nice event. Only a dozen or so tourists came to it. But many employees of all the motels and hotels, whoever could be spared, came.

The evening began with a high-board diving exhibition given by Harley French, "who performed at the Steel Pier and is one of the foremost divers in America today," according to master of ceremonies Hal Baker of the Montauk Yacht Club.

This was followed by an open bar and wine and cheese and crackers on a buffet table, and music and dancing to the Four Tones with special guest singer Lauri James, lent to the proceedings by Giordano's Lakeside Inn.

Then, for the grand finale, came the beauty contest and the crowning of Miss Montauk by Mr. Baker. The winner was Marjorie Bellis, a waitress at the Westlake Inn. Runners-up were from the Surf and Sand and from the Sands Motel, both of them maids for the rooms.

George and I leaned over our drinks. Sol Richer came over.

"I think you guys did just great," he smiled. "We learned a lot. And I think we can re-think this for next year." He actually seemed, still, genuinely happy at what we had done.

"Probably a good idea," I said.

And I thought, well, but not by us.

THE MacKENSIE SEAGULL WHISTLE AD

On the Next Page: *Printing presses have to print pages for a tabloid newspaper in multiples of four. You plan for it in advance. But what happens when at the last minute, a full page ad cancels? Here's what appeared in* Dan's Papers *on such a page on April 23, 1975.*

Introducing...
The Remarkable New

MacKensie
Seagull
Whistle

Only two inches long and made out of stainless steel, it is a MUST for anyone owning a four-wheel drive vehicle that might get stuck in the sand.

THE MACKENSIE SEAGULL WHISTLE has two notes. Blow soft for note one, blow loud for note two.
NOTE ONE "Seagulls Come Here"
You can't hear it but note one will attract every seagull within half a mile to your four-wheel drive vehicle stuck in the sand.
NOTE TWO "Seagulls PUSH"
On command, you have a veritable army of birds, each the equivalent of 1/100th horsepower pushing your car out of the sand.

 NEVER CALL THE WRECKERS AGAIN

With the MACKENSIE WHISTLE you will never again have to put up with sarcastic comments of the wrecker mechanic, nor will you have to put up with his fat towing bills.

THE MACKENSIE SEAGULL WHISTLE is handsomely designed by a Swedish designer, sturdily built, rustproof and guaranteed for as long as you own your car.

Be sure to fill out the coupon below and mail it today.
Don't delay! Supplies are limited.

Please send me more information about the MacKensie Seagull Whistle.
I enclosed a stamped self-addressed envelope. Do not send money.

My Name: _____

My Address: _____

My City Address (if any): _____

My Income: _____

Mail to: BIRDPOWER c/o Dan's Papers
Drawer AR, Bridgehampton, NY 11932

Adelaide de Menil

~~~~~~

I met her because we were the only two people standing by the side of the Montauk Highway in front of the East Hampton Post Office, watching workmen move a private home down the center of the street. Houses often get moved from one place to another in the Hamptons, so it's not that big a deal.

This house, called the Purple House, was being moved right through town, from the place where it had been on Main Street next to the library for hundreds of years, down the street and out of town to some private estate on the ocean to the east. Of course, I was there to take pictures of the move for *Dan's Papers*, now in its thirteenth year and at this point including an edition in East Hampton. I had no idea what she was doing there, but she had a camera on a tripod.

She was about the same age as I, maybe a few years older, a handsome, very well-dressed young woman in stylish khaki work clothes. Was she there working for another newspaper? It wouldn't surprise me.

At this particular moment, the house, an enormous old wood-shingled saltbox that took up almost the entire width

ADELAIDE DE MENIL
(Courtesy of Adelaide De Menil)

of the street, was stopped behind its tow truck. Men working for Kennelly Movers were trying to deal with a traffic light held high above the white line in the center of the street by a steel wire crossing the road that was not high enough for the house to pass under. And the light, unaware, was going through its paces. Red Green, Yellow Red. Red Green, Yellow Red. Although, because of the house, there were no cars in the road to instruct.

"Taking pictures for a publication?" I asked her.

"No," she said. "Just for pleasure."

We watched as the traffic light, being lowered by workmen, came, very slowly, straight down toward the ground on a cable. There was a man on the white line below. He grabbed it, and with wires swirling around it, began to look to see where he could take it.

Red Green, Yellow Red.

I thought this a wonderful scene and trotted out into the middle of the street in front of everything and took its picture. Then I ran back.

Now I noticed the camera on the tripod the woman was using. It was very fancy. Without the woman touching it, it made a loud *Click*. Then, after ten seconds it made another *Click*. And now the house, with the traffic light stowed on the sidewalk, was on the move again. The woman turned the camera just the slightest little bit. *Click* it went again. And then another ten seconds passed and there was another click. And now I knew what she was doing.

"You're making a stop-action film of the house move," I said.

"Yup."

"That's going to be great! A great movie."

The house had stopped again. And as it did, the young woman picked up the camera and tripod.

"Well, you'll have to excuse me," she said. "I have to get a new location." And with that, she was off, striding swiftly down the road alongside the house. It was moving, of course, at an absolute crawl. She could easily keep up with it.

Well, I had my shot. And it was a beaut: man holding a traffic light, still operational, looking around, quizzical look on his face, trying to decide where to put it. But I still had no idea who this woman was.

HOUSES ON THE MOVE AGAIN—2007
(Courtesy of Adelaide de Menil)

As I went back to my car, parked in front of the Post Office, I stopped briefly to talk to John Strong, who was standing by the front door of his real estate office next to our carriage house watching the proceedings.

"Do you know what this is all about?" I asked.

"I'm not in the real estate business for nothing," he said.

The house, he said, was called the Purple House and had been on the property where it had been built for 200 years. The library was built much later, next door. Now, here in 1973, the library was expanding. They'd bought the house and the property. And they said they'd tear this house down to build a new wing for the library.

I might note at this point that back during those years, it was no big deal to tear down an old historic house. Nobody cared much for history. Progress was what mattered, so neither John Strong nor I thought much in this conversation about the value of the Purple House. It was just one old house among many.

"Now here comes this very rich young woman named Adelaide de Menil," John continued. "And she's buying it and moving it off. She and her husband just bought this big oceanfront property on Further Lane. They're moving it there. Can you imagine?

"Who is Adelaide de Menil?" I asked.

"You don't know? I'm surprised, you being in the newspaper business. The de Menil family is from Houston. They are very active in the arts and they are great philanthropists. Lots of money. The mother is French. Dominique. Then there are the children Christophe and Adelaide and François. I don't know why they came to the Hamptons but they did."

"So that woman was making this movie for Adelaide de Menil?" I asked.

"That was Adelaide," he said.

Time goes by. The earth moves around the sun. Now it is a cold rainy day in January of 2007, and I am once again standing by the side of the Montauk Highway with a camera around my neck, watching a house being moved. But this time it is a much more elaborate proposition. There are thousands of people lining the sides of the road. There is a black helicopter hovering overhead. There is a parade of police cars, all with their lights flashing, in front of the house. But it is not just one house. Behind that first house are a second and a third and a fourth and a fifth and a sixth, an entire line of eighteenth century and nineteenth century historic homes and barns, a quarter-mile long, all heading very slowly—at the exact same two miles an hour—in a westerly direction, on their way to the grand front lawn of the old and rundown East Hampton Town Hall, not far from downtown. What a sight!

Among those there along with the hundreds of photographers and reporters were lots of people involved in making this incredible move, standing under umbrellas in the rain. There was Bill McGintee, the Town Supervisor, proud as could be, rocking back and forth on his heels in the rain, talking to reporters. There was architect Robert Stern, who would be designing a new Town Hall by making an assemblage out of these 200-year-old historic buildings. There was the Chief of Police, Eddie Ecker, and there was the owner of Davis Construction House Movers, now telling people about the new remote control devices that could steer the house with the press of a button because there were electric engines under the houses that responded to the clicks of the remote, rather than big trucks to pull the houses with tow lines at the front.

And there was the same Adelaide de Menil there, racing in and out among the houses, the Peach Farm House, the Hand House, the Hedges House, the Purple House, and several other houses and barns and other structures, all of which, over the prior years, she had saved from the demolition ball and taken over to her estate on Further Lane in our town.

This is a lifetime later, forty years and more, and she is dressed just as spectacularly, if not more spectacularly, than she was by the side of the road in 1973. She wears a black "witches" raincoat that flares to the ground over shiny black boots. A pointy black hood had been pulled up over her head to protect her from the rain, and as she runs around pointing at this, instructing somebody about that, she seems completely oblivious to everyone around her. From the curb, I wave to her as she runs by. She sees me for a brief instant, waves, and then she is gone, behind one of the houses.

Adelaide de Menil and Ted Carpenter had, in this interval, lived out their adult lives in this compound of what ultimately became twelve structures, including outhouses, toolsheds, and even a World War II submarine lookout station, the size of a wooden public telephone booth, which Coastguardsmen had paused in to warm up as they trudged the ocean beaches on two-hour-long shifts looking for Nazi invaders day and night through the long winters during that war.

All of these structures were not destined to remain on the forty oceanfront acres where the de Menils had placed them. There had been a trauma two years earlier. And the de Menils, in spite of themselves, were now in the process of saving these homes once again.

The trauma was real estate prices gone out of control. Wealthy and famous people had bought these big estates down on Further Lane during the 1980s and 1990s. They had paid $10 million for them, $20 million and even $30 million. By the year 2000, Ted and Adelaide were rubbing shoulders with Billy Joel, Jann Wenner, Bruce Wasserstein, Jerry Seinfeld and many others. Many were behind hedgerows and gates, accessible only by those who could punch in a code at a speakerphone on a pole by the entry gate, to get people inside to open the gates to let you go through.

I wondered for a long time how these historic buildings were arrayed at the de Menil's estate. Over the years, I'd run into Adelaide at art gallery openings and sometimes at nearby tables at restaurants, but I had never been invited to her home. Were they a little village, bordering some main street like at Disneyland? Were they all bunched together into one big house? Hadn't there been a house there, one they lived in, when they first moved here in the 1970s? How would this one house relate to the historic houses?

Sometimes, there were parties taking place at this compound, attended by successful people in the arts, music and financial fields. And finally I was invited to one. You passed through the gates and immediately drove up a gravel road and into a two-story barn building, in the front and out the back again, an exclamation mark declaring a new reality as you continued on along the winding road to the house.

One of the smaller houses was used as a shed. Another was a barn converted to a big gathering room. Two houses were attached by a glass breezeway near to the ocean, facing it, and it was these that comprised the domicile of the couple.

There was no recently built mansion on the property. In fact, there had never been one. This oceanfront acreage had been a potato field in the period before the de Menils had bought it.

Around 2001, however, Ted and Adelaide were reaching well into their sixties. They had had no children. What would become of this estate when they passed on?

Adelaide told me she had never put the house on the market. In that frenzied real estate time, however, offers came to her. One was for $55 million. Another was for $70 million. These were cash offers. In 2003, an offer for this property came in over $100 million, the largest amount ever offered for a home in the Hamptons, by a wide margin. Then another offer came in at $102 million. The price was going up and up.

In the end, in 2004, the de Menils, unsolicited, received an offer to sell the house for $103 million from Ron Baron, a wealthy Wall Street dealmaker. And they decided the time had come. The papers were signed, the money paid, and then Baron decided to do his own thing on the property. He offered them six months to find a new location for the twelve historic buildings on the property, after which, if they were still there, he would dispose of them.

Adelaide and Ted asked the library if it would accept the Purple House and put it on their property, next to where it had been in the 1960s. The library thought about it, but then said no. At that point, I really let them have it in the paper. The world had turned many times. They should have accepted it.

The heroes of this piece were Councilman Job Potter and Town Supervisor Bill McGintee. The old Town Hall was bursting at the seams. It was also in serious disrepair.

McGintee stepped forward and, at first, offered to just take all the houses and have them set up on that broad front lawn of Town Hall as museum pieces. But on further thought, he decided that perhaps these homes, the seven largest ones, could be put together in some artful way on the front lawn to become the new Town Hall.

He asked Ted and Adelaide about this. He asked if they would pay for the move, for some of the renovations and some of the upkeep. The offer was accepted. The Coast Guard warming house would go to the Amagansett Marine Museum. Other buildings would go to other locations.

"HOUSE COMING THROUGH"
(Courtesy of the author)

Two weeks prior to when the homes would be taken off their foundations on the estate grounds, a grand farewell party was held by Ted and Adelaide in a large tent at their estate. Hundreds came. The ancient homes were just so beautifully appointed. They were warm and historic inside. Fires burned in the fireplaces. Lots of people spoke. They were giving their farewells to the homes we had lost. People ate and drank. Some wept. But there would be a new day.

And so, as if it were a great Broadway show, the entire parade of historic houses left the property in a long line, and in one long day were moved to the Town Hall lawn and other locations.

A year later, an enormous cocktail-table-sized picture book appeared. It was, and is, *Further Lane*, and it documents the day of the moving of those twelve structures, as seen from the ground by various cameramen and from the helicopter above, where Adelaide's step-son Ian Carpenter was taking pictures for posterity of what might have been called a great public art moving event, with the assemblage of a new Town Hall at the end.

The job of saving these beautiful old historic buildings had been a success.

A job had been well done.

On the Next Page: *In the summer of 1988, the Village of Sag Harbor began to consider a plan to allow local artists to paint over the pale green forty foot tall steel ball in the center of town that had for many years been used for the storage of compressed gas. By this time* Dan's Papers *had become known for occasional fantasies and hoaxes that would shake up the community. Did Jackson Pollock really do a drip painting on that ball years earlier? From* Dan's Papers *on August 27, 1988.*

POLLOCK MASTERPIECE IS FOUND IN SAG HARBOR

The big steel gas ball that for years has dominated the Sag Harbor skyline may have a value in excess of $10 million, according to an art expert. Dr. Harrison Holly of the Manhattan Art Institute says that if this is the steel gas storage sphere that was built in Sag Harbor in 1952, and the company that owns the sphere, the Long Island Lighting Company, confirms that it is, then it has, under its many coats of paint, the largest and most spectacular Jackson Pollock drip painting ever made. "Pollock lived in the Springs," Dr. Holly said. "He made the drip painting standing on the top of this sphere in 1954, just two years after its construction. He was at the top of his form at the time, and the painting was considered a masterwork. Unfortunately, vandals painted over Pollock's work in 1956, just after Pollock's untimely death. It was a major loss to the art world at the time. I had no idea this sphere was still standing. Pollock's 'Blue Poles' sold at auction for more than $8 million recently. Pollock's paintings fetch more than those of any American painter of the 20th Century."

Dr. Holly said that whatever coats of paint have been put on top of the Pollock could easily be removed using modern restoration techniques. He said the possible existence of the sphere came to his attention because of newspaper reports about an East End group that wanted to paint the sphere as a replica of the earth. That plan, which was put before the Sag Harbor Board of Historic Preservation and Architectural Review last week, was unanimously turned down.

According to LILCO, if there is a Jackson Pollock under there, they are surely going to find it. "If this sphere is worth tens of millions of dollars, then we are surely going to take advantage of it," a LILCO representative said. "We may bring in a new sphere and remove this old one so we can work on it. We may put it up for auction. At this point, we don't know." The sphere was originally built in Sag Harbor by the local gas company that operated in Sag Harbor at that time. Owned by an erratic millionaire named Fester Blount, the East Coast Coal and Combustible Gas Corporation did its business just in Noyac, North Sea and Sag Harbor until right after the Second World War. At that time, Blount decided on a major expansion. He would have gas brought in by steamer, and he would distribute it up and down the east coast, from Maine to North Carolina. And he would build a big storage tank on property he owned on Long Island Avenue in Sag Harbor that would be large enough to serve the gas needs of the entire eastern seaboard. Blount hired Howard Horton Contracting to build him this gas ball out of steel plates and rivets—it was the largest of its kind at the time—and Horton complied. It was ready to receive gas by April 2, 1952.

Unfortunately, a week earlier, Blount was seriously injured when a tank of propane he was carrying from his car to his garage exploded in his hands. On his deathbed at his home in Sag Harbor, he was visited by, among others, Jackson Pollock, whom Blount had met at Jungle Pete's Bar on Fort Pond Boulevard in East Hampton. From the day of their meeting until their parting at Blount's deathbed, the two men were inseparable. Among other things, Blount was, along with Peggy Guggenheim, Pollock's major benefactor.

"Make my sphere your greatest work," Blount reportedly gasped to Pollock as his last words.

Before the summer was out, Pollock had made sketches, designed a concept and then climbed up to the top of the sphere to splash this

(Courtesy of the author)

most brilliant and exuberant drip painting down every side. It was a dramatic and unequivocal statement of Abstract Expressionism, visible for miles. Photographs of the sphere appeared on the covers of virtually every art magazine published at that time, with accompanying rave reviews. On the other hand, most of the Sag Harbor townspeople hated it.

One and a half years later, in August, with his wife in Paris, Pollock was driving two young women to a party at the home of Alphonse Ossorio in Wainscott. Ossorio was another abstract expressionist of sorts, and he had just returned from the Philippines and wanted to re-acquaint himself with all his friends. By four in the afternoon, when the party was to begin, Pollock was already drinking heavily and the girls had suggested they not go. Pollock insisted, however, and he began weaving his Oldsmobile convertible down Springs-Fireplace Road. As the girls continued to insist that Pollock was too drunk to go to the party, the painter became abusive, turned the Oldsmobile around, stepped on the gas and increased his speed to more than 60 miles an hour before reaching a bend in the road near Abraham's Path. The car lifted up, turned over and crashed into a tree by the side of the road. Pollock and one of the girls were killed. The other girl lived to tell the tale.

As for the sphere in Sag Harbor, it was entirely painted over in an aqua color during the night just one week later. No one was ever arrested for this desecration, and it was said that the Sag Harbor police, who along with the rest of the townspeople did not seem to appreciate either Pollock, his work, his girl friends or his drinking prowess, didn't try very hard.

The Long Island Lighting Company bought the sphere in 1962, when they consolidated all the small lighting and power companies on Long Island. And so it was almost ten years after its construction that the sphere was first filled with gas. Horton had built it well. There were no leaks.

From that day until this, LILCO has re-painted the sphere every eight years, always the same aqua color. Around 1975, the Federal

Aviation Authority passed laws requiring that all tall objects be painted in certain bright colors so they would not be dangers to pilots in passing aircraft. The aqua color was acceptable to the FAA.

Early this winter, a group of local artists formed an organization called the "One World Project," hoping to be able to paint the sphere as a replica of the Earth. Among those in the group were artist Bianca Rice from Sag Harbor, architect Eva Growney from East Hampton, Bill Smith, who is president of FISH Unlimited, and Barney Corrigan, president of Sag Harbor's Guild of Holistic Practices. They got the okay from LILCO to repaint the sphere so long as the colors were acceptable to the FAA, and on Monday, March 25, appeared before the Sag Harbor Board of Historic Preservation and Architectural Review to get approval from the Village.

The basic aqua color of the sphere would be left as it was for the various oceans. Land masses would be painted an FAA approved beige. Puffs of white clouds would be added.

Although the representatives of the One World Project brought in a petition of more than 165 signatures, many of them local Sag Harbor merchants who had to every day look out at the sphere, the Board was not satisfied that this was not some sort of "political statement" that ought to be better made in a demonstration or meeting. They voted the project down, unanimously.

Neither members of the Village Board nor members of the One World Project indicated they had any idea that underneath all of this was an original Jackson Pollock masterpiece.

"I had no idea," one One World Project member said, requesting anonymity.

Barney Corrigan, who left the meeting dejected after the Defeat, had originally said this was only the beginning of the fight and they'd present the proposal again next year. Now, with the new information provided by Dr. Holly, he said he would have no comment at the present time.

Elaine Benson

~~~~~~

One day in 1970, I asked Elaine Benson, the owner of a large art gallery and sculpture garden next door to the house that had become our new office in Bridgehampton, to write a column for this newspaper. It seemed a logical thing to do, considering that both the newspaper and the art gallery along with a nearby bar were pioneers in the transformation of Bridgehampton.

Until about 1970, Bridgehampton was just a three-block main street surrounded by farms and potato fields, really just an agricultural town, like any other in America. A popular summer event was for the largest potato competition. Another well-attended event was the antique tractor run. Agway was the big store. Farmers and farmhands were everywhere. Sunday, the downtown closed up. The farmers and their wives, all dressed up, went to church. Four churches graced Main Street. There were feed stores, luncheonettes—one was the Candy Kitchen (still there) where at the time, farmers assembled at 6 a.m. to discuss feed, grain, and potato prices

ELAINE BENSON
(Photo by Nancy Crampton, Sculpture by Molly Mason)

over coffee to start their day—a meat market with raw sides of beef hanging on hooks, two barber shops, and several taverns. Also, amazingly, in just those three blocks, there were seven gas stations, all of which fixed not only cars but also tractors and other gasoline-powered farm implements. The town even had a weekly newspaper, the *Bridgehampton News.* Around 1970, however, potatoes grown in Maine and Idaho began to dominate the market. Meanwhile, a new wave of artists, writers, sculptors, Wall Street people and others from the city were moving into town and building homes in some of the farm fields. And they were willing to pay high prices.

And then, along Main Street, there were us pioneers. First, in 1964, came the Benson Art Gallery. Elaine and Emanual Benson bought a large old Victorian home on Main Street and in the back, inside a large barn and outside in a field, exhibited sculpture and art from the abstract expressionists, the surrealists, and others. They showed the work of Willem de Kooning, Larry Rivers, Robert Dash, Fairfield Porter, all artists who lived in this community.

A second pioneer, a bar called Bobby Van's, opened in 1968 catering to literary types. It became a famous hangout for novelists and editors such as Truman Capote, James Jones, George Plimpton, Peter Mattheissen, Irwin Shaw, and others who had moved into the community.

And then came me. My entry into town came in 1970 when I moved the offices of *Dan's Papers* to Bridgehampton's Main Street, to a house directly next door to the Benson Art Gallery. I also bought a home nearby on Lumber Lane in a residential neighborhood for my young family.

Of course, the day after my new newspaper office opened, I walked over to meet the Bensons. They invited me in for coffee. And, over time, I got to know them well.

Emanuel Benson was a formidable, scholarly man of about sixty-five who had been the director of the Philadelphia

Museum School of Art. Elaine, a beautiful, graceful woman of forty, was his wife. I, at twenty-nine, considered them both wise elders.

Art was everywhere. The talk at the gallery was of literature, travel, Europe. I learned that at one time before they got married, Elaine had worked for Mr. Benson as his secretary. They had both been married at the time. There were children involved. But they had eloped to start someplace new.

And I'd see Elaine and Emanuel about one thing or another just about every day. Artists, writers and dealers came and went. As they knew everybody, why not, I asked her, write a weekly column in the paper about society and art. We discussed what I would pay. I told her an amount, she said she paid her cleaning lady more than that. I said I would pay what she paid her cleaning lady. That column ran in my newspaper over the next thirty years. Occasionally, she'd tell me that her cleaning lady got a raise, and I'd give her a raise.

One day, Elaine told me a story about a Texan and an angel. There had been a pre-opening party on a Friday night for sculptor Bill King, who had carved a series of three-foot-long wooden angels. Most were in flying position, Superman fashion, hanging on wires from the ceiling inside of the gallery barn.

In the middle of that party, Elaine became aware that a big, expensive Cadillac car had pulled up in front of the sliding-glass doors to the barn. The headlights shone in. But nobody got out of the car. This was really rude. She went to the slider and opened it. There was a man behind the wheel wearing a cowboy hat.

"I'm sorry, this is a private party," she told the man.

But the man insisted he be allowed in. It would be worth their while. She gave in and told him move the car first. And he did. After looking around, he bought one of the angels flying overhead. He put down a $3,000 cash deposit. The remaining $3,000 would be sent in by check after he had informed Elaine where the wooden angel was to be sent.

Two weeks later, a letter arrived with the remaining check for $3,000. The letter gave an address in San Antonio to send it to. But there was a request. "Have the penis cut off it," the letter read. "It's offensive to people down here in Texas to be looking at that."

Elaine showed this letter to Emanuel, who said send him back his money. And so she did. In today's money, that was about $30,000 to keep a penis attached to an angel in the name of artistic integrity.

And so beginning in 1971, with Emanuel running the gallery and Elaine assisting, acting as hostess and writing her column—Emanuel ruled that she was to never was to write about him—time moved forward. And then Emanuel Benson took sick and within six months died of cancer. This left Elaine, who really had just been her husband's assistant, the daunting task of trying to figure out how to run the gallery—which she soon did. Not only was she a quick study in learning the mechanics of running the gallery, she also had a remarkable eye for good artwork.

She also went on a campaign to remarry. Although my wife and I did not socialize much with her because of the generation differences, she wanted us to meet one suitor after another. To each, Elaine seemed restrained though amused, interested and encouraging. She was learning, or so it seemed to me, the quality that people have remarked was to be the keystone of the rest of her life—how to listen, and how to encourage the best out of people. I remember one such suitor who had the demeanor of a game show host. But she remained positive.

Then, one day, she was asked out by Joseph F. X. Kaufman, a man her own age who had a summer residence in Water Mill. Kaufman was an American raised in Paris, a bibliographer and historian, and a World War II veteran. European in manner, he was born wealthy but seemed to have lost most of it in a series of marriages and divorces that resulted in each of his ex-wives getting half. Now he wanted peace and quiet.

On that first date, Elaine told me, the two argued loudly about an arcane historical literary point. Thus, Elaine said, Joseph F. X. Kaufman was the man for her.

And so, from 1974 forward, Elaine ran the gallery—it was the Elaine Benson Gallery now—and arranged the couple's elaborate social life and business affairs. Joe was quite happy with this. A voracious reader, he would much prefer to stay at home, but he would grumble curmudgeon-fashion about having to go out and then would go, where, he would find, in spite of himself, that he was having a good time. His only request was that when he wanted to go home, they would.

They also became world travelers, since the gallery was only open from May to September. For more than a decade they owned a home in Portugal. But ultimately, their favorite city was Paris.

I recall feeling sad every autumn, when the gallery closed and they went away, because I knew they would be gone until spring. But I could always call up the gallery and hear her glorious, imperious voice on her answering machine whenever I wanted. All I'd have to do was call.

"The gallery is closed for the winter," the voice said. "Our artists have been selected for all of next year. If you are interested in the year after that, please contact us in the spring."

Over the years, Elaine also became my confidant and advisor. As my personal life went through a tumultuous series of marriages and business advances and reverses, I could count on her being there for me. Something would happen—an opportunity, a setback, a catastrophe—and who I would run to was Elaine. We'd talk over coffee. She was concerned, interested, analytical, encouraging. She was never critical. I put her up on the masthead as Faculty Advisor. I could think of no title more accurate to describe what she was to me, to my life.

Over the years, of course, we shared many experiences. A major fire burned much of the interior of her house consuming the couple's beloved dachshund. Also consumed was much of the research for a book Elaine was planning to write . . . on the history of underwear. (Eventually, she re-assembled the research and it appeared, published by Simon and Schuster, to much success.)

Another time, in the middle of the night, a man driving home from a party up island fell asleep at the wheel, jumped the curb, bashed through and shattered the *Dan's Papers* sign, the *Elaine Benson Gallery* sign, and, weaving merrily across front lawns and through shrubbery, continued eastward. To judge by the tire tracks, the driver missed a huge twelve-foot metal sculpture on Elaine's front lawn by inches, just missed the front porch of the barber who lived on the far side, and continued on through some bayberry bushes until he hit a chain-link fence, which wrapped itself around the front end of the car and acted as sort of a sling shot, slowing it to a halt just four feet from the side of the Pulver Gas Building. That fence saved the car from a collision with the side of that building, which could have blown up the entire town in a mushroom cloud of propane gas. Instead, the driver, still asleep, was found snoring at the wheel when the authorities, alerted by the ruckus, arrived to find a huge four-by-four post from the Benson Gallery sign speared through the front windshield to pass just inches from his head. He had slept through it all. On being awakened, he said he was just returning from an evening of bowling. He was uninjured. They removed him with a jaws-of-life machine.

On still another occasion, Elaine and Joe went to the beach with the well-known cartoonist Charles Addams and his wife Tee. Elaine was a longtime friend of the Addams's. They were going to meet Joe for the first time. Elaine gleefully told me what had happened that afternoon. In the course of it, lying there on the beach the four of them talking, Joe came to the amazing realization that years earlier, he and Charles had been married to the same woman, though obviously at different times. At that moment, Joe decided he'd keep that information to himself.

Toward sunset, Joe walked down to the water's edge and stared out to sea for a while. And then Charles came down to stand beside him. After a few moments of silence, Charles quietly asked Joe a question.

"What did you think of Barbara?"

Joe thought about it carefully and then replied.

"Which Barbara?"

And then there was a visit from Elaine's mother. Elaine wrote a column about it. I had gone over to see Elaine, but she wasn't there. An older woman answered the door.

Can I tell her who was calling? she asked. I told her. She seemed not to have heard it, so I said my name again. Later in the day, Elaine told me that her mother had told her a man named Sam the Cleaner had come calling. Elaine could not figure this out at first, but then it dawned on her. It rhymed with Dan Rattiner.

After fifteen years of friendship, I learned, for the first time, something I had not known before. Elaine had been a runaway wife. Before Emanuel, she had been married nearly twenty years to a man named Bill Goff, who was in the advertising business in Philadelphia. They had had four children. Yet Elaine had fallen in love with the elderly director of the Art Institute, the man she worked for, and simply had run off, leaving the children, who were between six and twelve at that time, with their father. I was amazed at this. Why had she never told me? I asked her. It was something she did not think it was necessary for me to know, she said.

Indeed, now, with her and Joe fully settled in Bridge-hampton, the children appeared, finally, to pay their wayward mother a visit and perhaps patch things up. They were teenagers now, high school kids, college kids. It had been a long time ago. They seemed to straggle in to Elaine and Joe's world, one by one, a sort of new act in the drama of Elaine's life, from my perspective.

Two of them, at one time, worked for me at the newspaper. Neal worked as a reporter and wrote about his adventures trying to enter the Miss Southampton Pageant, something difficult

ELAINE (MRS. JOHN) STEINBECK, ELAINE DANNHAUSER
(A REAL ESTATE BROKER), ELAINE BENSON (ART DEALER),
AND ELAINE (MRS. WILLEM) DE KOONING
AS JUDGES OF THE *DAN'S PAPERS* KITE FLY
(Courtesy of the author)

to do, since he was a man. I personally wrote a story about another of Elaine's sons, Bill, whose girlfriend Betsy water-skied one day all the way from Sag Harbor to Montauk. I was in a second speedboat so I could take pictures. A daughter, Kimberly, opened a dress shop in town.

In any case, all of them, according to Elaine, hated to have their names mentioned in her column. She wrote about them anyway. Now it was Elaine's rules.

Once I asked her what her maiden name was. Klebanoff, she said.

I pondered this. Elaine Klebanoff Goff Benson Kauffman.

Elaine become a major force in the community. She was on the Board of the Hampton Jitney. She became, as a part-time employee, the public relations director of the Southampton Hospital. She held an annual spring fundraiser at her gallery for the John Steinbeck Room at Southampton College. Other fundraisers at her gallery raised money for East End Hospice, the Retreat, the Nature Conservancy, the East End Gay Organization, and the Group for the South Fork and the Bridgehampton Child Care Center. It's been said that through her efforts, more than half a million dollars were raised at various times.

But now, celebrities and the masters of the universe were moving into town in droves. Newspapers would call wanting stories about these people. They'd call me at the paper. Or they'd call Elaine at the gallery directly.

As for the newspaper, Elaine's column continued, and her title of Faculty Advisor continued. But now she was also a participant at the once-a-week round table editorial meeting this newspaper still holds. Almost invariably, I was late for this meeting. I'd arrive, breathlessly, muttering apologies to the upturned heads.

"Well, Mr. Rattiner, I see you've decided once again to arrive," Elaine would say. Discussion would then proceed about the news of the week in the community, about coming events, about local authors or painters who were being honored and about other things we might assign to our group of eager writers. Elaine proposed much of it.

And then, one day, twenty-four years later, suddenly, there was a disturbing message on my answering machine.

"Please call me," Elaine said. "I think the time has come for me to tell you something."

I could hardly imagine. Joe had just passed away. Was it something about him? I called her. "I haven't much more time to live," she said. "I have non-Hodgkins lymphoma. I've had a good, exciting life. Everything I could have wanted, except maybe not the part about being a runaway wife. I'm not in any pain. I'm being well taken care of, though I'm having some trouble breathing now."

I was just about speechless. Just a week earlier she had been at the roundtable. Nothing was wrong.

"I had chemotherapy after they made the diagnosis," she continued. "Lost all of my hair, which was bad." (I had noticed for a while that she wore a wig, but she said she was writing a new book about hairpieces). "But I decided if I had to go through chemo again, I wouldn't. A personal decision. I'm at home now. But I'd rather not accept visitors. I'm sure you understand. Anyway, I will write one more column explaining why I won't be writing any more columns. You'll have it Monday."

Later that afternoon, I sadly searched the office, looking for a photograph of the two of us from when we had first met all those years ago, more than a quarter century. I couldn't find one. Finally, I took one of just me from thirty years ago, taken at the newspaper office. I wrote "Me When We Met" on it, put it in a frame, and I went to her house and rang the bell. I could see Elaine's car was there. For a long time, nobody came to the door. Then, there she was.

"Hello," she said, trying a smile. "I'm really not accepting visitors, you know."

"I know," I told her. "But I wanted you to have this. It's the year we met. You've meant a great deal to me."

"Thank you," she said.

I turned and left, and that was the last time I saw her. She died just four days later at the age of seventy-four.

———～～～———

But she can't be gone, I thought to myself, after reading her obituary in the *New York Times*. I'll see her at Friday's editorial meeting. I'm sure of it.

Audrey Flack

~~~~~~

Young Audrey Flack appeared on the New York City art scene in the 1950s making realistic still life oil paintings that were so astonishing as to be almost indistinguishable from photographs. She called her work photorealism, and she is considered one of its founders. She painted portraits of Marilyn Monroe during the 1970s and 1980s that are considered near genius. In 1966 she became the first photorealistic artist to have work accepted at the Museum of Modern Art in New York. Her paintings soon were in collections at the Metropolitan Museum of Art, the Guggenheim, the Whitney, and other museums around the world. She is considered one of the East End's great painters, which is quite an honor since they include Larry Rivers, Fairfield Porter, Jackson Pollock, Willem de Kooning, and others.

I met Audrey Flack in the summer of 1981 when she came to my house in East Hampton uninvited. At the time, I was hosting covered-dish jam sessions in our living room on occasional Saturday nights. I put classified ads in the paper inviting musicians to come. These jam sessions would

AUDREY FLACK
(Courtesy of Lou Meisel Gallery)

usually last three hours and would often consist of a half
dozen musicians, a half dozen significant others, a few friends
and neighbors, and a half dozen children and dogs running
around. We'd play Oh Susannah!, Wabash Cannonball and San
Francisco Bay Blues, laugh, talk, and eat the strange combina-
tions of random covered-dish food people would bring; and
we'd drink and argue and watch the sun set over the harbor
across the way. I remember these nights with great fondness.

Occasionally strangers would arrive at our front door
saying a friend of a friend had told them it would be fine
to just show up, which it was.

Audrey was one of those. She came—a small, intense and
attractive woman with a close cropped head of black hair, a

banjo, a covered dish containing a casserole and her husband Robert Marcus.

At first when she joined in with the song "San Francisco Bay Blues," she sang very loudly. She loved to sing. It was also shrill, which was fine, but when it was shrill and loud she tended to take over the song, drowning out the regulars. I told her about it, and she was more careful after that. By the end of the night we were asking her to come again next week.

After that, our families became friends. We occasionally went out to dinner with them, or we went to their house, or they came to ours. Bob Marcus was quiet and retiring and thoughtful, a perfect counterpoint to Audrey. He seemed amazed at how successful she had become. Often, when we were at their house on Cottage Lane in the Georgica section of East Hampton Village with other friends she'd invited, she'd ask one or another of the guests to perform. It might be reading a story they wrote. It might be a performance on a piano. I came to see what Bob and Audrey were doing as a kind of literary salon. I very much looked forward to attending. Sometimes, we'd ask her to lead us out to her studio to explain what she was most recently working on and what it was all about. That was a real treat.

But then, beginning about 1988, more and more, her work consisted of statues of women—some life size, some smaller, but all in some strong, fabulous, proud kind of inner female beauty that seemed very special to Audrey.

In 1993, Audrey entered a competition to build a statue of a fifty-five-foot-tall woman on the rise of a hill at Hunter's Point, Queens. It would stand right on the shore facing the

East River in New York City, a gift to the city from the Government of Portugal, paid for with $2 million, to celebrate the princess who grew up to be the Queen after which the Borough of Queens was named. She was Princess Catherine of Braganza, who later married King James II of England, thus becoming the English queen.

Audrey was ecstatic when she won this competition. We were all ecstatic with her and for her. The State of Liberty, a gift from France, would face the harbor on one side. Audrey's statue of the Princess from Portugal would be on the other.

One day, in her studio, we saw the first small model of what would become this statue. It was three feet high.

Here stood the Portuguese Princess Catherine of Braganza, dressed in a flowing gown, with bits of bronze, jewels, and gold leaf around her neck and in her hair to accentuate her great beauty. The wind appears to blow her long hair behind her. She holds a magnificent glass blue gazing ball in her outstretched hands—the new world—that welcomes those arriving at New York Harbor aboard their ships.

And Audrey had taken liberties with the Princess's appearance.

"There are oil paintings made of this Princess," Audrey told us. "We have a good idea of what she looked like. But I decided to design her in a more multi-racial way. She is politically correct, proud, an everywoman. She has a broad nose, full lips, and long curls that could be dreadlocks. She is the symbol of proud young immigrants who came to America."

"Did the Government of Portugal object to this?" I asked.

"Not at all. I think it is what won me the competition."

Years went by. Audrey built a six-foot statue in her studio in East Hampton. She worked on the twelve-foot one there. And then we didn't see her for a long time. She was, she told us by phone, up in Beacon, working on the full size fifty-five-foot woman, which would be cast in bronze. Soon, it would be done.

But then, in the autumn of 2005, the news media began reporting problems arising from the imminent arrival of the Princess. The statue had been approved by Queens Borough President Claire Shulman. Now people were speaking out against it.

"This statue's hands are bloody with the murder of millions of Africans," a woman named Betty Dopson, the head of the Committee to Stop the Statue, told the press. "Do we really need a statue of a slave mistress? To erect this monstrosity shows disrespect to every African-American whose ancestors were raped and shackled and shipped off."

Suddenly, news came to the fore about American Presidents who owned slaves. Thomas Jefferson owned slaves. So did George Washington. In New Orleans, the George Washington High School said it would change its name. It was confirmed, through the newly discovered advance in medical testing, that the claims of people who said they were the descendants of Thomas Jefferson and his slave girl lover were correct.

Borough President Shulman said she had no idea Princess Catherine was a slave mistress. To confirm it, she contacted Dr. Frank Melton, a historian, a writer, and an expert on Princess Catherine of Braganza and professor of History at the University of North Carolina. He said it was true that in the seventeenth century many Portuguese traders were involved in bringing slaves to the New World, but there was no evidence at all that the Princess had anything to do with it. In fact, he said, her will actually left a sum for the "Redemption of slaves as is customary to do by the religion of the Holy Trinity."

Borough President Shulman continued to defend her decision to allow the project to go through. She referred to the friendship she had with the Mayor of Lisbon and how she had been his guest in Portugal at the time of the announcement of the competition in 1989.

"The project will proceed toward its unveiling in the spring of this year," she said in the summer of 2005.

But that was not the end of it.

"American ideals are not based on statues of a monarch," said Thomas Paino, an architect and another officer in Dopson's group. "Consider the ironies. This statue will overlook a Revolutionary War battleground."

He was referring to the Battle of Brooklyn where slave-owner George Washington defended our right to independence, but, on that day, lost and retreated to New Jersey.

The battle over the statue swayed this way and that. Borough President Shulman reminded everybody that the project had been endorsed by Jimmy Carter, Senator Alfonse D'Amato, Mario Cuomo, Governor George Pataki, Governor Christine Todd Whitman, Donald Trump, Mayor Guiliani, and former Mayor David Dinkins. All had joined the honorary committee to raise funds here in America for the statue.

The Rev. Charles Norris, executive secretary of the Southeast Queens Clergy for Community Awareness, said that the way the statue faced—it was to face the United Nations across the East River—all anybody in Queens would see was the Princess's back.

"Claire Shulman would not accept a statue of Eva Braun or anyone else associated with the Third Reich," Ms. Dopson waded in again. "Well, to us, Catherine would be a black swastika. How can she expect us to accept that?"

As for me, I expressed my opinions in the paper.

"Are we to take down every statue, every icon that exists in America about every person who made an important contribution but who has a mark against them somewhere? Shall we put a gag in the mouth of any person who tries to say what borough Claire Shulman is President of? What will be left?" I asked. I would defend any present or former member of our jam session to the death.

On December 11, 2005, Ms. Shulman called a meeting of all those in favor of or opposed to the statue. She would re-evaluate her position. In Beacon, New York, at the foundry where they were just about to pour the bronze into the mold to begin the final phase of construction, work stopped.

The meeting was held and it was a disaster. It became a shouting match. And when Dr. Melton explained again that there was no evidence that Catherine either owned slaves or profited from them, those opposed to the project got up from their chairs and stormed out of the room.

And with that, Ms. Shulman changed her mind.

"I had no idea the depth of these people's feelings," she said.

She signed an order withdrawing her approval of the Hunter's Point site, which is publicly owned. She signed a further order that the statue was not to be placed on any publicly owned land in the Borough, effectively killing the project.

"I can't tell you how sorry I am about all of this," she told a reporter for the *New York Times.*

All of this time, those of us who knew Audrey expressed hope that it would indeed go ahead. She was understandably very angry. It was hard to talk to her about it, and most of us did not.

"I gave six years of my life to this project," she told the press. "I designed this statue with healing and positive values. I cannot believe this is all going to wind up in some barn in upstate New York." But it did.

It did not deter her, however. During the years she was building the Princess, she created statues that today stand in many other cities around the world. There are statues, almost all of variations on these magnificent women, in public places in Berlin, Germany; Knoxville, Tennessee; Gainesville, Florida; Rock Hill, South Carolina; Roanoke, Virginia; Tampa, Florida; and Nashville, Tennessee. She continues to do this work to this day.

Most recently, she and a group of musician friends formed a folk music band called "The History of Art String Band" which performed at the John Drew Theatre in East Hampton.

As for the Princess, she lay in pieces at the foundry for many years, but now, I've been told, has finally been melted down.

Houses on Stilts

~~~~~~

In the late 1960s, because of severe erosion, the Army Corp of Engineers began a vast project to armor the entire Dune Road barrier beach in the Hamptons with jetties. Each jetty would stick out from the dunes at the back of the beach and into the ocean several hundred feet. They'd be a half a mile apart. Along this stretch, from the west side of the Shinnecock Inlet to the east side of the Moriches Inlet, a total of thirty-two jetties would be constructed. After these sixteen miles were built, the Army Corps of Engineers would consider armoring Fire Island, and from Southampton to Montauk, for another forty-five miles of new jetties. This would be some project.

The bid to build the first part was won by Herman Bishop, a politically connected fellow with a construction company in Westhampton Beach. The project began not at either end, but in the middle. The first of the jetties would be built on Dune Road in Quogue and would march westward to end at the Moriches Inlet. Altogether, that would be twenty-two of the projected forty-two jetties. The federal government

HOUSES ON STILTS
(Courtesy of the author)

would pay the vast majority of the cost, with the rest being paid by the Suffolk County and the Town of Southampton. Officially, it was a Suffolk County project.

The jetty construction began in 1963. For five years, big trucks with huge boulders chained to the flatbeds in the back would make their way out from Maine to Quogue and the beach front.

I am sure many of you know of, and some of you older people even participated in, a nationwide convulsion of protests and demonstrations during the late 1960s and early 1970s—to end the war in Vietnam, to create equal rights for women and blacks, and to allow for a much wider interpretation of

free speech and free love. People also demonstrated to legal-
ize marijuana.

Here on eastern Long Island, many protests were also
held to stop the construction of a radiation-emitting nuclear
power plant at Shoreham. That demonstration was successful.
Construction was halted. The ruins of this $6 billion plant,
completed but never opened, remain today in the woods
between Shoreham and Wading River.

Less known were the demonstrations against Herm Bishop
and his jetties. The taxpayers of Suffolk County, nearly 98
percent of whom live inland, would be paying to protect the
homes of the privileged 2 percent. This was totally unfair.
And so, around March of 1969, after many protests, the
County shut down the project and the workmen left with
fourteen jetties in place between Quogue and the western end
of Westhampton Beach. Eight more, covering the remaining
four miles, would never be built.

The vast majority of the people out here rejoiced when the
project was halted. Even the people in those last four miles
favored abandoning it, because there really was no problem
with all the little homes, about 350 of them, side-by-side,
sitting at the top of the dunes along that stretch. Much beach
separated them from the sea. What could go wrong?

It took another ten years before it became apparent that
just about everything was going wrong. During that period,
from 1971 to 1981, the fourteen jetties in place began to
capture the sand that naturally drifted with the current along
the beaches from east to west, from Montauk to Far Rockaway.
This sand was filling in the spaces between the jetties, just as

it was supposed to. The beaches, where the jetties were, were now more than 200 yards wide. What wonderful beaches! Indeed, they are wonderful today. Those little homes along that stretch have every protection imaginable against erosion.

In Westhampton, however, something awful was happening. The sand, piling up at the jetties, was no longer appearing in the west. A great gouge of beach formed to the west of that last jetty. The small oceanfront houses there were losing their beach. The ocean was now up to the dunes.

Soon this gouge washed up into the dunes, flattened them, and took away the three homes on stilts nearest to that last jetty. And it wasn't stopping there. By the end of that first year, the ten homes next to the first three were washed away.

Those who were losing their homes, and those who could see they were about to lose theirs, complained to everyone they could think of. They complained to the Town of Southampton, to whom they paid their real estate taxes. They complained to the County of Suffolk, who had authorized this project. And they complained to the Army Corps of Engineers and the federal government. Indeed, with the loss of now forty homes, there was soon a tangle of nearly 200 lawsuits from forty individual homeowners that would probably take ten years to resolve and require the services of thousands of lawyers.

I went down to the end of Dune Road during this time to report on what was going on. The end of Dune Road was no longer at Moriches Inlet. It went only to the last jetty. There you faced a barrier and a town police booth with armed officers. You could go no further. But you could see the remains of houses—bathtubs, sofas, chimneys, cesspools, bedframes, bookcases, decks—all lying in the sand along where Dune Road should have been. At this point, the pavement of Dune Road was buckling. The telephone poles going out alongside it were either at 45-degree angles or lying on the ground. There was no longer telephone or electric service beyond the last jetty. The water lines, we were told, were broken. The fire hydrants were dry. And there were no houses for half a mile. Beyond that, some were seen tipping or leaning this way or that. Beyond that, there were homes still standing, but abandoned. You could not see to the Inlet.

This place was a war zone. And like any war zone, there were angry homeowners who often went out to the police booth, desperate to continue on to what had been their homes to scavenge and save what they could. But they were prevented from doing so.

Seared in my memory is the scene of a woman pulling up in her car and getting out with her seven-year-old son to scream and cry at the police officers. They could not console her. And it was no use. The only people who were getting out there were vandals, arriving by boat late at night, unseen by the police, to steal whatever they could find of value. It was a very dangerous business to be out there in the wee hours of the morning.

In 1988, Mayor Andon of Westhampton Beach invited me, along with a dozen other newspapermen and other officials, to go with him by boat to see the wreckage out there. The boat, it turned out, was what they call a Duck, a steel boat with wheels under it. We climbed aboard on the beach within the jetty field, then sat tight as a diesel engine bumped us noisily down the beach and through the surf to the open sea. There, we turned west and chugged along through the water toward the Moriches Inlet.

"You will see where the sea first came up at the last jetty, and how it has now broken through to the bay." The Mayor said, "This is a new inlet. It makes where we are going an island. We are thinking of naming the new inlet Pike's Inlet, after Otis Pike, who served as a county legislator from Riverhead for many years."

Soon we arrived at this abandoned island. There had been 350 homes on it. The easternmost 140 of them had been washed away. Most of the rest, still standing, awaiting their fate, were looted clean. We walked around. There had been one nightclub on this stretch of Dune Road. The local residents in years gone by had tried to get rid of it—it kept them up at night. But they had failed. Morgan's White Cap had soldiered on for more than two generations.

Now, however, Morgan's White Cap looked like something out of a horror movie. Abandoned, it had also been overrun by drifting sand. Only its damaged roof was visible, with the sign *Morgan's*, crooked, on the eaves. Morgan's, one of my former advertisers, was being buried in the sand, gone forever.

At this point, the 140 oceanfront lots, each about a quarter of an acre, were under the ocean. For $5,000 you could own one. A year after our boat trip, I was offered one for that amount. I declined. "Not a better buy than the Brooklyn Bridge," is what I replied when offered.

But then a meeting was held at the home of Gary Vegliante, a man who owned several restaurants in western Long Island but also owned a summer home in this affected area.

His home did not face the ocean, however. It was on the bay. And on the bay it was intact, just a hundred yards into the disaster from that last jetty, the last house on the mainland remaining standing. From that house, Vegliante could look out onto the bay to the south and to the west where Pike's Inlet now abutted his property.

At this meeting, which several lawyers attended, an innovative way to deal with this mess was agreed upon. They would gather up the names and addresses of all 350 homeowners within this disaster, nearly half of whom had property underwater, and send them letters asking if they would spend a few thousand dollars to form an incorporated village.

An incorporated village could have its own Village Hall (Vegliante's home). It could have its own police force, its own highway department (there was no highway), and its own clerk and court system. The application went out. Within six months, the Village of West Hampton Dunes was born.

The first thing the village did was to consolidate all the individual lawsuits against the town, county, and country. Then they pointed out to the county that their lawyers had found, deep in county records, a law requiring that the county take over any property that defaults on its taxes. This mess would then be the direct responsibility of the county, from the default forward. They'd even be responsible for the Village's legal bills! The third thing that the new village did was write to the federal government on Village stationary. The letter was addressed to the President of the United States.

"Help," it said. "Our community has suffered a terrible disaster."

Learning that a village had been destroyed by the ocean, the feds rushed to the aid of West Hampton Dunes. As for the county, it turned around and offered all assistance to get this place rebuilt.

In the end, the Army Corps of Engineers had each of the last three jetties shortened, so the sand long caught up in the tines of the jetty field could begin to roll in. The Army Corps of Engineers then brought in a huge wall of corrugated steel that they pounded thirty feet into the seabed parallel to the shoreline. It also rose up thirty feet above sea level. It ran the whole quarter-mile across Pike's Inlet, plugging it up forever. Then tons and tons of sand were brought in, using the steel wall as a backbone, and the new island was now linked to the mainland. Soon after, the utilities and road were restored and the place was back in business.

Today, the police booth is gone, replaced with a grand sign reading *You Are Entering the Village of West Hampton Dunes.* There is no police blockade. You drive down the new Dune Road, passing beautiful two- and three-story wood-shingled houses, all on the same little quarter-acre lots where the one story bungalows on stilts had sat before. They sit thirty feet up on the underground steel spine, very close to one another. They front on an artificial beach. The parcels sell for a million and more.

All of these people today are now living securely in their homes, and there is not a trace of the horrific convulsion that shook this part of the Hamptons all those years ago.

May this never happen again.

Three Mothers

~~~~~~

Today, if you drive about 300 yards down North Main Street in East Hampton, you will come to the most celebrated and chic restaurant in the Hamptons, Nick & Toni's. All the rich and famous eat here at some time or another in the summertime, and to score a table by the front door is to be at the very top of the pecking order—for it is here that you not only get to be seen by those coming in, but you get to *see* who is coming in. It could be Steven Spielberg or Sarah Jessica Parker or Martha Stewart. Everybody eats at Nick & Toni's.

When I go there and come up to the front door, however, I think of Ma Bergman. You'd walk in. She'd be there in her white apron smeared with some spaghetti sauce, and she'd greet you and your family with this wonderful smile. The place would be full of diners, however, all local people. And so she'd turn and, raising her voice a bit so her ten-year-old daughter sitting at one of the tables could hear, and shout "Loretta, could you finish your homework upstairs. We could use that table." And Loretta would push together all her papers and stuff them in her knapsack, wave, and head off.

It was not Nick & Toni's then. It was Ma Bergman's, the restaurant before Nick & Toni's bought that establishment and remodeled it into something reminiscent of a place in Milan or Florence. Ma Bergman's, in business from about 1955 to 1980, was a landmark favorite, not of the summer people, there were very few summer people, but of many local families in town. After that last year, Ma Bergman, together with her maître d' husband, closed down the place and retired. And Nick & Toni's moved in.

There were, in those days, three different establishments in East Hampton that I knew had very motherly women running them. A fourth was in Southampton, at Balzarini's Restaurant on Hampton Road. When I'd walk around town into any one of these four places selling advertising, it was the women to whom I sold. All of them were about fifty-five, all were a bit overweight, all had raised families, and all of them were warm and friendly and wanting to know all about me and my family and friends whenever I walked in the door for any purpose whatsoever. Honestly, I felt like I was the only one they treated that way. But the truth was that they treated everyone who came in that special.

They don't make them like that anymore, in the Hamptons, anyway.

Perhaps the most widely known of any of these women was Mary Damark, who ran Damark's Deli on Three Mile Harbor Road. I guarantee that even today, all these years later, there will be people reading this who will, at the very mention of her name, break out in a warm smile. *Oh yes*, they will think.

I still remember the first day I met Mary Damark. It was 1975 and I had just bought a small house on a hill up the street. I walked into the deli, with the little sleigh bell over the door going ding-a-ling, and she just looked up from where she was behind the counter. I'd come in there to buy some milk.

"I've been waiting for you," were the first words that she said. "What took you so long?"

"What are you talking about?" I asked.

"People are talking about your moving in here. So you bought the Miller house up the street?"

"Yes."

"And you publish *Dan's Papers*? Everyone likes you, you know, and everybody wishes you well. But what I want to know is—when are you getting married? A nice handsome man like you."

"I just got divorced," I told her. I was thirty-five years old.

"You'll have no trouble," she said.

And that's how I met Mary Damark. The deli is still there. And though the official name is Damark's Deli and it is owned by a Hispanic family, everybody *still* says, "I have to go down to Mary's to pick up some tall kitchen trash bags" whenever they are out of tall kitchen trash bags— whether they had ever met Mary or not. And fifty years from now . . . well, you get the picture.

The second woman I would like to salute was an older Italian woman named Alicia Guglielmi. In 1969, she bought the old Amagansett Inn, a gin mill on Main Street in that town, and converted it into a spaghetti restaurant with checkered tablecloths, Chianti bottles, and candles. She called it Guglielmi's. Her teenage son worked there. And, just like Mary or Ma Bergman, when you walked in, she doted on you. That included a hug and a grasping of an arm to lead you to a seat.

Mrs. Guglielmi's time as a doting mother, busybody, and merchant was much shorter than either Ma Bergman's or Mary Damark's, but I remember her nevertheless. Her restaurant lasted only seven years. I learned that at the end she had become ill with emphysema and could not run it anymore. I called her and spoke to her in the hospital. I really loved her. And I knew she liked hearing from me.

Mrs. Guglielmi was a lot different than either of the other two, however, in the sense that she was not only interested in you, but she was also interested in telling you about her. It was not so easy being her.

She had been married to O. Louis Guglielmi, the well-known surrealist painter, and for twenty years they had lived in a house down at the other end of Main Street, where Louis painted in a converted garage and Alicia raised their son, Kevin, who was now right there in the restaurant at the age of eighteen, working for her.

Louis had died in 1956, and Alicia, who had mourned him and missed him, decided to jump right into something new to keep herself busy. Because people said she could cook great Italian food—and boy, could she—she had bought the old Amagansett Inn and opened her restaurant to all comers.

She spent most of her time out in the dining room, talking to her patrons. She knew enough not to bother them while they were eating, but between the ordering and the arrival of the food (by Kevin), she'd let you know how happy she was that you were there. And she'd return later, asking about more family news as you were sipping coffee. She also told stories.

One September, I learned that she planned to stay open all winter, so she'd need for her ad in my paper to continue. She had not done this the year before. She would be returning to West Third Street in Manhattan, she said, where she still had the apartment, but Kevin, her son, would stay out for the winter running the restaurant.

"I don't see how he'll do this," she said, "but we'll see. I'll come out for weekends sometimes."

The restaurant did not stay open the entire winter. In January, it closed. And in May, when I saw the place being fitted out by her for the summer, I went in to talk to her again. And she explained what happened.

"I came out every weekend," she said. "He's only nineteen. But it was going well. Then I didn't come out until the middle of January. Kevin was fine. He hadn't been back to the city since I left. But he looked happy. And there was business.

"He said, 'Ma, I found this wonderful place. Bay Shore. It's really jumping in the wintertime. You wouldn't believe it.'

"And I said . . ." and she looked at me, this woman who lived a city-country existence in Amagansett and in the City ". . . Kevin, we're closing up. Anybody in my family who thinks Bay Shore is something, well, forget it."

Then there was this woman, Marge, who owned Balzarini's Restaurant in Southampton. She also fit this mold. She was also in her mid-fifties, interested in everybody's business, a bit overweight, somebody who made all her own pasta, somebody who welcomed everybody with open arms.

I recall waiting for her in the kitchen of the restaurant one morning while she made a business call to a wholesaler who was selling her wine or parmesan cheese or pasta or something. I knew to come to see her in the mornings. She'd open at 12 for lunch, then remain open till midnight, serving dinner.

In that kitchen was the most elaborate espresso machine I had ever seen. It occupied much of one wall, and had black and white gauges along its side amidst this beautiful sterling silver steaming pot. It had instructions in Italian on it. I imagined it being brought here by boat.

There were children and dogs running in and out. Her husband sat in a folding chair in there, reading an Italian newspaper. But every once in a while, he would look up and follow her bustling and scurrying around with interest. He did not have much to say to me. I thought, "Maybe he doesn't speak English."

She was a hard bargainer. She wanted to know if I would eat there more often, if perhaps we could trade advertising for food, which was a common thing to do back then. I would decline because I lived half-an-hour away in East Hampton and had little kids, and they'd be whiny and restless if we went out that far to eat.

Once, Marge asked me a question that really took me by surprise.

"You're in the advertising business. I want to change the name of the place. Balzarini's could use a rest."

The first thing that came to my mind was the obvious, which was something you did sitting on a toilet. I never liked that name. But that's not what I replied to her.

"Balzarini's is very respected," I said. "But perhaps there might be a better name."

"Tell me."

"I'd have to think about it."

I did come up with three or four ideas, but she never did change the name. In the end, she explained to me that Balzarini's had been the name of the place since 1923. It seemed to work, after all. But thanks for trying.

Today this is a chic restaurant until 10 p.m., and then an even more chic nightspot called Red Bar. Designers and models pull up in Ferrari's about midnight.

If the food at Balzarini's and also at Guglielmi's was good, I can still, in my mind, taste the spaghetti and meatballs that was served so cheerfully by Ma Bergman all those years ago. It was only one of three things on the menu. I had made the serious mistake, one year, of agreeing to take out the value of her advertising in dining there. I had a wife and three kids by this time—Marge was delighted with my little family, and always told them so when we came in—and it seemed we could eat it off.

The trouble was that the amount of advertising she bought, which was in the neighborhood of $1,100, was almost impossible to eat off. The prices were rock bottom. An entire family of five could eat there for less than $30, including Coke and tip. Divide it up. That's eating there forty times a year.

"Do we have to go to Ma Bergman's *again*?" the oldest, who was about nine, would cry.

"Bring your homework," I'd say.

The spaghetti and meatballs were good. But after all this time, we were just not happy going there. However, we'd dutifully eat there about twice a week, chewing well and swallowing everything down with lots of tomato sauce and parmesan cheese, trying to work off all that advertising.

"Hello, little family," she'd shout happily as we'd come in the front door. "Maya, that is such a pretty dress."

Maya was the eleven-year-old.

Today, Nick & Toni's only takes reservations after 11 a.m., and then probably for a week ahead. And no, there are no guarantees about a table by the door.

When you arrive, the manager, a tall New Zealand woman of about thirty-five, very much in charge, scans the room, noting that Jon Stewart might be over here and Renee Zellweger over there, and she'll say, "Let me see what we have in the back."

Dick Brass

~~~~~~

In 1974, *Dan's Papers* was still being published only in the summertime. It had expanded quite a bit, however. We were, by that time, publishing summer editions not only in the Hamptons and Montauk but also on Block Island. We had hired a woman on Block Island who would write up the articles that should go in that paper, and then, on a Tuesday, she'd appear in our office in Bridgehampton with a stack of the stories, written on a typewriter, held together with paper clips and inside a manila envelope. She'd work with our editors to get all the articles edited and re-typed and, with rubber cement, pasted up on boards to be gotten ready to go to the printer up the island.

The place reeked of rubber cement. We'd heard that kids could get high sniffing rubber cement. But none of us ever talked about that. We rather liked the smell. And nobody seemed high. Anyway, this was the only way you could do it. If you pasted something down with rubber cement, then later decided to move that story to another page, you could just peel it up and move it.

I first met Dick Brass in 1974 when he came into my office looking for a job. It was April of that year. The buds had begun to appear on the trees and you could just feel the season changing. I'd need a much bigger staff within a month. My secretary brought Dick up to my office and introduced him to me. He was twenty-three, a little on the heavy side, and rather loud and affably boisterous. He reached across my desk and shook hands with me vigorously, then arranged himself in the chair across from mine.

"Where did you go to school?" I asked him.

"Cornell," he said. "I was the editor of the daily paper there."

We talked a bit about what sorts of things he liked to write, how much he knew about the East End, which was not much, and how he worked with others. My judgment of him was that he was not only full of himself, but he was quite charming.

"I've got openings for three Associate Editors that I need here by May 10. It's going to get very busy. You're welcome to be one of them. None of it pays very much, and it would be only for the summer."

"I could do that," he said. "I'd *like* to do that."

Dick Brass fit right in. He worked with the other two editors writing stories, editing them down, typing articles and doing headlines, helping with paste-up, answering the phones, and attending the weekly editorial meeting. Brass had many suggestions for things we should cover. He went to art gallery openings, lectures, news briefings, events. He was good at what he did. His approach was filled with curiosity, asking questions and looking for answers. He had been a good choice.

This was about the time that technology was beginning to be a very big deal on Long Island. We had landed on the moon only five years before and a Long Island firm, Grumman, had produced the moon lander. The Brookhaven Lab was banging atoms together and coming up with new theoretical approaches. As for computers, well, they were refrigerator-sized. Some companies had them and they were the coming thing though ten years away. And people were now also talking about something called an Internet. It was some sort of communications thing that traveled through the air like radio waves, but only the government and the military were making big use of it. A lot of work was being done on it at universities.

One day, we got into a discussion at the editorial meeting about a new advance in this Internet thing. There was now a registry where private individuals could register a business name. When you registered the name, you owned the name on the Internet. You could use it to go into business.

"I wonder if any of this work is being done on Long Island," one of the editors said, suggesting it as a story.

"Oh, this is a long way off," I said. "And who owns a computer? They cost a fortune."

Apparently, however, this piqued the interest of Dick Brass, who was at the meeting. He was not interested in writing about it, it turned out. He was interested in doing something about it.

"Dick is registering names," one of the other editors told me later. He seemed worried.

"I bought 'dictionary,'" Dick said. "And I bought 'thesaurus.' You buy them with the term 'com' after them—Thesaurus.

com. You should buy some, too. They're cheap. You can get them for $45 each. When you own one, nobody else can use it. It's yours."

"Are you going to go into business as dictionary.com," I asked.

"No. I'm just going to hold onto it. People are going to want that name. The price is going to go up."

Dick continued on his buying spree. He bought 'Spell.' He bought 'encyclopedia.' He bought 'dictionary.' I don't know what else he bought. And I don't know where he got the money. He was a college kid working for me at the time for about $11 an hour.

"You really should buy some, too," he repeated to me not long thereafter. "There's plenty of names to go around."

But there was, I thought, something wrong with doing this. If you weren't going to use the name, then you were, like, holding it hostage. I told Dick this.

"It's up to you," he said. "It's not about hostages. It's about investments."

Dick's tenure at the newspaper ended on Labor Day, and he left to go to work in New York City as a reporter for the *Daily News*. But considering what went down during the following years, I began to realize that Dick Brass was something of a genius. Indeed, when people would ask me who among the people I employed I thought was the most interesting, I would answer Dick Brass. I often thought he must have become a millionaire by the time he was thirty. But I never knew because I no longer was in touch with him.

About ten years later, however, I got a call from him. He was married and staying with his wife at the Grandview Manor in Montauk for the weekend and would I like to come out to see him? I said sure, and I went.

Dick Brass by this time was working on founding some sort of wireless telephone company. There were no wireless phone companies at this time. His wife, a physician, was lovely and seemed a good match for him. She was as much interested in innovation as he was. I thought about his naming spree of the years before, but I didn't bring it up. I presumed he'd made a bundle. If he'd bring it up, fine. He didn't bring it up.

About ten years after that, however, I heard from him again by telephone. He was thinking of me and the paper, and wanted to know how we were doing. He was now living in the Pacific Northwest. He was a vice president at Microsoft. He was leading a research team. "Anytime you want to come out here, stay with us," he told me.

I told him I thought that was a wonderful idea, and indeed I did think that was wonderful. His boss, Bill Gates, by this time was living in a giant mansion high on a hill and had accumulated about $10 billion. I thought Dick and his wife must have a really nice place, too. But I never got around to going.

Over the next few years, it was with great pleasure that I saw Dick Brass in the news. He had developed the world's first online spell checker. He invented the first online thesaurus. He was demonstrating the new tablet he was working on. It would revolutionize the computer industry, he said. At one point, I saw him on TV at a conference, holding up a working model of the Microsoft tablet. He said, "The last print edition of the *New York Times* will be in 2018."

But the tablet never came out. Or else, if it did, it fizzled. What I thought was, "This is not like Dick Brass."

Then, in the fall of 2009, the Apple iPad came out to rave reviews. It was revolutionizing the computer industry. Tens of millions of them were being sold. And suddenly, on February 4, 2010, there was an op-ed piece in the *New York Times* by Dick Brass.

Dick Brass had been a Vice President at Microsoft from 1997 to 2004. His Microsoft tablet was supposed to have come out eight years before Apple's. But it had not. And he wanted everyone to know the reason why.

"MICROSOFT'S CREATIVE DESTRUCTION" was the title of his op-ed piece.

"Why (is it that) Microsoft, America's most famous and prosperous technology company, no longer brings us the future?" he asks.

He makes his case.

"It employs thousands of the smartest, most capable engineers in the world. More than any other firm, it made using computers both ubiquitous and affordable."

But then it stopped being creative, he reports. He writes of its stumbles. They included web browsers, high-end laptops, smart phones, personal music players and lots of other things. Why?

"As the fellow who tried (and largely failed) to make tablet PCs and e-books happen at Microsoft a decade ago, I could say this is because the company placed too much faith in people like me. But the decline is so broad and so striking that it would be presumptuous of me to take responsibility for it."

Brass talks about creative people with new ideas unable to get them past established executives running other divisions in Microsoft. Plans for a higher pixel computer screen got scuttled—it hurt the eyes, one executive reported. Plans for integrating the tablet with the rest of the offerings got scuttled—it won't work said the executive in charge of the Microsoft Office line, refusing to allow its use.

This letter in the *Times* created quite a stir in the computer industry when it came out.

Today, creatively, Microsoft is on the move again, at least a little. I like to think Dick Brass, who early on got his chops at Dan's Papers, had something to do with it.

Nick Vasilli

~~~~~~

Late in the summer of 1975, I got a phone call from someone who told me there was a commune in the Hamptons and perhaps I ought to go visit it and write an article about it.

I was certainly intrigued by this. This was in the middle of a time when America was going through dramatic change. People were protesting against the war in Vietnam, against secrecy in government, against the persecution of blacks, against censorship, against the subjugation of women, against the military-industrial complex and anybody over the age of thirty. It was a time of hippies, drugs, and freedom. A time for going to India and sitting with gurus.

Personally, before even visiting this commune, I felt it calling my name. My personal life had become a mess. After seven years of marriage, my young wife had begun to call me a dinosaur and, three months before this phone call, told me she wanted a divorce. Maybe more than just a story would happen when I visited this place.

NICK VASILLI
(Courtesy of Eric Cohen)

Journey, as this commune was called, was in East Quogue, up a long gravel road through some woods to a huge old farmhouse in a clearing. This was a seven-bedroom farmhouse. Nearby on the property there was a cabin where more people from the commune lived. And in other locations in East

Quogue, I soon learned, there were other houses where still other people from Journey lived, one on Lewis Road, another on the north side of the Montauk Highway. There was also a crafts store in downtown East Quogue. There was a Journey School. The commune was home-schooling their offspring, and people from the area could also school their children there. They offered from pre-K to third grade.

I drove up there on September 15. Outside, on a lawn between two vegetable gardens and alongside a pen filled with chickens and ducks, there was a man in his mid-twenties building a doll house. He had saw horses, piles of lumber, and a power saw. He waved, I waved back and then went over to talk to him. I told him I was from *Dan's Papers* and I had been invited to come over at this time to write a story about the place.

"I'll take you to Nick," he said. And so that's how, in the farmhouse, I met Nick Vasilli, the leader of the commune.

Nick greeted me with a smile. He was a small, Greek man about five years older than me and maybe ten years older than anybody else I was to see around that place. He had a dark, pencil-thin moustache and a full head of black hair. He had piercing black eyes, and an air of authority about him. But he was friendly enough.

He showed me around. There was a living room full of children running around; there were people everywhere. They had been there two years, he said. They were a group of thirty people who four years earlier had decided they wanted to live together, combine their resources, and spend the rest of their lives together. After a year in some loft spaces in Manhattan, they decided to find a place somewhere out in the country.

"Do you know Bill Swan?" he asked.

"I don't," I said.

"He owns a lot of land out here in the woods. Also farmland and farm houses. He inherited it from his parents. Anyway, he approached us in New York City about renting out here. So here we are."

He looked me up and down.

"Tell me about you," he said.

Two months later, in mid-November, I moved in. I was introduced at dinner one night. Everybody gave me a round of applause.

I have such wonderful memories of Journey. It was not a commune in the free love sense, which I suppose I had secretly hoped it was. It was more like a community or an extended family, although no one was a relative of anybody else. This commune was based on friendship, love, loyalty, hard work, family and friends, and an ethical code that might be best described as doing in any particular situation what you should for the higher good. There were married men and women with their children, small children in this case, with more on the way during my time there. And there were single people living there. I was one of them. What a place this was.

Here was a typical day at Journey. We'd wake up, eat breakfast with whoever was in the house we were in—I lived in a house on the Montauk Highway—then either head off to work in the community, at a store or ice cream parlor for some, or go to the main farmhouse to see what needed to be done there. At the main house, after breakfast, there was often a sing-a-long alongside the piano. After that, we picked beans, planted tomato seeds, drove a tractor, whatever. We had one horse, Rusty. In mid-morning, I would drive my van—I had a big red van with the words *Dan's Papers* on the side—to my office in Bridgehampton. The paper did not publish in the wintertime then. And so I'd go to the office maybe once a week for a while. When we got through that winter, though (more about that later), I went more often. Soon I was back to working in the office full time, but in the evening I'd drive back home to the commune.

It was on one of those evenings that Bobbie went into labor. Bobbie was the wife of Eric, who I had first seen making the doll house on the lawn, and they were having their first child. Both Bobbie's and Eric's parents were sometime visitors at the commune, as were the parents and grandparents of many of the people there, and Eric's grandfather had given Bobbie and Eric an old car so they would have transportation to the hospital when the time came. But one of the single people, a woman named Kay, had driven it into a tree one night.

"Tonight's the night," Eric told me. "Can I ask a favor?"

We all knew about Kay's accident, which had totaled Eric's car, so I already knew what they wanted. "Throw a mattress in the back," I said. "You can drive her to the hospital."

And so, at 3 a.m., off they went, all the way to a hospital in Manhattan where Bobbie's doctor had her practice. A week later, a friend of mine wanted to know if I was expanding the paper to New York City. He'd seen the big red van in there. I had to tell him no. And thus, Lauren was born.

When Evelyn, Dennis's wife, went into labor, it was a whole other story. She would be having her child right in one of the bedrooms. There was a midwife who came. More than two dozen people, including me, sat worriedly in the living room, occasionally asking to help. We brought in wet cloths and pitchers of water. And then we heard the baby cry.

The commune had a mechanism to work out problems between people, or just problems in general. I sure had a problem. Divorce. We had these "sessions" in the evenings. Six or seven people would sit in a circle. And one after another each person would talk about his or her problem from the center of the circle while others would offer support. Nick led many of these sessions.

"Get in there," someone urged me. I got in the middle. I still vividly remember this. Someone handed me a tennis racket. Others stacked up some pillows.

"Now get that anger out," someone said. "Beat the hell out of those pillows."

I whacked and I whacked. "I HATE you," I said to the imaginary wife who'd just left. "I am FURIOUS."

"You're not furious," Nick said. "Keep it simple. Hate. Hate." And so I did and the hate came up and the pillows died and I cried it all away.

We were following the tenets put forward by Nick, who was taking everybody on this journey. He had learned them over the years, working at a drug rehab named Daytop in the city and another called Encounter.

Journey's school for the commune had expanded to the community. Little kids from town were now going there. In the summertime, we had a farm stand on the highway. We sold produce from our farms to wholesalers.

Birthdays were a very big deal. With all the people there, we had a birthday with presents, cake, and singing about once a week. One day Bob Blumenkrantz married his longtime girlfriend, Susan Silverman, in the pastureland where Rusty lived. They had brought in a rabbi. About a hundred people attended, standing around. Afterwards, we carried Bob and then Sue high up on a chair around and then had a big feast and barbecue with rides on Rusty for the kids.

One day, an old man with a backpack arrived at Journey. His clothes were filthy grey, he had long white hair and a big white beard. He also carried a walking stick. I happened to be in the living room, playing with the little kids, when he arrived. Everybody rushed over to him, to greet him as a long-lost friend.

"Spence. It's you."

"How are you, old man?"

"How long are you staying?"

"Oh, I don't know," he said.

He sat down on the couch. He was introduced to all the kids, and he made comments on how much they had grown, and he was introduced to me.

He spoke slowly and softly, as old men do. He did not have all his teeth. But he explained to me that he had been there at the founding of Journey and that he had passed on his beliefs, which he said came from an Indian teacher named Sree Sree Thakur, to Nick.

"Where do you live?" I asked.

"I just live everywhere," he said. "I get up in the morning and wherever I am, I head out. I trust that fate will take care of things. I never know where I will end up at the end of the day."

He also told me he didn't believe in possessions. He picked up things along the way, he said, but at the end of every day, he'd give it all away or would try to. He never kept money.

"There's nothing in my backpack," he said, his eyes twinkling and smiling at me as he opened it to show me. "I just keep a toothbrush," he said, patting a pocket.

He spent the night, and the next day he was gone. He did not return, at least not during my time there.

As it happened, the fall and winter of 1975–76, in spite of all efforts by Journey, were among their very hardest. Nick explained it to us at dinner one night.

"We didn't plan our harvest right," he told us. "Next year will be better. But now all we have is squash. We can get a few other things, too, I think. But squash is what we will be eating this winter. We'll find imaginative ways to prepare it. And we should be thankful that at least we have that."

I thought that he couldn't be serious about this, but he was. The women—I almost called them the womenfolk—slaved away in the kitchen all winter, slicing and dicing, broiling and frying, stewing and boiling. We ate squash every way imaginable. Occasionally there would be a treat of something else—chicken, sometimes—but for the most part that is all there was. I tried to imagine myself being thankful for the squash. It was hard.

Finally, the spring of 1976 came. And indeed Nick did have a better plan. We planted early, worked the fields, and soon were distributing cucumbers, peppers, green beans, wax beans, and all other manner of vegetables to the wholesalers nearby. We re-opened the farm stand. I designed, and painted, a new sign.

But Nick's biggest project was a very special kind of organic vine-ripened tomato. He had it planted, nearly a dozen acres of it, on one whole side of the property near to the house. "People will come from miles around for these tomatoes," he said. "We will become well known for this crop. This is our ticket to the future."

It was during June, when things were really blooming, that I moved out of Journey. I had been offered the use of a houseboat for the summer in Three Mile Harbor in East Hampton. It was a former touring yacht from the 1930s, fifty-four-feet long, all trashed and abandoned but still floating in a marina there. I imagined myself alone on that yacht and I loved the idea. I had had enough of people for a while. I had had enough of just helping out and being told what to do. I wanted to be back on my own, fully divorced, with my kids, who I knew would just love this yacht.

But I did not forget everybody at Journey, twenty miles away in East Quogue. All that summer, I went there once or twice a week to help out or just to have dinner with them all. The commune had opened a restaurant on Montauk Highway in Quiogue that summer. It had for a long time been a barbecue and ribs place called Sherman's. But Sherman had gotten old and wanted to retire. Journey took it over and made it into a really excellent Greek restaurant, in honor of Nick's heritage. His family had come from the island of Paros. His father had owned a restaurant there. I remember one night there, standing with Eric, who was one of the main chefs of this restaurant, looking out from the kitchen at 150 people eating in the big dining room. Eric turned to me. "I cooked for all these people," he said, smiling happily.

But the big thing that summer were the tomatoes. The other vegetables had been harvested and sold, but the tomatoes still remained on the vine. Nick wanted to let them stay there until they were at their very ripest and juiciest.

And then the worst thing happened. On the morning of August 30, a hot rainstorm came up, bearing what appeared to be salt water. It was the advance signal of a huge hurricane, Hurricane Belle, which arrived the very next day. We didn't know at the time that this was the advance storm to the hurricane—weather forecasting was not great back then—but it's arrival was enough to get Nick off his seat at the breakfast table and out there in the garden, where he proceeded, in the driving rain, to shake his fist and curse at God for this salty deluge which, in one stroke, was ruining his entire crop of tomatoes.

Right then and there, he called everyone in the commune to come on out there and help him gather up as much as they could, and we did. But we hadn't been able to bag more than a few bushels of them before it was apparent that we were now in a deluge, that it was all over and the rest of the tomatoes would simply rot on the vine from it. I never saw Nick Vasilli in such a state, not before nor since.

On November 16, 1978, two years later, 918 people in a commune known as the People's Agricultural Project in Jonestown, Guyana lined up and said goodbye to one another after their leader laced gallons of Kool-Aid with poison and told everyone they had to drink it. I was still dropping by Journey when I was in the area at that time, but it seemed to me that when that terrible tragedy was shown on the TV, a certain amount of energy went out of Journey. And soon thereafter, everyone went their separate ways.

But, as you can imagine, they have stayed in touch with one another for almost forever.

Friendships like these are not easily unmade.

In the fall of 1977, when I bought a former fishing cabin on Three Mile Harbor Road, overlooking that body of water, I posted a wooden sign out on the street facing the sunset. It had on it, in bright red with yellow rays, a sunrise. There was a word under it. *Naoussa*. Naoussa is the capital of Paros.

And even more wonderful. When my son Adam, who was one year old when we were at Journey, got to be a junior at East Hampton High School, he invited his sweetheart, Lauren, who had been born after being whisked off to Roosevelt Hospital in a red *Dan's Papers* van, to his junior prom.

Tina Fredericks

~~~~~~

In the early 1980s, when the price of real estate began to go through the roof, the kind of people who were in the real estate business changed. Earlier, you could be just anybody. Now you had to have flair and style and be part of the Old-Boy network of well-bred socialites. And it wouldn't hurt if you were just a little bit outrageous.

The broker who set the bar for that and for all future brokers of that era was a woman named Tina Fredericks. She was, and still is, a stunningly beautiful woman with elegance, good manners, and a touch of some sort of foreign accent, possibly European.

A classic story about Tina involved some broken glass. A couple listed their house for sale with her. They did not come out that weekend, and when they came out the following weekend they found that a pane of glass in the kitchen door had been broken so a person could reach in, turn the knob, and let themselves in. There was a note.

"A client wanted to see your house," Tina wrote, "but it was locked and the key was not where you said it would be. Have the glazier send me the bill."

TINA FREDERICKS
(Courtesy of Stacy Fredericks)

A month later, the client bought the house.

It seemed to me that Tina Fredericks would be particularly hard to get to know personally, but somehow, as it happened, we became friends. One day, early on in this friendship she invited me to Bobby Van's for lunch. As she had just brokered the sale of the largest private residence in the Hamptons—the

60 acre Ossorio estate on Georgica Pond—I considered it a celebration lunch, and so I decided I would celebrate by letting her pick up the check. I think the conversation at this lunch might be a good way for me to introduce you to her.

We were taken to a table, and after getting settled, Tina told me she had recently been going to doctors.

"Nobody seems to be able to find out what's wrong with me," she said.

"You have something wrong with you?"

"You didn't hear about my accident? I was driving back from Noyac from my exercise class about nine at night and I woke up to find myself on Route 114, not on the asphalt but driving alongside it on the grass. I turned the wheel to get back onto the road and the next thing I am going across the road into the woods where there are all these trees whizzing by. Then there was a lot of noise and then the car turned upside down."

"This was in your Range Rover?"

"This *was* my Range Rover. It was totaled. The light on the ceiling was down by my feet, the telephone was dangling upside down, the windshield had kind of pinned me to the seat, and the radio was playing."

"Were you hurt?"

"No. What I remember most was the Beethoven. It was so wonderful on the radio. The headlights were on and there were all these trees everywhere in these wonderful colors and the music was really so majestic and, it seemed to me, appropriate. But then I thought I really ought to get out of the car. I tried the door. It was jammed shut. I couldn't move."

"What did you do?"

"I called my friend Norman. He said he would come right over but he also said why didn't I call 911 and I said I didn't think of it and so then I did."

"And they found you."

"Oh yes. Ed Geiss was the first one there. While we waited for the fire department to come, we talked for a while and he said from the looks of things it appeared I had plowed down enough trees to start a new residential development."

"The Range Rover is quite a car."

"Well it's gone now. Anyway they got me out and they had an ambulance and asked if I wanted to go to the hospital and I said certainly not. All I had was this little tiny cut on my finger which was nothing. I was already late getting home."

She showed me the cut. There was a tiny scar half an inch long on the back of her right index finger.

"So why have you been going to doctors?"

"People said I ought to find out what caused this. What if I was driving and had somebody in the passenger seat and I blacked out again? I went to Dr. Burrescanno and he examined me and said I did not have high blood pressure and I did not have a stroke or a seizure and I ought to go to a heart doctor in Southampton, so I went there and they put a monitor on me and said my heart was fine but what they really wanted to do was put a long tube in my groin up through a vein into my heart and I said I'd really rather not do that. So then I went to my doctor in New York and he examined me and all the reports and he said it seemed I just fell asleep at the wheel, which is what I had thought in the first place."

Tina and I ordered virgin Marys and salads. Behind a potted palm affixed to the wall near our table was a plaque with a brass plate that read *The Ladies of Bridgehampton*. Under it were four brass plates, each engraved with the name of a well-known Bridgehampton woman. There were Shana Alexander, Gloria Jones, Tinka Topping, Barbara Hearst. We both knew all of these women but we had never heard of the organization. Was it an organization? Or just a list of those who lunched? We asked the waiter.

"It's the ladies of Bridgehampton," he said. "Some ladies who live here year around. But if you want I'll ask somebody else about them."

We asked him to do so and he did. A woman came over to assure us it was just a plaque of some year-round residents. And then another employee came who repeated it.

"If you want to know more, I could find out," he said.

We decided that was enough.

The food arrived, beautifully displayed, and we ate. We ordered some wine.

"Summer help," Tina said. "Nobody knows anybody. Which reminds me of this house I heard about that might be on the market. I called the owner and was told to call his son. So I called the son and he said the house might be for sale or it might not be for sale but in any case only a limited number of brokers would be handling it. I asked him if I was on the list and he said no. I asked him if he ever heard of me and he said no. I asked him if he read the *New York Times* and he said no. I asked him if I could have the listing and he said, 'Send me a resume.' A resume to get a listing to sell a house."

"Probably never heard of *Dan's Papers* either," I said.

We finished our lunch, noted that it seemed it was going to be a very interesting summer season, walked out to our cars together—Tina showed me where the paint was strangely chipping off her brand new Ford Windstar minivan—what an inappropriate car for such an elegant lady. I thanked her for lunch and we went our separate ways.

Later in the day, I went to Leo's Barber Shop on Main Street in Bridgehampton for a haircut. Leo is new to this area, an immigrant from Russia. He was a barber there and he is a barber here. He gives me a wonderful haircut.

"I had somebody in yesterday," he said, "who told me he's rented a six bedroom house for next August for forty thousand dollars. Big bargain. Apparently it was fifty thousand dollars and he got them to give him a discount."

Neither of us talked for a while after that. I wondered if Tina had this listing.

About a month after this, I was driving from my Bridgehampton office around 6 p.m. to meet my wife for dinner at the Laundry Restaurant in East Hampton on Race Lane six miles away. We had a lot to talk about. About a month before, the Berlin Wall, a ten-mile-long concrete structure that had divided that city since the end of World War II had begun to come down. It was an extraordinary thing. On the eastern side, the Soviet Union and the Secret Police controlled life. On the western side, the Americans, French, and English occupied the city. But now the Soviet Union was collapsing, and Germans on the western side had brought ladders over to their side of the wall and had begun chipping away at it with hammers and chisels. The Germans on the Soviet side were doing nothing. They were just waiting for their fellow citizens in the west to come through.

New Year's Eve was approaching. I had time to take a two-week vacation. We had decided that New Year's Eve at the Berlin Wall would probably be the most exciting place to be. We knew no one there, but we were up for this adventure.

As I drove along on that snowy evening, I became aware that a car was following me. I would turn, it would turn. After a while, I thought I'd lost it. I arrived at the restaurant, went inside, and sat down. My wife would be coming along from our house in Springs in her car. But she had not yet arrived.

Shortly, Tina came in and sat down at another table. She was alone too. I waited. She waited. Apparently she was waiting for someone too. I walked over.

"You here alone?" I asked.

"I'm waiting for a client. He'll be along shortly."

"I'm waiting for my wife."

"Well let's talk awhile. Did you know I was following you?"

"You were?"

"I was behind this car that had a Sarah Lawrence sticker in the back window. That's my alma mater. So I followed it."

"My daughter went there," I said.

"I remembered that when I saw you get out."

We talked briefly about the owner of the Gay Real Estate Agency in East Hampton who was being sued by a Jewish man for refusing to show him a house he knew was for rent, and then I got to talking excitedly about the trip my wife and I were about to take to Berlin.

"When are you leaving?" Tina asked.

I told her.

"I was born in Berlin. It's time I went back there. Could I come with you too?"

"Of course you could."

"When is the flight?"

I told her.

"I'll make the reservation," she said, and with that, she got up and went to the pay phone in the back of the restaurant. After a while, she came back. She had not only gotten a seat for herself on our airplane, but also for her daughter Stacy, who lived in New York City and who I had met once at her house.

"I'm sure Stacy would love to come," she said.

At that point, my wife arrived and saw me sitting at Tina's table. She came over and I introduced her.

"Tina's coming with us," I told my wife. "And she's bringing her daughter, who's about thirty as I recall."

"That's about right," Tina said.

The two-week trip to Berlin was to become one of the highpoints of my life. Tina took over the job of making accommodations for us all because, as she said, she still had kept touch with some of her childhood friends in that city. She had been born and raised there. Turned out there were apartments that Berliners rented out to visitors. She'd found one for my wife and me and one for herself and her daughter not far away. It would be much more pleasant than staying in a hotel, we'd see how the people lived, and it was also cheaper.

The flight over took six hours and, during the flight, my wife and I got to know Stacy better and more about Tina. This would be the first time Stacy had been to Berlin. She had married a college professor and had a daughter, and her husband would be looking after their daughter while she was away. As for Tina, she had left Berlin in 1937 with her father and mother when she was twelve. She had never been back. Among other things, she'd try to visit the house where she'd grown up.

"My father was the publisher of the *Berliner Post,* the daily newspaper in Berlin," she told us. "We had a beautiful home, gardens and grounds, servants. One evening my father went to the opera and sat in a box next to one occupied by Hitler and his propaganda director, Goebbels. He overheard them talking about Jews and the next morning he came into my room just before breakfast and said 'we're leaving. The servants are packing. We leave tonight.'

"I remember that all the books from my father's library were packed in wooden crates which were lined with cork. If the ocean liner sank, the crates would float and at least the books would be safe."

"You're Jewish?" I asked.

"Yes." Didn't you know?"

"Your last name is Fredericks. You live among the WASPs. All the wealth in this town is controlled by them. You certainly look like one. I always thought you were one."

"I was married to John Fredericks before we moved out," she said. "He was a WASP."

During the day in Berlin, we visited the wall and watched the local residents on ladders chipping pieces off this twenty-foot-high wall with hammers and chisels. It went on in both directions as far as the eye could see. I will never forget the metallic sound of this activity. Streetcar tracks led up to the wall and ended abruptly at it. The wall crossed main avenues. This city had been cut in half for forty years.

On our first morning, we met and had breakfast at a nearby restaurant and Tina, after asking about our apartment, told us about theirs.

"We are on the second floor of a townhouse. It's nicely furnished. When I was five years old, my father, who really was quite famous in Berlin, published a children's book that became famous in Germany, illustrated by an artist friend. It was a favorite of mine. Last night, I saw that very same book on the night table besides the bed. I could hardly believe it. It's still a bestseller today. This is so wonderful. It's an omen of some kind that I'd see it first thing."

On New Year's Eve, the four of us walked through Checkpoint Charley, manned by the police who, in former times, stopped people and turned them back, and now just waved everyone through. That night, we joined 600,000 people jammed into the Pariser Platz in front of the Brandenberg Gate to have the biggest New Year's Eve party ever. Disco music boomed from giant speakers. Fireworks went on for nearly an hour, lighting up the Gate, the wall beyond, and the Reichstag beyond that. Many people sat eighty feet up atop the Gate, and at least one, I learned later, fell off and died. What a time.

The next day, Tina, accompanied by her daughter, went to see the house she grew up in. It was in the American Zone up a long driveway and it was occupied by an American officer and his family who greeted them and graciously showed them around.

"I hardly recognized it," she said later. "It had been so differently decorated. But there was one thing. In the hallway, when you came in the front door, my father had built into the wall a glass case lined with red velvet which was lit from behind to display an antique vase or sculpture. It is still there. But I remember it at eye level. Now it seemed so much lower."

"Was there anything on display?"

"Nothing was in it."

Five years after this trip, Tina bought two acres of woods abutting Georgica Pond in East Hampton, probably the most expensive residential property per acre in the Hamptons. It was a stretch financially for her she told me, but she had done it. She did not want to build there, though. She wanted to keep it natural. She was perfectly happy to be living in the home she owned on Georgica Road. She had her office there, with a separate door to the outside and a parking area for staff and clients.

What she did have in mind to build on her Georgica Pond property was a small open-air Japanese tea house by the water's edge. She could go there to reflect on summer afternoons. She could have guests. She submitted plans to the town.

"They say a pavilion like that is illegal," she told me soon thereafter. "It has to be an 'accessory' structure to a house. So you have to build a house first. Do you believe it? I'm appealing this."

She lost. A year later, visiting Tina at her house on Georgica Road, I saw a beautiful little dollhouse-sized model of a fancy modern home on a wooden platform. Little trees were on three sides, the water on the fourth.

"I thought I liked the work of this particular Japanese architect," she said. "He flew in from Osaka and walked the property. Then he went back home and sent me this model. But I don't like it. I think I have to find someone else."

In the end, Tina did build a house on the pond. It's a grand cedar-shingle three-story rendition of a nineteenth-century English manor house. It sits in her woods some distance from the pond and looks like something from a Grimm's fairy tale. It has an indoor swimming pool, a stone entryway, towers and turrets, and odd windows here and there, but its most interesting feature is its elevator. Though the house is just three stories up, it's a split level, so the elevator stops every five feet and opens by a door opposite from where it was before, with the levels numbered one to seven—the seventh being a roof deck.

In addition, inside the elevator, on a wall that does not have a sliding glass elevator door, there is a small glass window that looks out onto the elevator shaft just one foot beyond. Through this glass window, the shaft wall appears to move as you go up, but when the elevator stops at any of the seven levels, a handsome oil painting on the shaft wall appears in that window.

I think it reminds her of Berlin.

Ted Kheel

When I started out publishing *Dan's Papers*, I often did "barter." People would advertise but they wouldn't pay for it in cash. They'd pay for it in kind. You might get fifty dinners at a restaurant for a full-page ad. Although there was often no official accounting, there was usually somebody keeping score somewhere, and when the fifty dinners were used up they'd tell you and it was time for another full-page ad.

I recall at the time reading an essay Mark Twain wrote when, as a young man, he took over a weekly newspaper in a gold-rush town in Nevada. He got the staff together in one room, stood up on a box and announced that henceforth there would be no more cover-up stories about the mayor's drinking problem, there would be no favors sought and none accepted, no more stories swept under the rug. They would instead run an upstanding newspaper devoted to truth, justice, high moral standards, and honesty. There would be no stone left unturned in that pursuit.

He ended the essay this way. "Now that you know about these changes, I want to know who here now gets the free opera tickets. From now on, they come to me."

TED KHEEL AND HIS WIFE ANN
(Courtesy of the author)

Of course, there can be a downside with barter. Once a travel agent offered me a free one-week vacation for two in a beach resort in the Dominican Republic in trade for fifteen weeks of advertising. Of course I took it and went.

We flew from New York to Santo Domingo, the capital of the Dominican Republic, to be met by a man in an old beat-up six-passenger van who drove us for five hours over rutted, dirt roads through the jungle to the other side of the country. There we came upon a small resort on the south-western tip of that island nation. Things looked pretty good as we rattled into the property. There was a main lodge with a dining room, a series of ten thatched-roof cement cottages along a beach, a stable with horses and ranch hands, and a small swimming pool next to an outdoor bar.

But the flies swarmed around, the kitchen staff was on strike, the food was awful, and at sunset you had to quickly get indoors because along the beach there would soon come two enormous anti-mosquito trucks with huge hoses on the back that men used to spray the entire resort with a billowing mist of DDT to kill the bugs.

After that stink drifted away, there was nothing to do but play cards for a while, either with the few other guests or with the manager, who told us how they were working so hard to solve the kitchen rebellion any day now, because the owner of the resort was expected down from America so they had to have it fixed up by then.

Then it would be off to bed in the cottages, until midnight came and we'd be awakened by the thundering hoof beats of all sorts of wild animals just outside—hogs, mules, goats, ponies, cows, horses, and other beasts who, having survived the DDT trucks, had apparently been let out of their pastures to spend the rest of the night snorting, honking, and frolicking in and around the cottages, where we lay fearful they might smash through the door.

We stayed three days, hoping that things might get better, but they didn't. So we left, our week only half up. Later, when my travel agent asked how everything went, I forced myself to say just great and thanks for everything and I did honor the rest of his advertising. So barter doesn't always work out, at least not the way you expected.

All this took place in 1977, however, and I had no idea that fifteen years later, when the paper was prospering, I would discover a new friend and a connection to this long-ago trip. I kept that information to myself, at least at first. This man didn't need to know.

The man I befriended was Theodore Kheel. About 1990, I had begun to write interviews with many men and women who were rich, famous, or very accomplished and who were increasingly finding their way, much to my astonishment, to home ownership in the Hamptons. Two years into this, I interviewed Theodore Kheel.

"You should get to know him," one of my friends told me. "He's probably the most famous labor lawyer in America. He has advised five different presidents. For one, Truman, he faced down a crippling national steel strike. He negotiated a railroad strike for President Johnson. He also did work for Presidents Kennedy, Reagan, and Clinton. He was hired by New York Mayor Lindsay to negotiate the city's way out of a teacher's strike. He knows everybody."

"I have to meet this man," I said.

I called him one weekend. He invited me to come to his house in East Hampton.

I arrived to his house on Drew Lane, a dead-end street off Lily Pond Lane that ends at the ocean, noted that the house was rather modest compared to the giant ocean mansions alongside it, and knocked on the door. Mr. Kheel's wife, Ann, answered, and told me to come in but that he was out in the backyard up in a tree house. I could wait till he came down.

"Why don't I go up there?" I asked.

She shouted out the back. A man's voice yelled back, "Send him out," and so I went. It was a big tree. I glanced up and there was this man, a handsome robust fellow about seventy-five years old, ten feet up, with wood and a hammer, banging shingles into a tree house wall.

"Come on up," he said.

And so I did, pad and pen in hand, and we sat up there together on a narrow bench for the next ninety minutes and talked, with only one interruption when Ann brought us some lemonade, which Ted climbed down and got.

Sometimes friendships are made in situations like this. This was one of them. The man I found up in that tree was a delightful, cheerful fellow who, in a kind of Will Rogers way, was full of ideas and great stories. Here's what he told me about his negotiating with the fiery Mike Quinn, the head of the New York City teacher's union.

"We did the negotiations in Mexico City," he said. "Don't ask why. That's where it was. We each had a hotel suite. We each had been assigned a limousine with a driver. One Sunday, we did not have negotiations. Around noon, Mike calls me and asks if I would like to come with him to a jewelry store. His wife told him about it. He said my wife might like some stuff from there, too. I asked if that was appropriate, the two of us, adversaries, going off like that alone, and he said, 'Why not? We're not adversaries today. I'll have my driver pick you up in half an hour.'

"So we go to this jewelry store, way, way out of the city in a small Mexican village, and after getting lost several times trying to find it, we get there late in the afternoon, pull up in front and park. 'Now when we get inside,' Mike says, 'let me do the negotiating.' I say, 'Sure.' So we get out of the car and, as we do, this fat woman is coming out from inside to pull down the steel gate of the store. She is closing. She's got it halfway down. Mike runs over—he's a little guy—and persuades her to stay open just a little longer because it will be worth her while and we go in.

"Inside, Mike takes a piece of jewelry over to the counter and asks how much, and she tells him so-and-so many pesos. He brings another piece over and gets the next price. Then the next. Then the next. Each time she totals it up into a new price. Then, finally, he's got about ten pieces on the counter and he puts his arms on the counter all around them and says, 'Okay, now what's your best price for *All* of them.' And so she tells him the total she had just added. And Mike says, 'No I want your best price,' and she says that's it. He points out she's added them up and taken nothing off and he needs a discount for so many and she tells him that's it, it's the best price. So finally he turns to me and he whispers, 'Okay, watch this,' and he turns to the woman and says, 'Okay, that's it, we're going,' and we walk quickly under the half-closed gate and back out to the car, and she's still standing at the counter.

"So we get in the car and he closes the door and he turns to me again and whispers, 'Watch. She's going to come out.' But she does not come out. And it is at this point that I see Mike has a cut on his forehead that's bleeding. He'd banged it going under the gate. He puts a handkerchief up to the cut. And he turns to me and, holding the handkerchief with a hand, says, 'We wait.' And we waited and waited and finally Mike takes a deep breath. 'We go back in,' he says, and so we go and he pays exactly what she told him it would all cost."

Finishing the interview, we came down to sit in the living room with Ann. He'd really taken a shine to me, I think. I was about the age of his son. So he told me more about his trip to Mexico City.

"It was on that trip I came to buy this enormous tract of land in the Dominican Republic. I don't know how I got talked into that. It was after the negotiations ended. I had a friend, a businessman, with me, and he said there was this land for sale, hundreds of miles of jungle along the ocean, and would I like to see it with him. We could take a plane and fly over it for the day before heading home. We went. We flew over fifty miles of oceanfront and wild horses. There was an occasional little village. Some rivers. And it was certainly cheap. I said I'd do it with him. But when we got home he backed out, so I went ahead without him. We've built a small resort way down there on the beach. If you ever want to vacation down there, let me know. I'd be happy to put you up."

"You fly into Santo Domingo," his wife said. "We go down there once a year. Ted has to bring his checkbook, so they are very happy to see him. It's six hours in a car through these bumpy dirt roads. But we have to go."

She said that like *"He really has to drag me there, but I go."* I said nothing. This was the resort we had stayed at.

In the years that followed, Ted frequently called to ask me to write about things he was doing. He took me to the United Nations once. He'd started a daily newspaper called

The Earth Times, which was circulated free to the delegates there. The U.N. was giving him an award for his efforts.

He also began inviting us to his annual Christmas party. It was held in New York City, in the Sky Club penthouse of what was then the Pan Am Building (now Met Life.) There were usually about a hundred people there, and he'd use the occasion to showcase an author he wanted people to know. At one of them, I met Loida Lewis, the wife of entrepreneur Reginald Lewis, the chairman of the conglomerate Beatrice. She spoke of her newly published how-to book about emigrating from the Philippines to America.

On other occasions, I attended parties on the lawn of Kheel's house in East Hampton—once, I recall, to celebrate the work of a sculptor whose work he had assembled there.

Ted went to the Rio Conference about global warming as part of the American delegation. He asked if I could publish a cover of *Dan's Papers* with the painting he had asked Southampton painter Roy Lichtenstein to make as a poster for the conference. There were signed prints made. He gave me one. I put it on the cover.

About ten years into our friendship, I decided I ought to have an "advisory committee" for *Dan's Papers*, which would consist of five prominent people living in the Hamptons. When it came time to decide on a "chairman," I offered it to Ted.

"I will absolutely be the chairman," he said without hesitation. "And who else is on this committee?"

I told him. Alec Baldwin, Christie Brinkley, Billy Joel, Roy Scheider.

"How often are there meetings?"

"We've never had a meeting," I said. "But everyone advises me."

It was at this point that, without going into a lot of detail, I told him I had once stayed at his resort in the Dominican Republic.

"We've torn down that old place," he said. "You owe it to yourself to see it again. We've built a lovely new one in its place. And we've got a paved highway all the way down to it. It's just an hour-and-a-half drive from Santo Domingo. Give me a date when you can come. I'll book you in for a week."

I went with my wife for a long weekend. It was really quite beautiful now. There was a bar on the edge of the pool. You'd sit on stools just underwater. It was professionally run. They had changed the name of it. Now it was called Punta Cana.

Ted was, at this point, one of this country's premiere environmentalists. In New York City, he bought a brownstone and rebuilt it as a completely self-sustaining office building, with plants, solar panels, everything he could think of, with no compromises. He then put parts of it out for rent, but the project failed because it just never could pay for itself.

And then, one day, Ted told me he had made a deal with the President of the Dominican Republic to build a small single-runway international airport at his resort in that country. He would try to get various owners of the other resort hotels interested—give them oceanfront property on a 99-year lease. In fact, he'd gotten his first one signed.

"It's Club Med," he said.

Today, Punta Cana consists of over 200 hotels on four miles of beachfront and is one of the world's major resorts, rivaling Cancún. It's all on property leased originally from Ted Kheel and his partners.

Six years ago, Ted proposed that private cars be banned below 86th Street in Manhattan. It would clear up traffic. His proposal did not catch on, but it did inspire Mayor Bloomberg to clear Times Square of cars at certain intersections, a project that is gloriously in place today.

Five years ago, Ted, who was now well over ninety, called to ask me if I would go partners with him to sponsor a book party at his house. He would hold it to help out a *New York Times* author who had written a book about the environment.

"You do the ads, and write a story. We'll do everything else. It will be 'Dan Rattiner and Ted Kheel present. . . .' It's the least I can do for being the chairman of an advisory board that in twenty years has never met."

"Will I have to make a speech?" I asked.

"Yes," he said.

When Ted Kheel died two years ago at ninety-six years of age, he was widely mourned. He was perhaps the most fascinating man I ever met in the Hamptons, and I miss him.

Fannie Gardiner

~~~~~~

On a Saturday afternoon in June of 1978, a group of summer people with sailboats in Sag Harbor decided to hold an impromptu regatta beginning at 5 p.m. A horn of some sort would be sounded at that hour. And whoever showed up at the starting line, which was marked off by a white buoy in the harbor, would be in it. The rules were that there were no rules. Any size boat with any number of people on board could enter. And the winner would be whoever could get all the way down to another white buoy and back three times.

This regatta was so successful that the yachtsman decided to hold it every Saturday at 5 p.m. all summer, and when they did that it became a story for the newspaper.

When I went down there to the harbor to cover it, pad in hand, I was startled to hear, exactly at 5 p.m., not the simple sound of a compressed air horn but the very grand sound of a cannon being fired from somewhere. I asked about it.

"We're now using a cannon. It starts the event."

"They have a cannon?"

FANNIE GARDINER
(Courtesy of the Gardiner Family)

"Oh yeah," the man said. Then he chuckled.

The chuckle made me think, This must be some cannon. I imagined that it looked like a Revolutionary War cannon. People would put cotton in their ears, light a fuse, then turn away and clap their hands on the sides of their heads. What did I know?

A few years later, I came to learn that a regatta cannon did not need to be anywhere near that big. I was not in Sag Harbor, but on Shelter Island, at a cocktail party in the main dining room of the Shelter Island Yacht Club. The sun was setting. As it did, a very loud cannon was fired from the deck of the Yacht Club to celebrate that fact.

Curious, I wandered out to look. The cannon was about two feet long and one foot high, and the man who fired it had pulled a string attached to the back of it while holding one foot on the top of it to keep it from jumping around.

And now I thought, I ought to have a cannon at my house. I live on a hillside. A road passes down below in front of the house, and on the other side of that road, backing almost right up to it, there are boats rocking in their slips. Beyond that, across one mile of water, the sun sets every evening.

I have kids age 15, 12, 6, and 4, is what I thought. And I'm a kid, age 47. From the time the oldest was in a stroller, we had gone to Disney World every year. They'd love a cannon.

And so I bought one.

I got it at Preston's Nautical Store in Greenport—the only store on the East End to sell cannons—and when I did, I told this skinny kid who was my salesman that I did not want to have to put my foot on the top of it when I fired it. It seemed undignified and unfair to the cannon.

The kid looked at me funny. He was chewing gum and he blew a bubble. "It does have quite a kick," he said.

"What if I bolt it to the deck railing?"

"You could do that. Just make sure you use strong steel bolts. You might want to brace it with some metal pole, too. You don't want it to tear your railing off. I would recommend a bolt at least a quarter-inch. They could also sell you a metal pole. There's a hardware store just across the street."

"How far away can you hear it?"

"With ten gauge shells?" He blew a bubble. It popped. "Four miles. You have a yacht club?"

The cannon he sold me was made of chrome-plated steel with its main feature a two-foot-long barrel on metal wagon wheels. It came with ten-gauge shotgun shells, earplugs, and a whole lot of other gear and instruction books.

At 4 p.m. I drove home by taking the little ferry ride from Greenport to Shelter Island and then, after crossing Shelter Island, another ferry ride to the Hamptons. I was very excited. I had a cannon in the back.

Sunset, here we come.

My four kids were all for this. Their mother was not. She folded her arms. But the kids raced around, fists in the air, whooping and hollering as I described where on the deck railing I would put it and just how loud it would sound.

"You can hear cannon fire from four miles away, the salesman told me," I said.

"Yippeee!" the four-year-old said.

"Don't worry," I said, addressing their mother. "It will be bolted down." I showed her the bolts and the drill. "It will only be fired at sunset. And you can keep the shells in the filing drawer with the lock and key."

That seemed to satisfy her.

During dinner, the kids repeatedly asked me if it was time to fire off the cannon. Each time, I pointed at the sun to note that it still had a ways to go. They were pretty impatient about how long it was taking.

Finally the time came for what would be the first firing. This was a few minutes before eight.

"Earplugs in?"

All the earplugs got put in. Everyone was standing around in a big semicircle. The four kids, the mom, and the two dogs. I fiddled with the cannon, cocking the trigger, sliding the shell all the way in.

"Step back, please," I said. "I want everybody far away from this."

Now the sun was right at the point where the last ray of it was about to set behind the far shore. I gripped the string, closed my eyes, and pulled.

WHAM!!!

I heard screams and howls. I blinked open my eyes to see a cloud of white smoke and two midsize animals that looked like my dogs go barreling past me and out into the yard and up the hill. The younger kids were bawling. The mother was holding them tightly to her.

"Cool," said one of the older kids.

Out on the street, I saw a car that just happened to be passing by when I pulled the string, pull over.

"Everybody inside," I shouted.

This man get out, looked around, apparently didn't see the white smoke that was still hovering there, and then walked around his car, a white Toyota, examining all four tires. Then he got back in and drove off.

For the next six months I fired the cannon every night at sunset, except when it was either raining or all clouded over. Slowly, it began to sink in on the yachting community that there was some guy sending out a salute to the sunset every once in a while from the head of the harbor. Those in the immediate neighborhood, I suppose, could see the puff of smoke if they looked at the appropriate time. Those farther away would have no idea who it was.

I spoke to my neighbor about it. I only had one neighbor there. He was Cliff Townsend, and he lived on the other side of some underbrush that separated our properties. This was about 200 yards away. He said he rather liked it.

"You always know it's coming, maybe," he said.

There was a problem that came up after a while, however, with the yachtsmen who had the boats directly across the street. The yachtsmen were not there all the time, of course, only once in a while, either coming or going. After that, there'd either be an empty slip or an empty boat in the slip, bobbing around for another day or two. It was just that sometimes, the sunset would begin to set up just as some yachtsmen and their guests were messing around on their boats.

BOOM!!!

"Ahh, hey, guy hold off, would ya?" two of them shouted up at us the first time this happened.

Well, the sunset was the sunset. "It's all over," I shouted down. Then I thought about it. "Tell you what," I continued. "If we see you out there and the sun is about to set, I'll shout out a warning for you."

"Okay."

As for the kids, I now had a rule that everybody had to be inside, behind closed door sliders, when I fired the cannon. And the dogs had to be further into the house, in one of the bedrooms. The kids could take turns being with the dogs.

On the other hand, on the rare occasion when the sun did set and I would miss it because I was not home, what went through my mind on those evenings, exactly at sunset, was everybody bracing themselves and then wondering why the cannon had not gone off. Was the cannon firer all right?

In any case, emboldened by the success of the cannon, I thought to expand my connection with the harbor and the boating community by buying a two-way marine radio. I set it on the table in the living room, right where you could hear it and look out at the cannon and the harbor beyond. I connected it to a cable that went up to a steel needle aerial up on the top of the roof. And, on random occasions, when the kids got tired of playing games, I suggested we listen in to the nautical chatter. We could even respond if we wanted. But I told the kids not to, because that was only if we heard somebody in distress. I had set the radio to scan. We'd hear anything that might be said on any channel.

Late on a Sunday afternoon, the family was playing cards in the living room when I heard a distress call.

"S.O.S. Anybody there? Hello?"

I ran to the radio. It was a sailboat that had run aground on a bar just inside the jetties. I said I would relay their call to the Coast Guard, and I did.

"How about *that!*" I said proudly to the family when I had hung up.

Everybody thought that was pretty neat.

A few days later, in the evening just after sunset (and the cannon), I picked up a call from some boatmen asking if anybody knew where they could buy some gas. All the marinas were closed. I asked where they were and they told me.

"You're not too far from my house," I said. "None of them are open. But I have a tank of gas in my garage you could have. Could you motor over here? There's two slips with no boats in them. Just tie up and I'll meet you there."

They said they could.

In the garage, I found the red plastic six-gallon tank that had spare gas in it, and carted it down to the water's edge. Soon they arrived, thanked me profusely, and, after pouring my gas in their tank, offered to pay for it. I declined.

"Just do a favor for somebody else," I said. I felt really proud of myself.

This is very interesting, I thought as I walked back up the hill to my house. I am an important part of the safety crew for this harbor.

I know, I thought. I'll call the Town Supervisor, who I talked to about other things from time to time, and see if he'll make it official.

My conversation with Supervisor Bullock, held in his office, was one of the strangest imaginable.

"You want what?" he asked.

"Nothing really. I just saved some lives. And gave gas to some other yachtsmen this past Sunday. I think it would be a good thing to just deputize me in some way. Give me a card saying I'm a volunteer."

"You're a volunteer," he said. "And a good one. But I don't have any cards I could give you."

"Could you *make* one?"

"I don't think we have money in the town budget for that."

I left.

I'm really on to something now, I thought as I drove home. The kids love it. I fire the cannon. We listen to the harbor activity. Dan's House is becoming an institution.

Standing in the living room looking out on the boats bobbing in their slips, what occurred to me was, "Boy, we're up high here on the side of this hill. From up here, it looks like we're actually a boat, too."

The next day, at a hardware store, I bought a four-foot-long brass sign you could attach to a wall. It read *To the Lifeboats*, and under it, sort of underlining it, was a big arrow. I arranged it to point up the stairs to our bedrooms. I also bought a bunch of junked nautical gauges from one of the marinas across the street—they were all busted up, nautical nevertheless, barometers, wind gauges, humidity gauges, depth finders, etc.—and I screwed them into the wall next to the *To the Lifeboats* sign.

I bought a thirty-foot flagpole with a yardarm from which I could attach nautical message flags, and I had it installed directly behind the cannon. After the gun firing, we'd lower the flag, carefully fold it up and put it on the table next to the marine radio.

At one point, I considered buying everybody in the house a captain's hat, but after thinking about it, decided not to. Enough was enough. Well maybe it was more than enough. But I thought, what the hell.

The cannon firings went on, at sunset, all that summer. I really liked being part of the scene at the harbor.

In mid-August—this was now seven weeks later—a police car came up our driveway just ten minutes after I fired the cannon. The kids, who were now playing in the yard, looked at the officer wide-eyed as he got out of his car and, in his full uniform, came up onto the deck.

"Are you the people who are firing some sort of cannon?" he asked.

You could still smell the gunpowder.

"Yes."

"We've had a complaint. I can't tell you who. One of the neighbors. You can't be firing a cannon on Three Mile Harbor Road."

I stood my ground. "It's not like I fire it all the time," I said. "I fire it only once a day, at sunset. It's a sunset cannon. That's what they call it. That's what you're supposed to do with it."

He looked at it closely. It really didn't look like much of anything.

"It's what they have at yacht clubs," I said. "And it only fires blanks, of course."

That was a lie. It could fire live shells if I'd wanted it to.

He thought about it for a minute. Then, finally, he spoke. "Yeah, I guess that makes sense," he said. "Just make sure you fire it *only* at sunset."

"Okay," I beamed.

The kids cheered.

Just before Labor Day, one of East Hampton's town characters, Fannie Gardiner, driving a beat-up fifteen-year-old Buick sedan with three magnetized antennas on the roof, paid me a visit. She was about fifty years old at this time.

I was alone in the house, sitting out on the deck, watching the scene. It was about three o'clock in the afternoon.

I could see this very strange car in my driveway, and of course I knew it was Fannie's. She got out, readjusted the cowboy hat she always wore, nodded to me, and clomped over and on up the stairs to the deck in her cowboy boots without the slightest hesitation. This was the first time she had ever been on my property. And although I had seen her and her car around from time to time, I had never before spoken to her.

Everybody in town knew Fannie. Some had conversations with her. Some not. To the best of my knowledge, she never smiled. She was tall and slender, had short hair, piercing blue eyes, and always wore cowboy clothes. She lived in a tiny cottage further up Three Mile Harbor Road. And she always looked as if she had just come back from riding a horse, which, probably, she had.

But she was also rich. Or was at one time. She was a cousin to one of the wealthiest men in town, Robert David Lion Gardiner, the millionaire owner of Gardiner's Island, the largest privately owned island in the United States, which was just offshore of Montauk.

She had been born and raised in great privilege among the wealthy WASP set. But she had rebelled. She refused to allow her family to have a "coming out" party for her. She would not go to any damn cotillion. She would not hang around with any of those rich people. She would, and did, grow up to hang out with the blue-collar workers in the town—the Bonackers, that tribe of people who hunted, fished, clammed, and farmed, and whose ancestors came over in the seventeenth century from England, in the employ of her ancestor, the first Gardiner, Lion Gardiner, who founded the town and whose descendants she was now shunning.

She did not address me by name.

"You know, you're breaking the law having that marine radio on all the time," she said.

"It's not on all the time."

"It's against the law to have one of those, except on a boat. You could go to jail for that. Ten years. You take it down. Or I'll turn you in."

"That's ridiculous."

"The boat people don't want nobody on the shore talking and taking up their space on an emergency radio. It's a federal law. It better not be on anymore."

And she turned, clomped down the stairs and back to her car and, as she drove away—the antennas bristling on the roof of her car, and smoke coming out of the back of it—I thought that car of hers must be packed with *three* marine radios. Who the hell does she think she is?

The next day I saw Ralph George, who was the Harbormaster for the Town, in his police boat across the street. I went over to him. And he told me that indeed, that was the law.

"But you know, you're talking about doing what Fannie does," he said. "I think that's what this is all about."

I'm not going to fight with Fannie, I thought. I run a newspaper. What the hell is wrong with me? And so, later that day, I went into the living room, disconnected the marine radio, and carried it down in to the basement. Goodbye marine radio, I said to it. Don't tell anybody you're down here. I also went up on the roof and took the antenna down.

I told the kids what I had done. "I checked," I told them. "It's the law. And we obey the law."

"Are you going to keep firing the cannon?" the youngest asked.

"Yes."

I continued on with the daily sunset firing right through the autumn. But then I began to tire of it. At this point, it seemed to me, it was getting to be a job. There were no boats in the water. And there were very few motorists on the road to try to time the firing so as not to scare. As a matter of fact, the sun was now starting to set so early in the day that it was getting hard to get home to fire it with any regularity at the proper time. So, I was only firing the cannon when I happened to be home when the sun came down, which was four in the afternoon.

But boy did it make a roar when I fired it then. Without the leaves on the trees, it would make the big bang and then echo not once but twice up and down the harbor. It must be something you could hear for ten miles or more.

About the tenth of November, I gave up.

One day in early May of the following year, however, there was the most beautiful sunset imaginable setting up at the end of the day. I could not resist it. I closed all the sliders, got the dogs in the bedroom, told everybody to get the earplugs in, shoved a shell into the breech, looked left and right to make sure no cars were coming, looked down to make sure there were no people in boats—well, there were actually *no* boats yet for the new year—and then, WHAM! Another sun successfully set.

Welcome to the summer season of 1987, I thought.

Jeff Parsons

~~~~~~

In 1981, Jeff Parsons took me out to his barn and showed me the rock. It occupied the center of the barn, was in the shape of a giant four-foot potato, all smooth and curved, weighed about a thousand pounds and was made of granite. It had a concave area in the top that seemed to invite me to sidle over and sit on it. I sidled over, but then I hesitated.

"Go ahead," Jeff said.

And so I sat. Apparently there was a flat bottom to the rock. It was quite steady. I was quite comfortable. I liked the rock.

"This is my latest work," Jeff said. He stood next to a battered wooden table on which were hammers and chisels and other tools.

"It's been commissioned by Guild Hall in East Hampton," he said. "It's going to set out on their front lawn along with the other sculpture that is out there."

"That's quite an honor," I said. I wriggled around and made myself even more comfortable.

JEFF PARSONS
(Courtesy of Jeff Parsons)

"I call it 'Invitation.' "

"Well it sure is. Is it done?"

"I've just got a bit more polishing to do."

Jeff was one of my best friends. I'd met him ten years earlier, in the early 1970s, during the height of the hippie era. He was soft spoken, had long hair down to his shoulders, played wonderful folksongs on his guitar, and worked odd jobs while making his grand sculptures. He was certainly part of the art scene in the Hamptons.

In the second year of our friendship, Jeff married a beautiful woman named Maria, and a year later, fathered a little girl they named Maya. Quite by chance, Maria and my wife were in the Southampton hospital having babies at the same time. As it happened, we named our daughter Maya too. Our families soon became close.

Jeff finished his sculpture, but he never did get it placed on the front lawn of Guild Hall right on Main Street in East Hampton where everyone could see it.

In the back of my mind, I sort of knew this was going to happen. These are such small towns we live in. When the first sculpture appeared, just put there by this cultural institution without anyone asking permission to put it there—it was, after all, their front lawn—all sorts of people came forward to vigorously voice their objections to it. The object was not a building, it was not an accessory structure, it was not a cupola, what in god's name in the world of zoning was it? And where would it all end?

It had taken a year. But in the end, the officials from Guild Hall dutifully made some sort of application, appeared before the zoning board, and got permission to keep the sculpture, another half-ton piece, where it was.

As for Jeff's sculpture, apparently, according to Jeff, Guild Hall officials made an application for this second sculpture—after they commissioned him to make it—and it was rejected. They couldn't take "Invitation."

It was during this time that I was doing construction on the *Dan's Papers* newspaper office building, a former late Victorian residence on Main Street in Bridgehampton. We were too many people in too small a space now. I built a little addition on the side, with the approval of the South-ampton Town officials of course, and I completely enclosed the front porch. It was all fresh and new. New grass seed had just been put down on the front lawn. Come fall, it was all going to look quite beautiful. And it was at this point that Jeff approached me with a proposition.

"I was thinking," he said. "How would you like to have the sculpture 'Invitation' on your front lawn at the office? I'd just put it there. You wouldn't have to pay for it. But if people come by, and lots of people come into your office, and they ask about it, tell them it's for sale and have them contact me."

The Elaine Benson Gallery had already established the practice of putting giant sculptures out on their front lawn in Bridgehampton. So there was a precedent for this. And Bridgehampton was not East Hampton.

"Sure," I said.

Later that spring, with the grass grown in, Jeff and I walked around on the lawn and decided on a particularly artistic place to put it, halfway between the building and the street, and not far from a maple tree, whose branches and leaves would arch high over the rock in the summertime. And so, a month after that, a backhoe arrived with the rock in its scoop and we placed it just where we had agreed. The concave part had you sitting facing the street. You had been invited, and you could sit and contemplate the cars driving by. At your feet was a rectangular steel plaque set into the concrete pad upon which it sat. It said 'Invitation.'

In the years that followed, everyone got to enjoy the rock. We placed a picnic table between the rock and the house, and sometimes, you could look out from the office and see people, complete strangers, who had pulled over and parked and were enjoying a picnic at the table and the rock.

In later years—the decades were rolling by now and *Dan's Papers* had become quite well known—a number of famous people often stopped by to enjoy our outdoor facilities. Mark Feuerstein, the star of the HBO series "Royal Pains" was often found out there. He told us his day was not complete without a visit to our front lawn. He'd sit and read.

I do recall on several occasions people asking me who had sculpted the rock and I told them, and I told them it was for sale, but nothing ever came of it.

The rock remained. Around 1990, Jeff and Maria got a divorce and they both moved away, both to the wilds of northern California. There they set up housekeeping just a few miles apart from one another in the lumber town of Garberville on the side of one of the Atlas Mountains and they raised their Maya and two other daughters there. A few years later, I visited them out there. Maria had married a hippie farmer named Proud and was doing well. They had horses and crops. As for Jeff, he still had his long hair but was not doing sculptures anymore. Instead, he was making his living playing music in taverns and bars. He lived in a small apartment in town with a girlfriend.

"You know you really should pay me for that sculpture," Jeff said. This brought me up short. "You've had it out there for fifteen years."

"The arrangement was I'd try to sell it for you. So far it hasn't sold."

"I figure $3,000 and it's yours."

This was not what we agreed. So I wasn't buying it.

"If you want to have someone remove it, it's right there," I said, and that ended the conversation.

Honestly, I never thought there might be a problem with the rock in this way or any other. I was resigned to it either being there or not being there. If Jeff sold it, great; if not, great. But then, the following year, something happened that made me realize that having an extremely large and heavy object on your property might have a life of its own.

Down the street to the east about three miles, there was, and still is, a moving and storage company called "Home Sweet Home."

Not very long before, this place was in the news when a dozen canvases believed to have been painted by Jackson Pollock were found among the possessions of the late photographer Herbert Matter stored there before he passed away. It was like one of those classic stories about finding a million dollar antique at a yard sale.

But the story about Home Sweet Home that was also in the news that year was about these two enormous stone sculptures that guarded the front door of the establishment. They were eight feet high, made of granite, and were of two mythological beasts.

I had always thought, driving by Home Sweet Home, that the owners of this establishment owned these sculptures. But now there was a lawsuit. A woman in Maine had sculpted them. She had stored them there for many years. Now she wanted them shipped to her. Home Sweet Home refused. There was a storage bill owed in the tens of thousands of dollars for them. The woman needed to pay that. Instead, the woman sued. And that's what was in the news.

Today, the sculptures are still alongside the doors. The lawsuit fizzled, I was told. The moral was that hard-to-move giant objects often stay right where they are no matter what. It would probably be the same for me and the rock. And that was fine with me.

Until it wasn't.

In the summer of 2011, I realized that we would have to move out of our office in Bridgehampton. We were now nearly forty people working in a former two-bedroom home. It was very tight. Yet the property had been expanded as far as it could legally go. It would be best to sell it. The end of an era.

We found a new building in Southampton, nearly twice the size as our house in Bridgehampton, and I put the old place up for sale at the beginning of September. Within three months, I had a buyer, a builder named James McLoughlin who wanted the house for his corporate headquarters. The house would be sold on January 9, 2012, and, with the buyer's permission, we would move out to our newly fixed-up place in Southampton in April.

Of course, looking out my front second-story window every day, there was the rock.

I called Jeff in California, or tried to call him. His phone was disconnected. Then I called Maria who did answer and who told me she had a phone number for Jeff's girlfriend who lived with him there in Garberville, but she thought Jeff was now spending lots of time in South America.

"What's he doing in South America?" I asked.

"He loves South America. He's got a band and he's very good. I think he's in a resort town down there that loves him."

I called his girlfriend Rose Marie. Yes, Jeff was in a small town in Uruguay. But she'd have him call me. I gave her my number. And, soon, he did.

"Why don't you see if the buyer wants to buy it?" he asked.

This was in December. We had signed the contract. But so much can go wrong between a signing and a sale. I hesitated.

"I think that would be up to him to talk to you about it after he buys the property," I said.

"Can you find another buyer?"

"I can try. It's on my property until January. I'll make some calls. Tell me what you can about the rock and about you as a sculptor."

"I am in several collections. Alfonso Ossorio was a big collector. He has, or had, about ten pieces of my work. I've been shown in many galleries as you know."

"Any sculptures in museums?" I asked.

"No."

"What do you want for it?"

"$10,000."

"If I can't sell it, maybe I could just get it moved off the property."

"Sell it."

We agreed to stay in touch, but because of the cost of a phone call to South America, it would be through his girlfriend in California. He didn't have email in South America.

"We write letters to each other every day," he said.

Well, I tried. I called Lou Meisel, who owns a gallery in Manhattan and many buildings in the Hamptons, including the one next door to the *Dan's Papers* office in Bridgehampton. I told him what Jeff wanted for it.

"We could just slide it over there," I said meaning the business next door.

"I'll take a look," he said. But then he called back. "Nope," he said, "not interested."

I called a few other people I knew and I even called Guild Hall, but nobody wanted to pay anything for Jeff's sculpture.

I then called Lou Meisel back and asked him if he wanted to move the sculpture off to his private home in Sagaponack where he has a whole field full of sculptures, if Jeff would let him do that for nothing. He said no to that too.

At this point, I decided to call my brother-in-law, who is a lawyer. I wanted him to clarify the legal aspects of the situation.

"The legal situation," he said, "is that the sculpture belongs to Jeff Parsons, but he has left it in your care with your permission. It is a work of art. If it is broken up or destroyed, I think he could sue you and you would be liable for its value."

"So I am liable to have it shipped to California? To South America?"

"Maybe you could have it moved to your new location."

"Could I *bury* it?"

"I think you could. So long as Jeff knew where it was. And so long as you possessed the property."

On the day of the closing on January 9, as the ink was drying on the sale, I broached the subject of the rock with the new owner of the property.

"I like the rock," McLoughlin said. "I think I'd leave it there."

"Well then, you should contact Jeff Parsons and negotiate with him."

"Okay."

For the rest of that year after the sale, our old property was a construction site with canvas panels placed on a six-foot-high chain link fence surrounding it so you could not see in. Above the top of it, however, you could see that the building was not being torn down. It was being repaired and restored and you could see all new shingles and shutters and doors and windows and it looked quite good. And then, with the landscaping in, they took the chain link down.

No rock.

As I write this, they are still working on the interior and McLoughlin has not yet moved in. Last Sunday, with nobody there, I decided to come in the driveway and go around to see what they'd done in back.

There was the rock, in a wooden enclosure. Ready for Round Two. Whether Round Two means putting it back out front, shipping it to South America or California or to a rich man's mansion on the ocean, or burying it where it stands I do not know. Anyway, all seems well for the rock.

I'm thinking about contacting Jeff. But maybe not just yet.

Memorial Day

~~~~~~

In 1983, I bought a fifteen-year-old Volkswagen camper bus for the purpose of writing my stories for *Dan's Papers* down at the beach. Prior to that time, when it was just my wife and myself, I'd find a quiet place in the house to write, but by this time there were four kids running around plus my wife, and if someone were to come into where I was working all of a sudden, it would break my concentration and cause me to lose where I was in the story. It would put me in a bad mood, and that was not right for me or anybody else. I had to find another place to write.

The Volkswagen bus, even used, was a thing of beauty to me. Who cared that it only had a 48-horsepower engine and could barely climb hills? Inside it had all the comforts of home—cabinets for storage, frilly curtains, louvered windows with screens, a propane stove, a sink you could hook up to a water source, and a Formica table on a hinge that swung up and, when set on its fold-out leg, became a perfect place for four people to eat a meal. This was really cozy, because two padded seats faced the table to create a luncheonette booth experience. I'd work at that table, of course. And if I got tired, the roof popped up and became a tent. I could sleep on the mattress up there. Nobody would know.

There were no laptop computers in 1983. But what had come out that year, for the first time—which is why I thought about all this—was a "portable" computer. It was called an Osborne. It was the size of a suitcase and weighed about twenty-five pounds, but if you swung it up by its leather strap, you could set it on a table, unlatch one side and, on a hinge, a keyboard would open up and drop down to reveal a small four-inch screen, upon which your typing would appear as glowing green letters.

Of course, you needed to plug this thing in. But I'd figured that out. I went to the lumberyard and bought a small gasoline-driven generator, not much bigger than the Osborne. I'd rigged it up in the driveway. It sat on the asphalt outside the Volkswagen, puttering away, and the line from it went in through a connector on the side of the bus, and into the back of the Osborne inside, where I had heaved it onto the Formica table. This was made for me. And I knew exactly where I would go. I would drive down to the beach, Main Beach in the center of East Hampton, and write my stories for *Dan's Papers* there, facing the ocean. I'd stay for a few hours.

Thus, I would go into my little writing world. You might envy me for being able to write while sitting out at the beach. But soon after getting there, I'd get lost in my work and not even know where I was. I could be in Secaucus, New Jersey. Or in Indianapolis, Indiana.

I'll give you an example. Once I was writing a story about David Gardiner, who lived in East Hampton in 1688 and was trying to shield a woman who the townspeople thought was a witch. I had come to the part where a wooden ducking stool was set up alongside Town Pond and this woman, Goody Garlick, struggling against her captors, was being taken over and tied to it. They would dunk her into the pond, and if she died, she was innocent; and if she lived, she was a witch. Mr. Gardiner was racing down Main Street on horseback to save her when, suddenly, an East Hampton Town Lifeguard crossed in front of my van carrying a coiled rope.

Mostly, I'd write down at the beach in the middle of the afternoon. Sometimes, however, especially if I couldn't sleep, I'd get up in the dark around five in the morning and drive down. When I'd first arrive, the seas would be black, and all I'd see were the twinkly lights noting the locations of fishing boats and freighters out at sea. I'd set out my generator, set up my table and computer, and, by a light on the wall between the louvered side window and driver's door, begin to write.

As the morning progressed, the sun would rise and the people would come. They'd come and park by the beach to read the morning *New York Times* (or *Dan's Papers*) and they'd break out rolls and orange juice and coffee and have little one or two person breakfasts behind the wheels of their cars. Others came with surfboards. Still others came with fishing rods or with large dogs they'd let run around outside awhile. The laws against dogs on the beach really were not seriously enforced until 9 a.m.

Furthermore, the police were also very generous about not enforcing the 15-Minute Parking laws. Though these laws are prominently displayed on metal signs you see at the beaches, there is a long tradition of the local people driving down to the road ends to look at the ocean. No matter what the sign says, a mayor who ordered his police department to tell the locals to move on would be voted out of office in about the blink of an eye.

Early one morning in 1988, I arrived down at the ocean to write at about six in the morning. As usual, I went into deep concentration. But, looking up from time to time, I could see lots of things were going on. What were they? I'd only see things in this disjointed way.

1. Nobody here. Dark. Foggy. Noisy sea.

2. Sun coming up. Fog lifting. Lady in a BMW next to me reading the *New York Times Review of Books*. She's using the vanity light. Noisy sea is due to rough waves.

3. Big school bus next to me. Some kind of marching band getting out.

4. Soldiers with khaki uniforms, medals, gold braid, silver helmets, white gloves and rifles.

5. Huge crowds of bystanders. They mill around, talking, gesturing, mumbling something or other.

6. Everybody walks down to the edge of the ocean.

7. *Crack*. The soldiers, standing all in a row, fire a fusillade into the air. *Crack*. *Crack*. Now they stand down. The puffs of smoke drift to the west.

8. A man in religious robes says something. Sounds important.

9. What is going on here? The marching band has begun to play "The Star Spangled Banner." People have removed their hats, placed their hands over their hearts. Everyone is standing up. I better get out of the car and stand up too. I get out of the car and with my hand over my heart, stand there. This is very annoying, I think, because I was right in the middle of this part . . . where was it? Well, you can't stay sitting when they play "The Star Spangled Banner." People notice.

10. ". . . o'er the land of the free-e-e-e, and the home . . . of the . . . brave." People cheer. I hop back into the car and sit down. Now, where was I?

11. Four people, one of whom is the religious man in the robes, carry an enormous wreath down to the edge of the sea and throw it as far into the water as they can. It doesn't get very far and, in about a minute, it washes ashore.

12. Everybody climbs back into the busses. The busses start up, and everyone drives off. I get back into my Volkswagen camper.

I have gotten to the part in this story about the Shinnecock Hills Golf Club, where young Cornelius Vanderbilt, on the first tee, has made a million-dollar bet with his uncle that he could hit a ball more than 300 yards to the green.

If people fire any more rifles around here, I may have to go somewhere else. Then it occurs to me. It's the morning of Memorial Day. There's been a parade through the center of town, and now a wreath has just been thrown into the ocean in memory of all those who fought and died for their country.

Enough of this. Back to work.

John and Chris Lyons

~~~~~~

In the mid-1970s, radio commentator John Lyons called me to ask if I knew any interesting people in the Hamptons he could interview for his show.

"I don't mean exactly interesting," he told me over the phone. "I mean, uh, wacko."

John and his wife, Chris, had a popular show on WABC. I asked him why he was looking for these sorts of people in the Hamptons.

"Chris and I have been broadcasting from a van while driving around the country. We thought we ought to see if there was anybody out here where we live. And you're the man to call."

I had no idea the two lived out here. Turned out they lived on Skimhampton Road, right around the corner from me. Who knew?

I had heard some of the interviews. And I had seen some of them, as segments, on TV. In one, I remembered, he interviewed a man who owned a motel whose interior rooms were designed as caves. In another, they had interviewed a

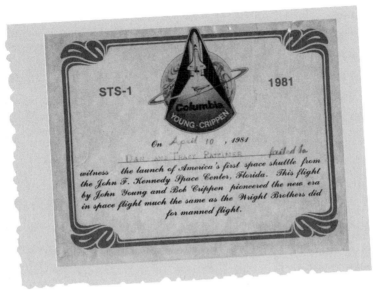

FAILED TO WATCH LAUNCH
(Courtesy of the author)

man who had built a rocket in his backyard in California. He was going to the moon.

"I can't think of anybody," I said. "No. Wait a minute. I can think of some people."

I then reeled off three different people I thought fit the bill.

"Great!" John said. He always spoke like that, at least on the air, with the enthusiasm of a fifteen-year-old boy, all filled with fun and excitement. I had just gotten a little of that.

As a result of this initial request, John and Chris soon became friends of mine. Who would not want to be friends with these people? John was a big guy, about six-one, 250 pounds. He had not only a teenager's voice, but a teenager's smirky smile, and his hair fell over his forehead. Sometimes remaining a teenager happens to people.

Chris was his perfect foil. An attractive blond woman, she spoke in a kind of monotone that made it appear she was trying, usually unsuccessfully, to restrain John's enthusiasm. What crazy thing was he up to next? But often she'd go along with whatever he was doing because, in spite of herself, she had to see what was next.

On a warm summer's day, six months later, John, carrying his camera, together with Chris, me and my wife, and our dog, walked across the street from our house on Three Mile Harbor Road to film one of these interviews. It was to be with me, though the actual word *wacko* had not been mentioned. But John had an idea.

"Okay," he said, "let's go to your boat."

What we were looking at there were the thirty-five boats that sat rocking in their slips, side-by-side, facing the house. These were all kinds of boats—sailboats, sport-fishing boats and pleasure boats—all somewhere between twenty and forty feet in length, all fitting appropriately in the long row of slips. All of this was in a small inlet. The inlet led out into Three Mile Harbor. The harbor led out to Gardiner's Bay.

"Over here," I said.

I led them to the right and along the boardwalk to where the dock ends. Beyond the last boat, there was a drop down from the dock, to a mess of beach grass, sand, water, flies, and dead crabs. I did not have a slip. My boat, a rowboat, was ten feet off of the wetlands, tied to a stake, and attached to the shore by a rope and pulley system. John handed the camera to his wife, then he and I climbed down from the dock to the shore, reeled in the rowboat, and John and I climbed in.

With some effort, we rowed out to just behind the big yachts, and just sat there in the rowboat, fifty feet from and parallel to the shore. John sat facing me, holding a portable microphone. On shore, Chris was setting up the camera and, with a zoom lens, aiming at the rowboat. My wife stood alongside with our dog.

"Try to shoot between the yachts," John yelled to Chris. "Don't want anything else in this picture, just me, Dan, and the rowboat."

"Okay," Chris said.

"Start with just our heads and the microphone, but not with the boat," John said. "Then, on cue, zoom out."

"I'm rolling."

"I am here with newspaper publishing tycoon Dan Rattiner on his yacht," John said. "He lives in East Hampton, New York, and owns a far-flung empire of newspapers on eastern Long Island. Dan?"

John pushed the microphone toward me.

"Well, after the original paper in Montauk, I started editions in East Hampton, Southampton, and the North Fork, and then on to Block Island."

"That's in another state."

"Yes, Rhode Island. We're making plans to publish in Martha's Vineyard and then in Nantucket."

"That's in Massachusetts."

It was at this point that John, with a little flick of his hand, made the cue to his wife on shore. In response, she zoomed out to show that the company yacht we were sitting in was actually a little tiny wooden rowboat.

"Do you just publish newspapers?" John asked.

"No, we also publish guidebooks and a map and we are planning to do a magazine one of these days. . . ."

"HALT! HALT!" John shouted to Chris. "Look at that!"

"What?"

"Behind us. A hundred yards behind us. Film that!"

I turned. Behind us, sitting in our shallow inlet was something I had never seen. It was an enormous 200-foot-long yacht. It was solid white. Up on top, a radar dish turned slowly. Just behind, on a top deck, was an automobile. After tying up somewhere, the feet of whoever owned this wouldn't even have to touch the earth.

The yacht was moving forward very slowly and carefully, staying between all the buoy markers, so as not to run aground. It was one of the biggest yachts I had ever seen here, and it had no business in such a shallow inlet.

"Just stay with it," John said to Chris.

After a while, the captain of this ship, probably on orders from its millionaire tycoon inside, came to a halt and began slowly backing up to get out. It had been a mistake coming in here.

"Okay, now pan down to us," John shouted. "Just do it. Just zoom in to us in the rowboat. Did you get that? Did you get that?"

"I got it."

"And don't worry about the sound. We'll dub sound over."

Two days later, John and Chris invited us over to see the segment. They had a small but cozy house set back in the woods. One of the rooms had been set up as a recording studio (much equipment marked "Property of ABC"), and we sat on some chairs to watch. We had seen other segments. Now we were to see this goofy segment about me and my publishing empire. But it did not follow the script John had described before we set out.

The first part of it was the grand white yacht, slowly sniffing its way forward. After a moment or two to allow the viewer to get used to this scene, John's voice came over. You were still looking at this yacht. The rowboat was nowhere in sight.

"I am here with newspaper publishing tycoon Dan Rattiner on his yacht," John said. "He lives in East Hampton, New York, and owns a far flung empire of newspapers on eastern Long Island. Dan?"

At this point, the camera pans down, crosses some of the water and refocuses on this little rowboat with me and John in it. John pushes the microphone toward me.

"Well, after the original paper in Montauk, I started editions in East Hampton, Southampton, and the North Fork, and then on to Block Island."

"That's in another state," says John.

Our friendship with John and Chris Lyons was to last many years. In 1981, John invited my wife and me to Cape Canaveral to join him in watching the launch of the first Space Shuttle.

He was going alone. He'd love to have us for company, and we told him we'd love to come. We would be sitting in the ABC press booth with him as he described his account of this event on-air. We'd be part of his press entourage. He gave us the scheduled date and the time of the launch, which was 6 a.m. We'd of course have to fly down from New York the day before. And, of course, we were so excited that we simply did not go to sleep at all either on the flight down or that whole night before.

And so, at 4 a.m, we were sitting with John in a large white press tent where coffee, donuts, cereal, bananas, crackers, and cheese had been set up on banquet hall tables. Outside, across a lawn, was the rocket.

"When the time comes," John said, "you need to cover your ears. It will be very, very loud."

Nearer to us, facing us on the grass in front of the rocket, was a large lighted digital sign that had numbers counting down the seconds, minutes, and hours. At that time, it read 02:00:12, then 11, then 10, then 9 and so forth. Around it, various exotic Florida tropical birds glided and swooped. Boy, would they be in for a surprise.

During the next two hours, not much happened, except that we ate a lot of donuts, drank a lot of coffee, and met an astonishing number of media people from all over the world. At one point, an astronaut named Kathleen Sullivan, not on this mission but in full astronaut garb, came into the tent and stood in a spotlight on a little platform at one end and answered questions that TV and radio people asked her.

Excitement built as the zero hour approached. Soon it was 00:07:15 and everybody was staring at the sign almost as much as they were staring at the rocket. But when it got to 00:06:59, just as dawn was beginning to break, it simply stopped.

There was a delay. A three-hour delay. Then, after that was over, a five-hour delay. And then, after that it was announced it might take off around 11 p.m. that night. It didn't.

At that point, having had nearly fifty straight hours without sleep and hearing that it was postponed once again, well, it sort of broke our hearts.

In the end, we never did watch that first space shuttle launch. As the sun was setting on the end of that second day, with our bodies exhausted, we gave up. We could do no more.

At the airport, in the lounge at 9 p.m., waiting for our flight to be called, we once again saw an astronaut being interviewed by some newsmen with cameras and microphones. It was Kathleen Sullivan again. She looked the picture of health. And she was wide awake. When her interview ended, I walked over to her.

"Are you giving up, too?" I asked.

"Oh, not at all. I just came out here to the airport to give some more interviews. Then I'm heading back."

"Have you had any sleep?"

"No."

"How can you look the way you do? We're exhausted."

"I'm an astronaut," she said.

About a month later, a package arrived in the mail from John Lyons. In it was a framed, printed certificate with the seal of NASA in full color, an airbrushed picture of the Space Shuttle aiming straight up, and the following inscription:

> On this day, April 12, 1981, *Dan And Tracy Rattiner Failed To* witness the launch of "Columbia," America's first Space Shuttle, piloted by astronauts John Young and Robert Crippin.

The words "Dan And Tracy Rattiner Failed To" were written in ballpoint pen on the certificate. Also, the word "witness" had originally been "witnessed," but the last two letters had been crossed out.

The 300 Pound Naked Lady

~~~~~~

The 300-pound naked lady, full frontal, six feet in height, and very overwhelming, stood front and center as a gigantic two-dimensional poster taped to the front window of the Penny Lane gift shop on Main Street in East Hampton. It was put up there in the spring of 1988 and it would remain there for three years: winter, spring, summer, and fall.

Ordinarily, I enjoyed Penny Lane. Four doors down from the movie theatre, you could buy coffee cups reading "Caffeine Freak," bumper stickers reading "They Can Send Me To College But They Can't Make Me Think," and candy and whoopee cushions that made funny noises and funny and sexy greeting cards and a whole bunch of other things that you might be in the mood to buy late at night after watching a culturally uplifting Arnold Schwarzenegger movie. But this poster was different.

Uh-oh, I thought when I saw the naked lady for the first time. The Ladies Village Improvement Society is not going to like this. Behind me, along this broad boulevard, the pedestrians walked down the brick sidewalk past the flowers and planters, the cars rumbled grandly along the street, under the shelter of enormous elm trees that rose to heights of sixty feet and overarched the road, their leaves rustling in the wind, protecting the propriety and good manners of this town. Swans paddled peacefully in town pond at one end of Main Street. The village green with the big wooden windmill sat at the other end.

And then there was this shocker. I stood there. The naked lady seemed totally unaware anything was wrong. Why she allowed herself to be photographed this way I do not know. But she looked out pleasantly enough. "This is me," she seemed to be saying.

Above there were two words in big black type. "Think Thin," they said. Along the sides in small print, were the names of various items such as chocolate brownies, marshmallow sundaes, and french-fried potatoes, together with the amount of calories in a portion of each. Was she obscene? Probably. She was disgusting. Wait 'til the Ladies Village Improvement Society see this.

These were the blue-haired ladies who took care of morals in this town by actively walking every day and conducting surveillance. They talked to merchants who had *Sale* signs in their store windows too big for the LVIS's comfort. They asked people dressed in Bermuda shorts to please put on decent clothes. They stopped people eating ice cream cones on the street. Please do not do that here. They even sometimes would call in the police to have them escort someone they thought completely inappropriate for this village out of town. And they saw to it that all the stores were closed on Sundays because it was the Lord's Day. They did this by intimidation.

They'd walk into a store if it were open and tell the owners that the store had to be closed. The next Sunday the store would be closed. And now there was *this*.

I went inside, that first time I saw it, to make inquiries about it. A salesgirl came over. The poster cost $10, she said. "It belongs taped to the door of a refrigerator. You wake up in the middle of the night and come down in the dark for a snack, turn on the lights, put your hand out to open the refrigerator door, and you see *this*. It scares the hell out of you. That's what it's for."

In other words, it was a health aid. It would be cottage cheese and carrot sticks for you that night. And maybe it would extend to all future nights you went downstairs to open the refrigerator. They could not have paid this naked lady enough to pose for this photo.

"Do you think it might be better on a back wall in the store?"

"You'd have to talk to the owner, Mr. Greenberg, about that," I was told.

"Is he here?"

"No."

I left.

A week later, I learned about the chain of events that happened over the next few days. A blue-haired lady had shown up at police headquarters on the first day. A woman had complained to the local police about her eleven-year-old son wandering in there on the second day, and the police, knowing ahead of time they were not going to get anywhere with this store owner if nobody else had gotten anywhere by now, turned the matter over to the county detectives, who then sent somebody in to purchase one of the fat lady posters and a few post cards with little tiny naked people on them, just for good measure. A summons followed. Alan Greenberg was in violation of County Law 1985-2 that prohibited the window display of sexually provocative material. It was going to court.

I really wanted to meet with the owner of the store at this point, and one day, after learning he would be in there, I did. He was surprisingly different from what I thought he would be. He was not a suntanned surfer, or an accountant type in tie and jacket, and not even a local. He was a middle-aged, New York City liberal intellectual with ill-fitting clothes and long straggly hair. He had dandruff and a pasty complexion, as if he had not been out of a library or bookstore in years. What was he doing running a novelty shop in downtown East Hampton? But that's not what I asked him.

"What's with the naked lady?" I asked him, motioning to her. He looked both ways, as if he was looking to see if anybody was going to overhear him, and then simply escorted me out the front door and stood with me next to a fire hydrant. There was almost no one around. We could talk here.

"What it's about," he said, "is intellectual freedom," he said. "In the 60s I marched in Selma, I protested in Washington, I was in Chicago for the riots. I am within the law. This is art. A meaningful, wonderful poster. And that some group of old ladies or anybody else would want me to get rid of it, well, they are going to have a fight on their hands."

"I guess you will be going to court."

"I have the Civil Liberties Union involved in this. We will take it up to the Supreme Court if necessary."

Later in the day, I asked the owner of the card shop four doors down from Penny Lane, someone I did business with, what he knew about Allen Greenberg.

"I've had my own feuds with Allen," he told me. "He is a fighter. He stands up for what he believes. And he doesn't back down. But I'm told he has been diagnosed with cancer. Don't be too hard on him."

I looked up the County Law. It was so graphic and specific that much of it would knock your socks off. It described just about anything that anybody could ever do sexually, using words such as bizarre costumes, bound and fettered, genitals of an animal or fowl, undergarments, masturbation, homosexuality, and deviate sexual intercourse.

Similar local laws regarding nudity and prohibited sexual behavior are tame in comparison to this one. This one went on for three pages. I thought at the time, as I began to write about this battle, that I could not publish even parts of this county law in this family newspaper.

Well, the battle in court went on for three years, at which time this county law got thrown out. After a lower court convicted Mr. Greenberg of being in violation of it, "providing dissemination of obscene material to minors, thus requiring the seizure and destruction of these materials and the criminal penalties for the display of offensive sexual materials," an action held up by a temporary injunction, the appeals court, the Appellate Division Second Department, voted unanimously, 4 to 0, that the law was unenforceable.

Oddly, the appeals court decision was made on jurisdictional grounds. The court noted that, though local communities have the right to make ordinances for their small areas, this right is not without its limitations. For example, a County or Town could not lower the legal driving age to fifteen. That is a matter for the State to decide.

The decision was written by a Justice Vincent R. Balletta who took ten pages to declare that in this case, the county law had overreached its bounds.

In other words, in 1990, when this appeal was decided, the truth was the "Think Thin" poster might be illegal after all but now we will never know. The matter had been prosecuted under County law when it should have been prosecuted under State law.

However, the real reason we would never know, was that the matter was no longer worth pursuing. Both Penny Lane and the Paper Place, were no longer in business. Paper Place could not make it. Penny Lane closed, taking the refrigerator lady with it, when Mr. Greenberg got more seriously ill and died.

Also dying, I believe, although I am not sure, was the fact that although no financial judgment was made in favor of the victor, Mr. Greenberg was, in fact, entitled to court costs. And so, the only real winners were Mr. Greenberg's lawyers, and the State of New York, whose claims of laws preempting the County and Town laws was reconfirmed. Nothing at all was ruled about the obscenity. And so, that was that.

Today this row of stores houses the fashionable Ralph Lauren, Rugby, and Sam Edelman Shoes. And if a 300-pound naked lady showed up on a poster, the fashionable New York housewives in high-heeled boots, big floppy hats, and sunglasses would just tear it down and rip it up.

Richard Klein

~~~~~~

In the early 1980s, I began for the first time to hire an advertising salesman to sell ads exclusively in New York City. But it was very hard to find a salesperson who could do this successfully. Although the newspaper was everywhere in the Hamptons, it was known only to the New York people who came out to the Hamptons, so a salesperson would often see a prospective client who had no clue what *Dan's Papers* was about.

Nevertheless, we plunged ahead. I'd offer a salesperson a 15 percent commission on whatever he or she sold, and for encouragement I'd pay an advance, a weekly amount that would be a loan, to be deducted against future commissions when they came in. But more often than not, no sales would be made, and I'd have to end the relationship. After that I'd always say, well, don't worry about the advance. You can keep it. You tried.

And then there was Richard Klein. He answered the ad I'd put in the *New York Times* for a city salesman in March of 1991. I invited him out to the Hamptons for an interview and he came to my office. He was about forty, pleasant looking, well turned out in a suit and tie, and he certainly could make a positive appearance. He told me a series of sales he had made for small publications in the past, brought out copies of them, showed me the ads, and then the proof that he'd sold them—full-blown insertion orders from ad agencies, orders to publish that were as good as gold. Furthermore, he declined to take the advance against commission. He was quite confident he would sell ads very quickly. Of course, I hired him.

I recall watching him out my second-story window as he strode out to his car, twenty sales packs under his arm, thinking, "Well, I'll hope for the best." He lived in Forest Hills, which was good. He would commute to Manhattan. His car was a Ford, modest, a sign of living within his means.

Once a week, I would call the city salespeople to see how they were doing. At the end of Klein's first week, I called him.

"Quite well," he said. "I think I should have something by next week."

"Really?"

"Yup."

"Who have you seen?"

"Several ad agencies. Spielvogel. Young and Rubicam. And Seagrams. I have a good line on them. I think I've got something."

Four days later, he told me he had sold Seagrams. It would be six insertions, full-page color ads, during the sixteen weeks of the summer.

"I had to give them 10 percent off," he said. "I'll fax you the insertion orders. The total is $14,500."

I was astounded. A new salesman selling a huge account in just ten days? This was incredible.

In the second week, Richard Klein faxed me insertion orders for $8,200 from Cartier and $12,900 from an agency that worked with BMW. There was nothing in the third week. But in the fourth week, there were orders from Saks Fifth Avenue and Blue Nun Wine. At that point, I asked Richard to come out to our start-of-the-year staff dinner. It was coming up in two weeks. Everybody would have a bit to drink and there was lots of camaraderie.

"I want to tell the staff what you have done," I said.

"I have no place to stay out there."

"You'll stay with us, at my house. I want you to meet my wife and kids. You're terrific."

"Would it be all right to bring my wife?"

"Certainly. We'd love to meet her, too. We're busy Friday night, but come Saturday afternoon for the party, then stay the rest of the weekend. Enjoy the Hamptons."

Richard and his wife, Adele, arrived in their Ford, rang our front doorbell, and when we opened the door presented us with two bottles of Absolut Vodka. I made a big fuss over them, introducing them to my wife and three boys, who were at that time 8, 10, and 16. My daughter, 20, was up at Sarah Lawrence.

Adele was a frizzy blond and was not only his wife, Richard said, but his best pal. We offered them something to drink, showed them to the guest room, then sat with them in the living room talking until it was time to head off for the party. I took Richard and Adele. My wife stayed at home for dinner with the kids. Our office party was a business affair, after all.

The next morning, after breakfast, Richard shyly told our kids that when he was younger he had a band and they'd had a hit single, which had gotten up to number eight on the Billboard charts.

"It was just that one song," he said. "We did others, but none of them hit. But this one did. We sold out a concert at Palisades Park."

Palisades was a big and very popular amusement park that existed in the 1950s and 1960s on the cliffs overlooking the Hudson River on the Jersey side. But it was closed by 1989.

"You were a *rock star*," my two youngest boys shouted in unison.

"Well, I guess you could call it that."

"What was your band?"

"We were Richie and the Rockets," he said. He turned to me. "Maybe you remember," he said.

"I think I remember them."

"Know what I have with me?" Klein said. "I have it out in the car. It's a cassette of our song, 'Tender Love,' as it was played on the Jimmy Carlock Show on WINS radio. There's an interview with me just before."

"He plays it all the time," his wife said conspiratorially.

"Go get it!" son David said.

And so he did. On this cassette tape, Jimmy Carlock is talking to this younger man and asking him about the concert at the Palisades and how they were doing, you know, now that they had the hit. You could hear Richie answering his questions. Sure sounded like him.

"Okay, everybody, I think it's time we played a little bit of this," Carlock says. "Here we go. Richie and the Rockets and 'Tender Love!' "

Honestly, it was pretty good.

We spent the rest of that Sunday morning at the house, and then I offered to take Richard and Adele off on a tour of the Hamptons. But Richard said they really had to be going. He had a client he wanted to see that afternoon, a big catering house in Glen Cove that was interested. And so, within the hour, this was about noon, we waved goodbye to them as they drove out of our driveway and headed west toward the city.

Later that afternoon, we found two empty bottles of Vodka in a trash can in their room.

The thing started to come apart about two weeks later. By this time, Richard had sent in orders totaling almost $35,000. He'd earned over $5,000 so far. This was a tremendous success. Or was it?

Late one afternoon, my traffic manager, Joe Harris, came up to my office to tell me there was a problem with Seagrams, which was supposed to begin running in three weeks. He had called them to get the proof copy for the ad. They said they couldn't find the paperwork for the ad going in *Dan's Papers*.

"Did you send them the order," I asked.

"I faxed it over. They are looking into it."

Later that day, with a copy of the insertion order on my desk, I called Richard to tell him there might be a problem.

"I'm sure it's just some lost paperwork," Richard said.

"It's signed by Fred Ferris," I said, looking at the insertion order.

"I know. I'll call him up right away. I'll get back to you."

But he didn't. Two days later, Joe came back to tell me they really could not find any record of this insertion order. The next thing he told me left me astounded.

"They told me they do have that insertion order number, but it's for another publication. And they said Joe Ferris never signed anything. Apparently, this was cut-and-paste."

"What?"

"It's pieced together from different insertion orders to make it look as if it was an order for *Dan's Papers*."

"Then it's a fraud."

"Yes, it is."

"Then they are all frauds."

"I guess."

Joe left. All I could think about was the company party we had had. I had stood up there, my arm around Richard Klein, telling the twenty-five people at the party what a great job he had done, what a hot-shot he was and how he was the best salesman we had ever had, bringing in what he did from this very difficult market. People had given him a standing ovation.

Then I comforted myself with another thought. The arrangement was that he would get paid when we would get paid. But now we were never going to be paid. And he had refused any advance. I had not paid him a dime. This was crazy.

And then I thought of Jimmy Carlock, Richie and the Rockets, and "Tender Love." Was that really Richard on the tape? This was AM radio, that's all we had back in the 50s. It was staticky at best. And he had saved this tape for thirty years.

And then I thought of the two bottles of vodka.

I did make one phone call, to the publisher of a small magazine for the auto parts industry that Richard had given me. Richard's name had been on the masthead. He had shown me the ads he had sold. I had called the owner and he had given me a pretty good reference for Richard.

"Aren't you aware of what he does?" I asked this man.

"Of course I am. That's why I let him go. He was seeing a psychiatrist about it. He couldn't help it."

"You never told me anything about this."

"We kept him for almost a year. He kept doing it. The psychiatrist even called us. Said it was a sickness. He'd get him over this, work with him."

"You never told me this."

"In this day and age," this man said, "you give somebody you don't know a bad report about somebody, you get sued. I do think I told you he had problems."

"It wasn't enough of a hint," I said.

Twenty years later, in 2011, I read an article in *Newsday* about a salesman who had been working for the small newspaper we have in Sag Harbor, the *Sag Harbor Express*. The newspaper was pressing charges against one of their salesmen, and the police, after conducting an investigation, were charging him with third-degree grand larceny and one count of second-degree forgery, also falsifying business records and scheme to defraud, also unlawful possession of personal information identification, a misdemeanor.

Yup. It was him. At it again.

John Keeshan

~~~~~~

I was sitting alone with John Keeshan in his small real estate office on the circle in Montauk, looking out at the town green. There was a flagpole on the green. A bandstand. But nobody was around. It was a quiet afternoon.

John was a slow talker, tall and slender and friendly. We were almost exactly the same age, he and I, born a month apart. But while I was chugging along through middle age, John, rather amusingly to not only me but him, was having a tussle with it. Out front was his Harley Davidson. He ran running races and sometimes won his age division, our age division, which was forty-five to fifty. He was not becoming a grown up easily.

John took big ads in my newspaper, when he wanted to do that. Sometimes he would, sometimes he wouldn't. But he was always very sure of himself when he spoke so there was no hemming and hawing about it, which was good. Thus, we sometimes did the business early and after that short time, just sat around talking about this and that for a while. While in business, John was sure of himself, about other things he was sometimes not. It was this gentle, quizzical part of his character I liked.

"Nobody in town today," John said. "Not a soul."

"Everyone's at the beach," I said.

"I've been wanting to ask you something."

"What?"

"After the air force base closed, did you sneak in and look around out there?"

When the air force base closed, we were both around twenty.

"I might have done that," I said.

"Would you want to do it again?"

The air force base was a big thing in Montauk in earlier years. It occupied about 1,000 acres way out at the tip of the island, adjacent to the Lighthouse. Lots of soldiers were there. And we enjoyed it being out there, even though it was off limits to civilians for security reasons. It was alive with activity and military people, many of whom were in town every day. This was when we worried about a Soviet nuclear attack.

But then, in 1962, they closed it. And then, instead of carting everything inside of it away, they just left everything there to rust away forever, putting a padlock on the gates of the barbed wire chain-link fence surrounding it and just walking away. Now, if you could sneak in, you could discover its secrets. And so, of course, we young kids at that time did sneak in. We'd cut the chain-link fence and then fold it back so you couldn't see the cut unless you unfolded it. In late afternoons, we'd go in and cautiously look around. It was such

JOHN KEESHAN
(Courtesy of John Keeshan)

a big place, you could take until dinnertime enjoying it. And then you'd sneak out and go home. You never told anybody.

Now, sitting with John in his office twenty-five years later, he said something pretty weird.

"How about we go out there and sneak in tomorrow," he said.

We were two prosperous businessmen approaching fifty.

"Okay," I said.

"But I can't bring the motorcycle," he said. "Too much noise. It would arouse suspicion."

"I'll pick you up here in my car at ten," I said.

"Pick me up at five in the afternoon. We could stay until dark."

All the next day, I looked forward to this adventure. And it did bring back memories of when it was open and when I was in there as a teenager. Yes, I got in there then. A few times. By invitation.

Once, my dad at the pharmacy in town had me go up there during the day to deliver a prescription to one of the officers. I drove up the little gatehouse with the white sign on the top reading "773rd Radar Squadron. STOP." There was a guard with a helmet and a rifle. I told him what I was supposed to do, showed him the little white pharmacy bag and he looked at a clipboard and pressed the button that raised the yellow barrier gate. I was to deliver it personally and I did.

The other way I got in had to do with one of the junior officers. One day down at the beach, when I had time off from working in the store, I fraternized with what turned out to be young officers off duty. They were just men in bathing suits at the beach, twenty-, twenty-one-, or twenty-two-years-old and, you know, in a bathing suit who knew? A few days later, one of them called and invited me to a party at the officer's club. Want to come? Of course I did. I'll leave your name at the gate, he told me. So much for security and the Cold War.

I got in, parked in a lot and walked along one of the roads inside the base. There were soldiers everywhere. There were not, however, any aircraft or runways. This was not an air force base where there were airplanes. This was an air force base with a ten-story radar tower that had a huge radar dish on top that turned slowly around twenty-four hours a day, looking for incoming Soviet guided missiles.

Once, when I was in there, I shopped at the PX, which is the little store where officers buy toothpaste and candy and souvenirs and other non-military goods. Prices were about half what they were in the real world. I bought stuff. I have to come here more often, I thought to myself. I didn't have very much money at that time.

The radar tower, of course was visible looming over the trees not only at the air force base but from everywhere else in Montauk. You could see it ten miles away. Also if you had a radio on anywhere—we only had AM radio then—every twenty seconds, the time it took for the massive metal dish on top of it to turn around once, there would be a buzzing sound lasting half a section. I asked my dad about it once. He often listened to classical music on a big living room radio console at our home.

"If there were anything bad about that," he told me, "they wouldn't do it."

There were rumored to be big sixteen-inch guns pointed out to sea, notched into protective reinforced concrete supporting structures set into hills at the top of a cliff at the air force base. Though I'd never seen them, sometimes I heard them. They boomed and shook the ground all over town when fired, aimed at dummy aircraft or ships out at sea.

There was a gymnasium, an officer's club, a series of office buildings, and a kitchen and dining hall, all built in such a way that if you were to look down at this cluster of buildings from above, say from a Soviet bomber, you would think you were looking at a fishing village. The gym had a "cupola" on it to make it appear to be either a school or a church. Other buildings had peaked roofs as you might see on homes in a small town. There was no mistaking the radar tower, however, which was across the street.

Most interesting of all, I thought, were the cottages, also designed as part of the "town," which were used as barracks buildings, not only for the officers but for their families. The cottages were nothing special but the water lines and electric lines leading to them were. They were neither buried nor on poles. They were jerry rigged. The electric wires were on six-inch-square wooden posts ten feet up in places, on tree trunks in other places. The water traveled in pipes several feet above ground. They rested precariously on cinder blocks in places and they'd march up and down hills from one building to another. In the dark, there were no street lights, so you'd have to watch your step so as not to trip over them. Very strange indeed.

When the afternoon before our middle-age adventure came. I decided to wear black, but I didn't have black. I did have dark brown, though. I wore dark brown pants and shirt and sneakers. It was going to be pretty dusty and dirty. This place had now been abandoned for twenty-five years. What I was driving at that time was an old Buick convertible. I came to pick up John at his office. He had also decided on black and he found black, and before getting into the car, on this very sunny day, he said "put the top up. We don't want people to see us." And so I did.

A half hour later, with the sun low in the sky, we parked on a dirt track in some woods off the road across from the abandoned guard house. We looked both ways before running across the street, and we went straight to where we remembered the break in the chain-link fence, fifty yards to the east of the guard house. It was still there and we wriggled through.

John looked around nervously.

"I see nobody," he said.

"Local publisher and real estate man arrested and awaiting arraignment for breaking and entering," I said.

"Shut up," he said.

We walked quickly up the road. It was paved, but in places the paving was crumbling, in pieces. We entered the "village" and went to the gymnasium with the cupola on the roof. The door was partly open, hanging by one hinge. We went in. Some of the windows were intact, some broken. There were the remains of a metal grillwork over some of them. Yellow light streamed in sideways from outside. Inside, the basketball backboards were still up, but the nets were in shreds, eaten away. More yellow light came through holes in parts of the beamed ceiling. There were nests of birds and small animals up there. As for the floor, the hardwood was cracked in places, planks pulled away in others. We left.

We walked down to the latrine building. Graffiti was spray painted on the concrete walls. We peered inside. The toilet seats were gone, ripped away. We walked on.

Alongside the ten-story-tall concrete radar tower, there were two nearly windowless buildings, very ominous looking, one larger than the other. The first had a reinforced concrete blast wall out front of where there had once been a heavy steel entry door. The steel door, maybe two hundred pounds, was off its hinges and leaning against the building. It was dark inside that opening, but after hesitating, I followed John in. There was a second, inner concrete wall. It was a building inside a building! So we went into *that*. And here, almost entirely in the dark, we found ourselves feeling our way around a serious military war room. As our eyes adjusted to the gloom, we could see rows and rows of heavy metal tables on which were the remains of thirty-year-old typewriters and green-screen television monitors with frayed electric circuitry. It was unmistakable what we were looking at, heavily vandalized as it was. I reached down to the floor and picked up a metal object in the debris, some sort of rusty switch. I put it in my pocket.

"This is pretty spooky," I said. "We're not supposed to be here."

"Well, we're here."

"I feel claustrophobic in here," I said. "I have to get out."

And so I did. And, after a while, John emerged too, rubbing his eyes.

"Anything else in there?" I asked.

"No," he said.

We looked briefly at the second building, which looked like it must contain more of the same. But we did not go in.

We did go into the radar tower building itself, though. This building was like a giant farm silo. It went way up. But there was a door we could get in through. Inside, once our eyes adjusted to the dark, we saw more of the same sort of thing we had found in the control room. But here there were also chalkboards and big gauges on the walls, with electrical cables leading up through a twenty-foot hole in the high ceiling. There was also a metal stairs that you could climb to get up to the next level with the promise of still more stairs going all the way up, but neither of us would go up there. It didn't look safe. Again, I took a piece of some rusted switch off the floor and put it in my pocket, and as I did, I heard a very loud metallic banging sound coming from high overhead. And I knew what it was.

"The radar tower dish up top must be loose," I said to John. "This is very dangerous."

And so we left there and began a brisk walk to the cliff and the ocean where we believed the big guns once were. I had seen pictures of them in the library. The gun barrels were about twenty-feet long, the size of guns you would see on a great battleship. But though we found the bunkers on the top of the cliff, there weren't any guns. The air force must have taken them. What we did find, though, were the heavy steel gun mounts, behind which were the remains of steel railroad tracks leading down a narrow corridor into the bowels of the structure. Walking down this corridor, we came to a huge empty underground room filled with a foot

BLOCKHOUSE BECOMES SUMMERHOME
(Courtesy of the author)

of water where the guns shells must have been stored at one time. There was graffiti and trash all around, though. There surely were midnight parties that went on here on Saturday nights in recent days, no doubt about it. We left.

And then, in a field we came upon a huge steel lookout tower that had a metal ladder going all the way up to the top. It wasn't as tall as the radar tower but it was pretty near, and from up top, at a platform with a roof, you could surely see everything going on in every direction.

"Let's climb this tower," John said.

"I'm afraid of heights. I can't climb it."

"Oh, come on."

"No. I'm serious."

"Then I'll climb it."

"It's too dangerous. It's rusted out."

And with that, he was off and climbing. I stared up at him. A middle-aged real estate company owner risking his life.

"How ya doin', John?" I shouted up.

"It's *great*," he said.

And so, indeed, in fifteen minutes, there he was, way up there on the platform, with the sun setting and the wind rising, and he began howling.

"Aaaaah Rooooo!!! Aaaaaaah Rooooo!!!!"

"Come on down, John."

"Aaaaah Rooooo!!! Aaaaaaah Rooooo!!!"

"That's enough John!"

———

In the spring of 1992, nine years later, a man named Don Preston published a book called *The Montauk Project* that became a nationwide sensation.

In the book Preston claimed that after the military abandoned the Montauk Air Force Base in the early 1960s, a group of scientists secretly moved in and succeeded in developing time-travel and thought-control projects. A Navy destroyer had been transported from one time to another, but people had died during the process. It was just too dangerous, and it had gotten out of control. The Montauk Project was then abandoned. And from that day to this, a government cover up had kept the whole thing hush hush.

I thought—been there, done that.

Also, when I meet up with John Keeshan every once in a while—we are now in our early seventies—he looks at me with a twinkle in his eye.

"When are we gonna climb that tower out there again?" he asks.

On the Next Page: *After the publication of* "The Montauk Project," *people came to Montauk just to get a sense of what a secret government program involving time travel had done to the town. Was everybody here spooked? Here is a hoax I wrote and published in* Dan's Papers *on March 17, 1994.*

RADAR TOWER AT ABANDONED MILITARY BASE TURNED 90 DEGREES LAST TUESDAY NIGHT

Last Wednesday morning, police received a call from a citizen who lives in the Camp Hero housing development just one mile from the giant ten story abandoned military radar tower saying that when he woke up he observed that the dish atop the tower had moved about ninety degrees counterclockwise from where it had been the night before. When he went to bed, it was pointing to the northeast as it always has. When he woke up it was pointed to the northwest. It has not moved at all since 1962, this man said, since it had served its final day for the Air Force and was decommissioned. He thought it startling that the dish was now turned in another direction.

The call was transferred to the Montauk Police Annex in the center of downtown Montauk where an officer was dispatched to the scene. The dish was indeed pointing to the northwest. But, even though this officer was a longtime Montauk resident, he could not remember if that was different from the direction it always pointed. He thought that perhaps the caller was playing a trick on him and that it had always pointed to the northwest. He went to see the caller, a Howard Edelstein, who was adamant that he had seen it move. And so, the officer asked around. Nine people said that even though the dish looms over the landscape at one hundred and ten feet, they never noticed before which way it pointed. But one old timer, Max McLaughlin, said he remembered that it pointed northeast and when he was asked to look at it, he did and became agitated and said that it very definitely had moved.

This radar tower had been part of the cold war, designed and erected shortly after the Second World War to act as a deterrent and possible early warning system in the event of incoming Soviet nuclear missiles. Nearly 150 airmen lived at the base, monitoring air traffic with the dish, from 1956 to 1962.

Later that day, police made a further call to the New York State Park Commission Office in Sayville, who said it had checked the plans and since the radar tower and the support housing had been made into a state park exhibit in 2002, it had been pointed to the northeast.

The Montauk Fire Department was called to the scene since it was now believed that it had indeed moved, and that it might have come loose from its moorings up there atop its concrete tower. The concrete tower rises ninety feet with the steel dish twenty feet high and forty feet wide atop it. Ladders were put up to the side of the tower. But they did not reach far enough up, and so it was decided to abandon the fire department effort because the dish might be tippy and dangerous and possibly come down on top of everybody at any time and what could they accomplish up there anyway?

As a result of this, the fire department and police put a police cordon around the base of the tower until the Parks Department could dispatch experts to deal with the situation, which the Parks Department arranged for Friday.

The dish did not move at all on Wednesday night or Thursday, but on Friday morning it was found that the dish was facing southwest, another counter clockwise move of 90 degrees. Again, it had apparently moved during the night.

A team of 15 experts from the New York City Bridge and Flange Repair Company, arrived in three trucks on Friday about noon. It was a warm day and there was a big crowd of people behind the police barrier out there to watch. Men in helmets with climbing equipment and pickaxes spent an hour atop the tower and said the dish showed no sign of being moved whatsoever and that the heavy bolts, though rusted a bit, were still holding it in position fast and there was no danger of it falling or coming loose whatsoever.

"It's as solid as a rock," the foremen from NYCBFRC said.

At the suggestion of a Montauk War Veteran at the scene, Retired Air Force Colonel George Pincus, who said he had knew air force officers who worked at the Air Force Base in the 1960s, which he said was the 772nd, it was decided to put a call out to experts in the military who, with blueprints of the interior of the tower, could go inside to see what was causing the movement. To that end, the plywood covers of the doorframes to the tower were removed. A police cordon remained at the tower all Friday night and on Saturday morning, through the good offices of the Coast Guard Air Rescue Squadron at the Gabreski Airport in Westhampton, Army Engineers were contacted and, with the original plans and about a dozen experts, came out in helicopters on Saturday afternoon to go inside the interior of the concrete base to determine what had come loose in there.

The experts spent a day inside and came out with the report that everything inside was frozen solid and it was impossible for anything to move to make the dish turn.

"We are back to ground zero," said Chief Button of the East Hampton Town Police, who was leading the investigation.

Saturday night, a team of ten police officers and detectives remained on an all night vigil at the radar tower. The dish did not move Saturday night.

On Sunday night, the police took a different approach. Feeling that perhaps local teenagers were involved in this as a prank, the cordon was removed and plainclothesmen were dispatched to loiter at the scene all night, some disguised as campers on the beach, others as fishermen or hikers. Three went to some of the homes in the Camp Hero development where some homeowners had volunteered to allow them to conduct a vigil from the attic of their homes all night. It was hoped they would catch the perpetrators in the act. But once again, the tower did not move that night.

On Monday, East Hampton Town Supervisor Bill McGintee ordered the stakeout to be discontinued, "for budgetary reasons," is what he said. East Hampton Town finances are in a shambles. They need to save every penny. "Nothing is coming of this," he told a press conference Saturday afternoon.

On Tuesday morning, it was found that the radar dish had moved from southwest to southeast to point to where it almost was when all this activity began six days earlier.

As we go to press, everyone is waiting with bated breath today, Tuesday, to see what is going to happen tonight.

"Frankly, I'm scared," said Paul Peterson, who lives on South Edgemere Road in Montauk.

For up to the minute information about the movement or the lack of movement of the Montauk Radar Tower dish, go to danpapers.com.

(Courtesy of the author)

Shoreham and IBM

~~~~~~

In the summer of 1980, two men from IBM hauled three large boxes up the steep stairs to the bookkeeping office of *Dan's Papers* on the second floor.

There, they assembled this IBM 6110, a computer the size of an industrial-sized stove that I had bought for $17,400.

It was a wonder of the age. No longer would a mid-sized business need accountants slaving away with pen and ink entering business transactions in ledgers. With the 6110, all of this would be done automatically, through the wonder of computer technology.

The 6110 consisted of four units the size of steam radiators that bolted together into a giant cube. Three had large slots into which you would slide black plastic floppy disks eight inches in diameter. When you turned it on, they spun around in there like song records. Atop this was mounted the fourth steam radiator, which featured a keyboard just below a small black-and-white TV screen. I was a little concerned about the size of the screen, since it was only four inches in diameter. How could the bookkeeper see everything that was going on? But the salesman, who was one of the men now in my office, had assured me it would be just fine.

He also told me, quite proudly, that *Dan's Papers* was, that year, the first business on the eastern end of Long Island to computerize its bookkeeping department. As it turned out, I would live to regret the day.

It is really hard to realize today, when everyone has a laptop, an iPad, a cell phone and a half dozen other high tech devices, just how revolutionary and fascinating computers were in the 1970s. In the 1960s, computers were the size of elephants. You needed entire laboratories with technicians to run them. Even then, they only did anything if you had teams of people feeding the computers punch cards. Only big government, the military, and universities had computers back then. And they were able to share information over something called an Internet.

When the IBM salesman had come to visit me three months earlier to sell me the 6110, he took me out to lunch and, among other things, we swapped computer stories.

A story I told had taken place in 1965 and involved the single largest power outage in the country up until that date. Due to somebody accidentally tripping a switch in Queenston, Canada, the entire northeastern United States from Canada to New Jersey went dark and stayed dark for two days.

"I was in New York City when the lights went out," I told the salesman. "And after the two days when the lights came back on, people were just so happy. And all these stories went around.

"At the *New York Post*, before the blackout, the editor got a phone call from Columbia University saying that some

SHOREHAM PROTEST ON EAST HAMPTON TOWN GREEN
(Courtesy of the author)

scientists there had invented a computer that could play chess. Would the *Post* like to do the story? The editor went out to the city room and scouted around until he found a guy who could play chess. And he sent him there and told him to write about it.

"The reporter wasn't much of a chess player. But how good could the computer be? That evening, he went to this giant glass-walled laboratory where there were three white-coated technicians working an enormous computer that practically filled the whole room. They welcomed him. And after they shook hands all around, they sat him down at a table that had a chessboard on it all set up. He should make the first move.

"He did. King's pawn three to king's pawn four. A standard opening move.

"A technician wrote the move down on a punch card, pushed it into a slot at the base of the computer and they waited. The computer shook and rumbled and its lights flashed and after about four seconds, it spit out its own punch card on which was its own move. The technician read the card and made the move.

"So this went on and on for a while. And for a little while it seemed to the reporter that he might win this simple little game. But then he realized that the computer had led him into a trap. It was quite subtle. And he could not get out. What he did see, however, was that there was one wild move he could make with his queen that might, with a little luck, entirely turn the tables. It was a huge gamble. If it failed, he was done. He made the move.

"The move was written down, shoved into the computer and they waited. The computer shook and rumbled and beeped and it did this for an entire minute, and then two and three minutes. At five minutes, with the computer continuing on like this, the technicians became concerned. They scurried around, checking various dials and buttons, but nothing changed. At seven minutes, smoke began to be emitted out the back of the computer and then, suddenly, the entire northeastern United States went dark."

I have always loved that story, I told the salesman. We were good buddies by that time. The 6110 would revolutionize *Dan's Papers*.

About a half hour after the 6110 was assembled, the computer programmer I had selected arrived and immediately set to work on writing the software for our operation. This programmer was not from IBM. He was an independent contractor. As the salesman proudly explained, IBM was so good that the government, fearing the company would become a monopoly, passed a law prohibiting them from writing the software for what they sold.

About a month later, the software programmer was done. Late that day, he called me up to the bookkeeping office and there he showed me how all this would work. It was dazzling. He was standing alongside my bookkeeper who was seated typing data onto the keyboard.

"Okay, go out of entry mode," he said. And, apparently, she did. "Now press the sort mode." And she did that. The computer began to make a soft, humming sound.

"This is the beauty part of this," he said, proudly. The humming continued. "Okay," he said to the bookkeeper, "you can go home now."

The bookkeeper looked up at me, grinning.

What the 6110 was doing, the programmer told me, was sorting data.

"Everything your bookkeeper has entered this entire day, all the debits and credits, all the new customer information, and all the other things, has been saved onto one of the disks. It's a lot of data. Now, as she has pressed 'sort,' the computer will spring into action just as she goes home. It will add all the day's corrections into the proper places in all the customer folders overnight. And it will continue on until it is done. Then it will be ready to go for the next day's work."

"How long will this sorting take?" I asked.

"With the amount of data you enter every day? Much of the night. But don't worry. It turns itself off when it's done. And I've calculated the time it will take for this amount of data. It will be done in plenty of time before your bookkeeper comes in tomorrow morning.

The computer continued humming away. We left.

"Just don't turn it off," he said as we walked down the stairs.

You know, sometimes things happen that are just so unexpected and unrelated that you could not possibly imagine them having an effect on one another. Thus something did, right out there before our very eyes, compromise the 6110, creating a disaster so great it nearly caused the collapse of this newspaper I had created.

The seeds of this had been planted ten years before. In 1968, a businessman named Bob Uhl got the idea to build a nuclear power plant on eastern Long Island at Shoreham. Uhl was the CEO and Chairman of the Long Island Lighting Company, the multi-billion dollar business that provided the electric power to this Island. Long Island was growing. Power needs were increasing. And indeed, this community was at the extreme leading edge of modern technology. Here, they had built the Lunar Space Vehicle and the atom smasher at Brookhaven National Lab, and here they had explored the early physics that would soon lead to nuclear power, the provider of electricity for the future. Nuclear power was clean, magical, amazing, and it burned no fossil fuels.

I never met Bob Uhl. But I saw photographs of him in the business pages of the newspapers at the time, and I once saw him in a restaurant on Shelter Island where he was having dinner with Governor Hugh Carey. He was an overweight, bald, pudgy man of about sixty-five, a classic example of the "evil" sort of businessman that hippies—who were creating a whole new long-haired culture—would call "the enemy."

LILCO's nuclear power plant at Shoreham could be completed in five years. It would cost $300 million and it would ensure an adequate supply of power for Long Island for years to come.

No one thought that LILCO would have much of a problem with this when it was announced. But LILCO made the disastrous decision to build the plant themselves, rather than hire an experienced company to do it.

Construction started in 1970, but within a year workmen there reported that parts of it were being shabbily built. At one point, inspectors at the Nuclear Regulatory Agency had a whole section of the construction jackhammered out and rebuilt. It would set back completion by two years.

Things only got worse. In 1971, demonstrations were held around the country against nuclear power plants, which, the protestors said, created a radioactive waste that could kill millions if not disposed of properly. Indeed, the waste was not being disposed of properly. It was simply being buried in canisters in caves underground. It would be the problem for future citizens to figure out how to solve.

By 1972, a whole new set of requirements for the building of power plants was issued. As a result, still more of Shoreham had to be torn down and rebuilt. At this point, the costs were closing in on $1 billion.

In 1976, I personally participated in one of the many demonstrations against Shoreham. There were hundreds of us, carrying anti-Shoreham signs, climbing the chain-link fences surrounding the facility to meet teams of policemen on the other side who arrested us and carted us off to waiting school busses to be booked at the Shoreham-Wading River Police station where, the next day, charges would be dismissed. It was a wonderful time.

Soon after that, parts of Shoreham had to be torn out again. And so a further delay was announced. Then, in 1979, a reactor at the Three Mile Island Plant in Pennsylvania cracked and sent a plume of radiation into the air. Although nobody was killed, all plans for future nuclear plants were scrapped. Only the construction site at Shoreham soldiered on.

Sometime in early 1981, just as I was purchasing my 6110 bookkeeping computer, Uhl announced that the delays in the construction at Shoreham—many of them caused by the frequent demonstrations—would now mean that LILCO would soon have to struggle to provide an adequate amount of power for the Island. There might be blackouts. Surely there would be brownouts.

And so, on certain summer days in that year, the power demands made on LILCO exceeded capacity. Power grids partially shut down. Lights dimmed. Air conditioners stopped. Usually the brownouts would last for three or four hours.

And then there were the blackouts. It was later said, though never proven, that these brownouts and blackouts were fabrications, created by the executives at LILCO to turn public opinion back to Shoreham. Finish Shoreham! Now it needed to be finished without further delay.

The blackouts, to show how concerned LILCO was about their customers, were now scheduled to happen at night when everybody was sleeping. People would wake up in the morning to find their electric clocks telling the wrong time, or their houses hot because the air conditioners were off. But otherwise things were okay.

At *Dan's Papers*, when that happened, we came to work in the morning to find disaster with the 6110. The blackout would seize up the computer in mid-sort. And turning it on, which you *had* to do, scrambled everything. What a mess.

We called IBM, and they sent technicians but they could do nothing to stop this. Nothing could work without power. And the catastrophe hit our best customers the hardest. These were the merchants who so wanted to be in *Dan's Papers* that they bought everything we had to offer. We offered roadmaps, guidebooks, magazines, and newspapers in several different editions, as well as newspapers on Block Island and, at that time, on Nantucket and Martha's Vineyard.

There were maybe a hundred very big and enthusiastic customers at that time. And I had to meet with every one of them at the round conference table in our Bridgehampton office almost weekly so we could spread out all the different bills they had gotten from all the different divisions to try to figure things out. Some would bring their checkbooks to show us what and when they had paid. I called these situations "tangles." These customers were tangled up. We found that the only way through this was to return these big customers to manual billing, which created a whole new mess of accounting when we tried to merge the manual and computer bookkeeping entries.

To add insult to injury, just six months after they installed my 6110, IBM, with great fanfare, came out with the sensational PC desktop personal computer. It was the product of the year in 1981. It was on the cover of *TIME Magazine*. It was ten times as powerful as my 6110. It didn't require a "sort." It made my 6110 obsolete. And it cost only $3,100.

I called IBM and angrily demanded they take back the 6110, refund my money and instead sell me a PC. They said they would be happy to sell me a PC. But they would not take back my 6110. It was beyond the 30-day limit. If they did that for me they'd have to do it for everybody.

I was in a rage. I got nowhere. And in the inaccurate belief there would be no further blackouts, I decided that, having spent $17,500 with IBM, I'd spend no more, but would soldier on with what I had.

In this way, in 1982 *Dan's Papers* almost went bankrupt. The next year, I took the 6110 out to the back of our office and threw it in the dumpster.

As for Shoreham, its fate was sealed by the Governor of the State of New York, Mario Cuomo. I still remember listening to the Governor's speech. The Shoreham Nuclear Plant was a disaster, he said. It was true that it had essentially been completed, but it cost $6 billion and LILCO, to cover these costs, had now raised its rates per kilowatt to such a level as to make it the most expensive power company in the nation.

At this point, with everybody on Long Island hating Shoreham, hating LILCO, and hating the astronomic electric rates, the governor ordered the State of New York to buy Shoreham for the cost of its construction. LILCO would be dissolved and its stockholders, which included many of the citizens of New York, compensated. After that, the state would replace LILCO with a new quasi-public power company to be known as the Long Island Power Authority. And that authority would no longer mess with nuclear power. With that, he asked for bids to tear down and bulldoze the Shoreham Nuclear Plant.

And then something amazing happened. As the paperwork began to fly, LILCO, in an act of defiance, started up Shoreham. Nuclear power began to flow from it. For two days, it ran at full power without incident. And then they shut it down forever.

In the years that followed, I would often drive down Route 25A through a woods and past the entrance to the former Shoreham Nuclear Plant. You couldn't actually see the remains of the plant in there. Guarding the road was a chain-link fence, rusting and padlocked, and behind it a driveway that ran through the woods and presumably to the site of the abandoned plant on the Long Island Sound. I did wonder what it looked like in there with the whole complex bulldozed down.

And then, just seven years ago, in 2007, there was an item in *Newsday* which suggested that the former Shoreham Nuclear Plant be reconfigured as a coal-fired plant. It was just a suggestion. But LIPA was thinking about it.

SHOREHAM PROTEST WARNING SIGN
(Courtesy of the author)

I thought—"*What* nuclear plant? It had been torn down! No"?

Well, no. The bids came back. It would cost the State of New York $2 billion to tear down what $6 billion had caused to be built. And so, quietly, the state had done nothing. All those years I had been going by and imagining it inside as a pile of rubble, it wasn't.

It stands. The fuel rods are out of it. But one wonders. A generation has gone by. Most people don't even remember the battle for Shoreham. Would it be a good idea, considering the price of oil and the world situation today, to fire it back up? Beats me.

The Time Capsule

~~~~~~

Over the years, on various occasions, our various towns celebrate big anniversaries of their founding. And on those occasions, they sometimes bury time capsules which are to be dug up in a hundred years.

As a young publisher, I was never informed of when these things occurred, and, as a result, I felt sort of left out when I learned of it because nobody had contacted me about possibly saving a copy of *Dan's Papers*. But then I'd think, well, the paper is new and not well-established. Someday, along with other items, they'll want to put one of mine in with the other mainstream weekly newspapers. And so when the next opportunity came up, I went and called the appropriate authorities only to receive the ultimate rejection—don't call us, we'll call you. There you go, I said to myself.

It was, therefore, a great and wonderful feeling when, in 1990, I got a call from the Mayor of Southampton Village at the time, Roy Wines, Jr., who told me that to celebrate the occasion of the village's 350th anniversary, they were burying a time capsule alongside the pond down by the ocean off Old Town Road, and could I give them a copy of my newspaper?

The newspaper was now thirty years old. I considered it a sort of coming of age. I drove over to Town Hall with a copy of the paper and personally delivered it to Mr. Wines.

A month later, I attended the burial ceremony. It was a grand affair on the banks of Old Town Pond on a strip of grass along the shore. The capsule was to be lowered into the ground next to a bench where people sat to contemplate the meaning of life and feed the numerous swans that live in that pond.

Speeches were made by the Mayor and the Town Supervisor, and the Veterans of Foreign Wars Military Band, in full uniform, played the National Anthem as we held our hands over our hearts. The swans watched. The time capsule was a stainless-steel capsule in the shape of an artillery shell, and sat leaning against a pile of dirt adjacent to several shovels and a deep hole in the ground. There was also a big boulder four feet high with a plaque on it next to that.

When the speeches concluded, two workmen from the highway department lifted the time capsule and dropped it carefully down into the hole: eight feet down we had been told. The dirt was now shoveled over it. And then two more workmen came over and the four of them wriggled the boulder with a brass plaque on it over the top of the hole.

"Thank you all for coming," Mayor Wines said. And everybody applauded.

Well, eighteen years went by, and wouldn't you know it, on the night of June 7, 2008, somebody came down to where this capsule was buried, moved the boulder, and dug it up. They took out what was inside the capsule, then threw the capsule itself into the bushes, and went off. The details were in the local newspaper.

The crime was reported by Thomas Rewinski, an employee of the parks department, who got a call from a resident nearby who saw this big pile of dirt, the boulder moved, and the hole in the ground. Rewinski went down there, reported it to the police, then after the police investigated the crime scene, got a crew together—the robbers had dug the full eight feet down to get at the capsule—and filled the hole with dirt. Then Rewinski had the boulder and the empty metal shell hauled off to a building at the public works yard on Willow Street.

I found it hard to imagine why someone would do such a thing. It seemed like a particularly complicated business for big-time vandalism. But then I thought maybe it was someone who had something down in there he didn't want there—something that when dug up might embarrass or compromise him or his family or his memory.

Well, it was pretty dumb in the first place, it seemed to me, that on this boulder they put a brass plaque announcing that beneath this boulder lay a time capsule of stuff from Southampton in 1990 not to be opened up until 2040. The plaque itself had probably got a certain person thinking about it as he strolled by.

This crime has never been solved. But in any case, I would like to report what stories ran in the copy of *Dan's Papers* buried in this time capsule on New Year's Eve of 1990. We keep back copies of the paper. We have copies of the paper going back all the way to 1960 in a library room in our office.

One story was by Ellen Keiser, one of our reporters back then, who went to the private, off-limits, and nobody-allowed-in-without-a-permit Plum Island Animal Disease Research Center by pretending to be an employee there. She helped celebrate the fourth annual Family Day party. There was an article about the sharp downturn in real estate prices. A three-bedroom house on the ocean, on the market at $3 million had been sold for $850,000. The Shinnecock Tribe was fighting to get some Indian remains in a Southold museum returned to them for a proper burial. There was an article with the headline *Secret Paradise: The North Fork is Beautiful, Peaceful and Still Undiscovered.* Some of the advertisers included the New Moon Café in East Quogue, Bobby Van's in Bridgehampton (with Bobby at the piano), the Coach Factory Store in Amagansett, the Morris Studio in Southampton, and Reed's Photoshop and Studio on Newtown Lane in East Hampton.

As for the lead story that week in the paper, it was a personal letter from me to the future people in 2040. I had known this issue was going in the time capsule after all. So here is what I, as a pompous ass, wrote.

Dear Kids:

At this point, I know most of you don't think of yourself as kids. As I write these words in December of 1990, a good many of you are running around the sofa, peeing in your diapers, chasing one another with sticks, and playing Nintendo. You are listening to the Chipmunks on your cassette players, you are watching cartoons on

Nickelodeon, you are looking to see where we adults have hid the presents. If that ain't kids, I don't know what is.

Well, that's some of you. As for the rest of you, and if we are five billion people, you are probably ten billion, you aren't even a gleam in your parent's eye. You are future kids.

One reason I bring this up, you should know, is that we've been worrying about you. This is a new experience for us. Until now, nobody has really thought much about what things were going to be like for you people way down the road. We only worried about tomorrow. We did our best, and very largely succeeded, in making life a better place for ourselves and our families than had been a few days before. We called it Progress . . .

After this introduction, I went on a bit about global warming and how all the crap we have thrown up into the air has caused flooding, temperature rises, and other problems. I then expressed the hope that you in the future had it under control. I ended this way.

Well, maybe I'm wrong. Maybe I'm writing and you people in 2040 reading it are wall to wall from Montauk to Westhampton Beach all sitting in your automobiles with all the problems of global warming a thing of the past.

Anyway, come visit me. I'm a hundred and one years old here in the year 2040. I've very likely forgotten that I've written this little letter and no doubt, as I'm escorted by my beautiful young wife down the ramp of my private jet to the runway there at the Suffolk County Airport in Westhampton, having just returned from the International Conference I chaired in Paris, I would no doubt be genuinely amused to read what I had to say back in 1990.

Sincerely,
Dan Rattiner
Editor

Now, thanks to some thieves, these damn people in 2040 would never know what I wrote to them.

Ron Ziel

~~~~~~

The whole thing came about because some people I did not know were taking all their worldly goods from their old house in Southampton to their new home in Montauk and had stopped at our office in Bridgehampton. A Mayflower van was not far behind, they told the receptionist when they came in the front door of our office building. But the reason they stopped, they said, was because someone had told them that I was a collector of railroad memorabilia. In cleaning out their house, they had found a whole stash of it up in their attic, stuff left there by a long ago uncle, and it included several cardboard boxes of hardcover books, magazines, and photographs about railroading. They had them in the front seat of their car right on the street. Perhaps I would like them. Should they bring them in?

The word made its way up to my office and I immediately knew they had made a mistake and had confused me with an editor who had worked for me for many, many years—Ron Ziel of Water Mill. Whatever they had, Ron would love. He was a railroad buff who seized upon whatever he could find about railroading. He had ceiling light fixtures from trains in Calcutta, a brakeman's clutch handle from a train in Peru, a railroad crossing sign, now no longer in use, from a road in Translvania. He also had a vast photo collection, not only of old glass-plate negatives taken by others, but from photographs taken by himself as he had traveled all over the world. He had photographs of steam engines struggling to haul freight and passengers through the mountains in the Andes, across the Atlas Mountains in Bulgaria, up the Steppes in the Soviet Union. Often, when he returned from these trips, he would show me the photographs he had taken. He had stood on a ladder in a snowstorm nine miles west of Stalingrad after persuading a border guard to let him do that; the train was two and a half hours late, but he got the picture. His shot here was of a steam engine working hard climbing a hill west of Manila leaving a huge trail of white smoke, arranged in giant puffs hovering over the rest of the train as you could see. Give Ron the time, and he'd tell you more about trains than you might ever want to know.

As a matter of fact, the very chair I was sitting in at the desk in my office when the call came up was a birthday gift from Ron—a red leather easy chair stuffed with horsehair. Formerly, it had been bolted to the floor of a parlor car on the Long Island Railroad "Cannonball," the Friday night train from Manhattan frequented by the wealthy as they came out from New York City to the Hamptons in the 1920s. You've probably seen pictures of these great millionaire developers and robber barons, reading newspapers by the light of overhead chandeliers, smoking cigars, enjoying champagne served to

RON ZIEL
(Courtesy of the author)

them by black porters in white coats. He'd saved this club chair from the wrecking ball in a junkyard in Queens ten years earlier. It weighed thirty pounds, swiveled, and at the press of a button on the end of the armrest, the seat went back. I loved that chair. I still do.

Well, I told the front office, have them bring their cardboard boxes in and I would come down and make a fuss over them at the front counter and would then make a phone call to Ron who would undoubtedly think this was his absolutely luckiest day and come right over.

Four hours later, I was standing on the big deck in front of our office when I heard Ron's familiar voice hail me from out in the street. I looked over and there he was, waving at me from the driver's seat of his ten-year-old beat-up Mercury Meteor station wagon, about to turn out of the line of the bumper-to-bumper eastbound traffic jam into our driveway.

I don't know if it was the waving he did or what, but the right turn he made into the driveway was not sharp enough. He came to a complete halt, threw his car into reverse, and, without looking behind him, began backing up. I could just see in his eyes the enthusiasm and excitement that would soon be his as he became the proud owner of books with titles such as *Highliners: A Pageant of Trains* by that legendary bon vivant Lucius Bebe, or *Canadian Steam* by David Morgan. He had no idea what was behind him.

Directly behind him, in this line of traffic, was a young woman in a new black Mercedes. I judged her to be no more than eighteen and as she saw the rear end of Ron's old station wagon heading for her, her jaw dropped open and she slammed on her brakes. Then she put her car in reverse and began to back up a few feet, just as many as she could squeeze out of the situation before backing her own car into the car behind her, which had also come to a halt. Maybe she moved eight feet.

Well, Ron just kept coming. And so, unable to do any more, she just sat there and stared wide-eyed at the broad rear end of Ron's old Meteor bearing down on her. Both hands had come up and her palms covered her face. She was going to die. There was nothing further she could do.

Miraculously, Ron stepped on the brake just inches before hitting her. He waved again at me. He smiled. He still hadn't seen her. And then he lurched forward, grinding his gears and found that he *still* was not cutting sharply enough. And so he stopped and backed up again.

The woman's hands, which had briefly come down when Ron moved forward now sprang up again, this time covering her entire head. But again, Ron stopped with an inch or two to spare. And this time when he shifted into his forward gear, he came forward and had plenty of room. He pulled into the driveway and came to a stop right alongside me on the deck. He was completely blocking any future people who might like to drive into or out of our driveway.

"Hi," he said. "Thanks for thinking of me."

With that, he got out of the car leaving the driver's door open—he'd only be a minute—and he went inside to get his boxes of stuff.

It was at this moment that I got a good look at the young woman in the Mercedes. She was, I thought, too young to be some rich billionaire's trophy wife. She was, instead, I decided, the trusted daughter of a wealthy Wall Street magnate, coming into town to get, perhaps, a fashion magazine at the Bridgehampton Pharmacy and a *Wall Street Journal* at the Candy Kitchen. She had just experienced, or almost experienced, a fate worse than death—the smashing in of Daddy's Mercedes.

What is it they say—that if the front of your car hits the back of somebody else's car then you are the one at fault? The young woman now ran her hand through her hair, looked neither left nor right and, having somehow gotten control of herself, stepped on the accelerator, roared forward a few feet to catch up to the back end of the Audi in front of her and then lurched once again to a temporary stop. She wasn't about to mention a word of this.

Ron emerged a few minutes later carrying the boxes of books and magazines. It was a great find, he said. He was glad to have it, especially the Lucius Bebee book. Bebee had died in a plane crash you know. And then he was back in his car and heading, in reverse, back out the driveway. Ron and the rest of the Universe would make it through another day.

Robert's French Ice Cream

~~~~~~

At six in the evening on July 2, 1992, a very odd encounter occurred in Southampton at Robert's French Ice Cream. This was a place I loved to take my wife and kids. It was a tiny, one room wooden shack hard by the highway in the parking lot of a recreational complex where you could hit golf balls at a driving range, play miniature golf, or, around the shack, sit at some tables and chairs under an awning attached to this building and have a bad-for-you dinner of fried fish sandwiches, hamburgers, French fries, fried clams, and cakes handed to you through a window. And, of course, ice cream.

It was most famous for its ice cream, which was made right there on the premises. In fact, it had a national reputation. People came from all over to enjoy it, because in 1978, two years after it opened, owner Robert Skrogen got the idea of sprinkling M&Ms in his vanilla ice cream. A few years later, he began swirling raw chocolate-chip cookie dough into his vanilla ice cream.

These flavors, and several others he created, swept the nation. Before Skrogen, there were just the regular flavors.

Reporters from national magazines came to Robert's French Ice Cream to watch him make these new flavors and ask what made him think to do it. Clippings from newspaper and magazine articles were in both the multipage menu given you when you came to the counter to order and in picture frames above the freezers and sinks and ice cream machines that lined the interior walls of the place. Genius is where you find it.

On this July evening, the business was no longer owned by Robert Skrogen. He had moved on after selling it to Audrey "Bunny" Henry, a woman who was happily continuing the tradition. She was happy about it at least until that day at 6 p.m., when she received a phone call while on the beach at Fire Island nearby, visiting some friends. After the call, she immediately took the ferry back to the mainland and rushed out east. It wasn't pretty.

According to witnesses, at about 6:10 that evening, a large 18-wheeler semi-tractor-trailer truck driven by Edward Oliver came down the hill on County Road 39, about half a mile to the west of Robert's. Heading at him the other way was a young teenager driving a Buick Regal, who was driving in an alarming way, weaving in and out of his lane on the road. Now, to his horror, he was in Oliver's lane and coming right at him. Oliver was going to have to take evasive action, and fast.

It had been a hot, sunny day that Tuesday, and for much of it, business had been brisk. But now the shadows were growing long. At that moment, there was only one person in or around the building—nineteen-year-old Dutch exchange student Andrea Keepings, working the late shift until closing at eleven. At six, when she had a free moment, she reached down and plugged in the little row of tiny lights that bordered the awning of the building—Christmas tree lights. It was a gay display, on all summer after the sun went down to provide a warm glow of light for the customers who sat outside at the tables to enjoy their time there.

Earlier, at 5 p.m., Keepings had served a group of fifteen kids celebrating a birthday out there. They'd blown out the candles on an ice cream cake. But now they had left. At five of six, a car had pulled up, and a mother and son had gotten out and ordered two vanilla Oreo sugar cones, and they had left. Now there was nobody there but Miss Keepings.

Andrea Keepings, inside the shack, turned her back on the counter, the window, and the street. She began washing some of the dishes piling up. Picking up an ice cream scoop, she put it under the hot water in the sink.

At that moment, with a huge crash, the entire Robert's French Ice Cream building—a structure measuring twenty by twenty feet, with its counter, freezers, sinks, refrigerator, the big sign, the framed newspaper clippings, the menus, and outside the tables chairs and awnings—simply vanished from around her.

Keepings, who was not injured, stood there entirely alone for a moment, staring at the ice cream scoop. That's all there was left of Robert's French Ice Cream.

People, having heard the crash, soon arrived from the miniature golf course and the driving range and from cars that had pulled over. They found her, standing there, statue still, not a mark on her, staring at the ice cream scoop. She didn't say a word. A police car arrived. An ambulance arrived, and the people gently helped her get into the back. The ambulance drove off.

Soon thereafter, Bunny, who had arrived from Fire Island, made a phone call to the owner of Susan's Garden, a farm stand along the side of Montauk Highway in Bridgehampton, to tell Susan about the accident and that many of the ten-gallon tubs of ice cream were perfectly intact and still inside their respective Plexiglas and steel freezers now scattered along the roadside, all scuffed and scratched, their electric wires ripped from them but still cold inside and that it would be fine with her, Bunny, if Susan wanted the tubs. Just pick them up pretty quick. Susan called the Essay family, who sold ice cream under their own name and had freezer trucks, and they all came and met up and gathered what they could. Thus, tubs of these unique flavors were now at Susan's farm stand, still good and ready to scoop, to become the last Robert's French Ice Cream available ever. Susan put a big sign out front of her place to announce that fact to passing motorists the next morning.

Andrea Keepings stayed overnight at the hospital for observation, and the next day she left town. The day after that, she flew back to Holland.

Ed Oliver was the man who applied the brakes of the semi-tractor-trailer truck as he approached Robert's French Ice Cream. After shattering the building, he had wrestled with the wheel and come to a stop, and was soon found sitting in the driver's seat of his truck, a few hundred yards down the road, breathing hard but uninjured. He declined to be taken to the hospital. His truck had some dings and dents, but that was about all, other than various splatters of ice cream.

As for Bunny Henry, although shaken and now back in Holland, she swore that sometime, somehow, she'd be back in the same old stand when they got Robert's French Ice Cream rebuilt.

The morning after the crash, at breakfast, I told my kids what I had heard on the radio, and that everyone was all right, but we wouldn't be having Robert's French Ice Cream anymore because a truck had mowed the place down. They didn't say anything, but they looked sad for a minute or two.

I drove over there a few nights later. The driving range was filled with customers hitting golf balls off rubber mats out to where the markers that read 150 yards, 200 yards, 250 yards stood by sand traps and greens and bright floodlights. The huge forty-foot-high nets still surrounded the place, keeping the balls from going astray. Next to the driving range, there were families playing miniature golf, cheering good shots. Occasionally a bell would go off when there was a hole-in-one. But where Robert's had been in the parking lot, there was now nothing but this tan twenty-foot-square concrete pad, sitting flush with the black parking lot asphalt. Customers would back their cars up to it, or drive over it. This was where this famous place had sat for all those years. It seemed so small and insignificant to me, considering all the good fun that had gone on there all those years. But it also made me wonder what an extremely bad and dangerous decision this was, deciding to put up such a facility just there. The side of the road—there is no curbing here—was less than twenty feet away. Well, I thought, there wasn't so much traffic when they had built it all those years ago.

I also wondered about Miss Keepings. Surely, she suffered psychological trauma from her unsuccessful attempts to wash the ice cream scoop. She had, after all, cut her summer short to go home. But the fact is, a few years later, she returned to America. I learned this from Agnes Hansen, who along with her husband, Bill, had now bought the driving range and miniature golf course, where Robert's French Ice Cream once stood, from Bunny Henry. Agnes told me she had run into Andrea in downtown Southampton. Andrea is happily married and has put the whole thing behind her.

And then, in 1998, the Hansons made an application to the Southampton Town Building Department to rebuild Robert's French Ice Cream. They had architectural plans. They had the photos of the old place. It would be the same building that had been there for as long as anybody could remember, which was before zoning, and which was therefore grandfathered in and allowed to be rebuilt provided it was in the same place as before, a horrifying twenty feet from County Road 39. It was all legal and all the forms had been properly filled out and the applications made; the Town rejected the request anyway.

I drive by that twenty-by-twenty-foot concrete pad every once in a while. And when I do, I think of the Dutch girl, the 18-wheeler, the birthday party, and the ice cream scoop on that day in 1992 when all hell broke loose.

The Hamptons:
Behind the Scenes

~~~~~~

In the early spring of 1991, the 92nd Street Y in Manhattan asked if I would agree to conduct a bus tour through the Hamptons sometime in August. I asked them how they got my name and they said someone recommended me. I said they were probably looking for someone to lead a bus past all the homes of famous celebrities in the Hamptons and that wasn't the sort of thing I'd be willing to do. They said whatever I wanted to talk about was okay with them. They just needed an answer within two weeks because their Fall Catalogue was going to the printer listing all the performances, lectures, and tours the Y conducts during those three months and they had to make a decision.

I'd seen their catalogues in prior years. All sorts of important people gave lectures, taught classes, and played instruments at events at the Y. I wavered. But when they told me if I would do this they would need my picture for the catalogue and a mini-biography, I said fine.

The name of my tour, as I had requested, was "The Hamptons: Behind the Scenes." The bus would leave the Y at 8:30 on Sunday morning October 9, 1991, and would return at 7:30 p.m. The cost would be $55. And the capacity of the bus would be forty-eight. Also, I would be paid an honorarium which is shorthand for saying they are a charitable organization and they couldn't afford much. I told them they could cut me a check and I would write my own check to them to match it and give it to them as my contribution to the Y.

After agreeing to all this, I found there was a little hitch in what I had agreed to do. I live in the Hamptons. So I thought I could meet up with the bus when they got out from Manhattan at about ten, and then I could wave goodbye to them around 5 p.m.

We discussed this. They were willing to have me wave goodbye from somewhere at 5 p.m., but I'd have to show up to board the bus in Manhattan at 7:30 a.m. I thought about it. They were worried that they'd drive forty-six people out there and I wouldn't be there. I'd have to show up before they left. Okay, I said.

Before I went into the city to spend Saturday night there in anticipation of leaving early Sunday morning, I made a lot of preparations. I arranged with Brent Lynch and Tom Neeley of the Hampton Jitney for them to have a cooler of orange juice and muffins for forty-six when we arrived in the Hamptons to start the tour. I called on school teacher Hugh King and he had agreed to dress up in a Colonial American costume, complete with three cornered hat and breeches, and

BUS TRIP

meet the bus at 2 p.m. in front of the Clinton Academy in East Hampton for a 15-minute tour of the inside. And I had asked Don Spellman of the Sagaponack Country Store to say a few words when we stopped there.

The people who showed up for this tour at 8:30 that morning were mostly people who had participated in the Lexington Avenue Y programs in the past so they knew the drill. They ranged in age from late-twenties to one old man with a cane. They lived in the City or near to the City.

By a show of hands, all but four of them had been in the Hamptons before.

Some of the questions they asked as we were driving out:

"How did the early settlers get along with the Indians?"

"Will we see where Truman Capote lived?"

"How long have you lived in the Hamptons?"

Some of the questions they asked after we got out:

"Why are so few houses made of bricks?"

"Why are there so many people on the streets in East Hampton and so few people on the streets in Westhampton Beach?"

"Will we see where Truman Capote lived?"

I have to say there was something very exhilarating about leading a group of forty-six people—this was a sellout—wherever it was that I wanted to take them. I had a big shiny bus with a festive holiday mural on the side, I had a stewardess, an audio system, and a video system. I had a microphone over which I spoke and a bus driver named Fred, and I had a roadmap. If I told him to make a left over here he made a left over here. If I told him to make a right over here he made a right over here. We even had our own bathroom on board.

I had planned a considerable itinerary. And I had written it down and copies had been made and distributed. Also distributed to the people on the bus were forty-six biscotti. I had bought them at 7:30 in the morning at the cafe across the street from the Y to supplement whatever other sustenance we had. I'd win them over one way or another.

The thing is that I have been living out here so long I know all these fascinating stories and I wanted to tell them all or as many as I could, so I wound up talking from 8:45 in the morning until 5 in the afternoon when I got let off. After this, I met with my wife and kids for dinner at the Blue Parrot on Main Street in East Hampton and didn't speak hardly at all. I didn't speak for the next two hours.

"You don't seem to have much to say," my wife said as we were turning in about 11 p.m.

"Nope," I said.

The first stop we made upon arrival in the Hamptons was on Main Street in Westhampton Beach. I told everybody they could get out of the bus and stretch their legs for five minutes. I told them that I thought Westhampton Beach was perhaps the prettiest Main Street in the Hamptons and that during the Hurricane of 1938 it was under nine feet of water and roofs were blown off buildings and 345 people died and the official papers of the Village of Westhampton Beach were sucked out of Village Hall to come wafting down the next day onto an evergreen forest in New Hampshire.

My people got out of the bus with their cameras, walked around the village and then disappeared into the alleys. Some of them were gone for half an hour. We had to send out search parties. This was not going to be as easy as I had thought.

We passed the site in Quogue where a hundred years ago Thomas Edison and some partners had set up a factory to try to mine the iron that sometimes collects in a black film on the top of the beach sand. The factory failed. And we went to a beach pavilion in Hampton Bays. They loved the beach. They ran over the dune and down to the water and they walked around in the stiff wind blowing that day with their hands in their coat pockets. Then, their cheeks flushed red, they all walked back to the bus.

"This is great," one of them said.

I stopped in front of the old duPont mansion on Meadow Lane in Southampton and told the story of how Baby Jane Holtzer had swung from a chandelier there in a party many years ago and how somebody named Barry Trupin had spent about $6 million trying to restore it as a French chateau. He had failed. Now a New York real estate developer named Francesco Galesi was finishing the restoration.

"See the extension of the building sticking out to the west?" I said. "There is an aquarium inside. You can dress in scuba gear and dive in and swim around with the fish. Underwater there are spigots attached to the walls where you can refresh your oxygen tanks. You could stay in there all day if you wanted. I'm told there are two sharks."

We went past the Meadow Club—sitting up high in the bus we could see over the hedgerows as we passed—and we watched a dozen members in summer whites play tennis on these beautiful grass tennis courts. We stopped in front of the magnificent St. Andrews Dune Church and then the Southampton Bathing Association and I told all the passengers about these places.

In some ways, I felt like, if somebody should come by that I would know, I would duck down so they wouldn't see that I was conducting a tour. Tours and tourists and daytrippers are not what we have in mind when we think of what would be good for the Hamptons. We want a much more substantial clientele than this. (But this was for the Y, I thought.)

I took my gang past some of our beautiful summer estates and past our beautiful windmills—the one at Southampton College, the one on the Village Green in Water Mill, and the one on Ocean Road in Bridgehampton—and I talked about them and you know when you tell stories to people about things you see every day you begin to appreciate them more yourself. These were damn beautiful windmills.

Don Spelling told the hundred years of history of the Sagaponack General Store, about how they built the building one way and then turned it around 180 degrees because they liked it better the other way. Don leaned on the wooden railing on the front porch by the entrance to the store and my gang all stood on the sidewalk below him. Various dogs kept turning upside down on the ground there in the hopes of getting their stomachs scratched. Some of the gang obliged.

We stopped for lunch in East Hampton and I let everybody loose in the center of town for an hour and a quarter with a list of the various restaurants. If the cash grosses in downtown East Hampton were a little bigger that Sunday than they might have otherwise been, well, they were. My gang was making a major contribution to the town.

I tried to take everybody up into Springs to see the home and grave of Jackson Pollock but when we drove down North Main Street the bus driver braked to a screeching halt where the railroad trestle crosses over the road. The height of the bus was eleven feet. The trestle is has only ten feet clearance.

"There is more than one way to skin a cat," I said.

We drove back into town and past the Middle School to make a right onto Osborne Lane. We'd come down Cedar to get up into Springs. And I told the story about when the Middle School was the High School back in the late 1960s and some kids went out back at 4 in the morning and changed a railroad switch so that the 5 a.m. Cannonball from New York left the tracks and plowed up a huge swath of land before coming to rest just ten feet from the school cafeteria, which was what the kids hoped to have it hit.

We passed the turn on Springs Fireplace Road where Jackson Pollock, angry and drunk, had flipped over his convertible and killed himself. Also killed was one of the two young girls in their early twenties who were in the car with him. His wife was in Europe at the time. That was in 1954.

We stopped at the studio where Pollock lived. And we went to Green River Cemetery and walked around and looked at Pollock's grave and the graves of about forty other artists who are buried there.

"People are just dying to get in," I said as I led the group around. One particular grave is made of film reels but has no markings to indicate who might be buried there. A filmmaker one supposes.

We stopped where the sun was setting on Three Mile Harbor Road over the boats and, inasmuch as we were in front of my house, I had all forty-six people get out and come up on my lawn. They petted my dog who was up on the deck, they tried to pet my cat (the dog barked the cat off), they took pictures of my house and walked around it, and they watched the sun set. Several of them said that no bus tour guide had ever taken them to their personal home before and thank you very much.

We toured Sag Harbor for a bit and just before I had them drop me off at the Bridgehampton Candy Kitchen on that town's main street to end the tour, I had the bus driver pull over and everybody got out to silently stand alongside one of the kettlehole ponds on Scuttlehole Road, amidst the bugs circling around, to enjoy the farm fields and the ducks and geese flying overhead as the sun set.

"Is there a reason we are here?" somebody asked me.

"To watch the sun set, stupid," somebody else answered before I could.

As we watched, on the other side of the pond about a quarter mile away, two Labradors commenced to run at top speed along the shoreline. They came all the way around the pond, which took them about four minutes, just so they could get a few pats from forty-six tourists, one bus driver, one tour guide, and one stewardess. We patted them and they wagged their tails happily and from across the pond there came the long drawn out wail of a dog owner—a woman—calling to her two dogs to come back. After a while and quite reluctantly these dogs left us and raced back around the pond the way they had come.

Would I do this again? That was the thought that came to me as I waved good bye to them at 5 p.m. And at that moment, the answer I would have given was "no."

That night, however, I had a dream. I was leading all these people from a bus through some strange village in

Morocco where we went into people's houses and looked at the residents living there and these people were not happy about this and shooed us off and we dispersed and people ran off and we never were able to round them up again. In the end, I came home with only half as many tourists as we had gone out with. I woke up in a sweat.

So the answer was still no.

John Darden

~~~~~~

John Darden worked for *Dan's Papers* in the mid-1990s as our credit manager. People would buy ads, fail to pay their bills on time, and it was John's job to call them up and urge them to pay. He'd talk to people in his nice pleasant voice with its slight southern drawl, and no matter what anybody said in reply, nothing ruffled him. Often he got results where others could not.

John and I hit it off from the get-go. And in the course of things, I got to know him pretty well. Soon we started going out and playing golf together on weekends. Turned out we were a good match. We both played in the low 90s.

At this time, it was somewhat difficult to find a place to play golf in the Hamptons, even though there were plenty of golf courses upon which to play. This was something I resented. As a teenager growing up in New Jersey, I played golf all the time in the summer, just about anywhere I wanted. There were courses everywhere. And I was on the golf team at my high school. Here in the Hamptons, I found there were also many stunning private golf courses, but none would let me play on them. It was pretty widely known that three of these courses, all private clubs, did not accept Jews or Blacks. They were the Shinnecock, the Maidstone, and the National. At one point, when I moved from East Hampton to Bridgehampton, I applied to the nine-hole Bridgehampton Golf Club, which was not a particularly attractive course but at least I thought could be a course where I might play. To my astonishment, I was rejected. They too did not accept Jews or Blacks. This left me able to play at a few sort of worn out public courses in the area with John, which I did, reluctantly. Most were pretty flat and uninspiring. One, the Poxabogue Golf Club, was a nine-hole course but actually was only big enough for seven holes. The last two holes were just chip and putt holes of seventy-five yards or so. Nevertheless, it was always a good day in the sun, "a good walk ruined," as the phrase goes, as we talked and talked and tried to get a ball into a cup with the least number of swings.

One time we talked about how we came to play the game. John had gotten into the game because for twenty-five years, before he worked for me, he had worked for Grumman, the builder of Navy fighter planes. For more than two generations, this was the largest employer on Long Island.

"It was in the culture," he told me. "We worked hard. We spent weekends together. Grumman had several golf courses for us to play on. I really got to enjoy the game."

"I have an idea," I said. "Let's see if we can arrange our lives so we can play on the Maidstone, the Shinnecock or the National. Or even Bridgehampton."

"How do we do that?"

I told him that I was thinking about something I had read in a paper the year before. The Shinnecock Golf Club,

ME AND JOHN DARDEN
(Courtesy of *Dan's Papers*)

one of the three oldest golf clubs in America, had been the site of the 1984 U.S. Open. Now, in 1994, they had been invited to again become the site of the 1997 U.S. Open. But, I had read, times had changed and there was a catch. Before the Open, they would have to accept a black member. They agreed. And so, to get this event back, they accepted a black man who was a doctor.

Two weeks later, a small ad appeared in *Dan's Papers*. It was a photograph of the two of us, arms around each other's shoulders, smiling at the camera, each toting a bag full of golf clubs on our back. One of us, me, was white, Jewish, and I look Jewish. The other, John, was black, very black.

"Our Goal Is To Play Every Private Golf Course In The Hamptons. Dan and John—Golf Partners," was the headline.

Here was the copy under the headline:

We are both WASPs listed in the Social Register. Handicap approximately 15 each. LOOKING FOR INVITATIONS TO: Maidstone, Shinnecock, the National, Amagansett, Bridgehampton, the Atlantic, etc., Available for 8 am tee time every Thursday all summer. PLEASE CALL US. 631-537-0500.

The ad went in the paper for the first time on the Fourth of July. I ordered it run for the next ten weeks, until Labor Day, and it certainly created quite a stir. An account of our quest appeared in *Newsday*. Another account appeared in the *New York Post*.

Frankly, I did not know what to expect. Maybe we'd get nobody. But that's what we were getting anyway. One day, we got an invitation from a woman named Winnie Hatch, inviting us to play at the Bridgehampton Club which, earlier on, had rejected my application. We went and had a great day. Although only a nine-hole course, one of these holes is a par three that from tee box to green is a fabulous English garden with flowers in bloom over which you have to hit. Do it and you stroll down the garden path through the buzzing bees and butterflies on the fairway. At the end of that fairway, the green sits on a rise. Winnie Hatch hit the ball as well as we did, and when we asked her about it, she said she was a tomboy when she was a little girl and could do lots of things as well as boys. As it happened back then, however, the only sport open to her in high school was field hockey, which she played with gusto, eventually becoming captain of the team.

It was walking through this fairway garden that John told the both of us about his adventures at Grumman, not on Long Island, but in Iran.

"You remember when Iran was ruled by the Shah?" he asked. "Well, as the Islamist fundamentalists were trying to take over, Jimmy Carter sold the Shah half a dozen Grumman F-14 fighter jets to help him deal with the uprising. These fighters were the best in the world at the time, bar none, and a lot of people were surprised we would have sent them to the Shah. We hadn't sold them to anybody at that time, not even the Israelis."

"I remember when that happened," I said. "It was just six months before he was overthrown."

"So over they went. And over we went. These were very complicated aircraft. I was part of the Grumman team that was sent over to Iran to show them how to fly them."

"I've heard there are golf courses over there," Winnie said.

"There were two we Americans could play on. Both were just desert with sticks in the sand."

"Doesn't sound like fun."

"We made it fun. Anyway, few Iranians were willing to try to learn how to fly these planes. There's a rule in the Iranian military: if you break something, you have to pay for it. And if you can't, there is punishment. So—I didn't see this but I heard about it—one of the Iranians, sitting in the cockpit of an F-14 on a runway, pushed the ejection button by mistake. The cowl flew off, the seat flew up, a parachute opened, and he floated back down to the ground. They shot him. That's what we were told anyway."

"Did they ever learn how to fly them?" Winnie asked.

"Never happened. The Shah was overthrown. We had to get out of there fast. We picked up everything we could—the spare parts, tools, manuals, and flew home the next day. You can't learn to fly a plane without those things."

We arrived at the green. John and Winnie were on it, but I had hit my ball over it onto a grassy slope, so, as farthest away, I hit first. I hit it into the cup for a birdie.

A week later, I got a call from a representative of a major motion picture company who said he had seen our hilarious ad in the paper and believed there was a story line for a movie here. He came out from Manhattan and the three of us met in my office.

"James Earl Jones should play me, or Eddie Murphy," said John, whose ancestors were slaves.

I, a man whose grandfather fled the pogroms in Russia during the era of the Czars, said I should be played by Harrison Ford or Bruce Willis.

Subsequently, the guy wrote us a letter which says he spoke to his superiors and they were in agreement with him. But we never heard anything further from him.

Well, no further invitations came in for us to play one of the fancier courses for the rest of July. So we continued to trudge around on the weekends playing the public courses.

I have to tell you, playing on a public golf course is not at all like playing on a private course. The thing is, there is a whole lot of etiquette to golf. There is etiquette about who gets to hit first, where you stand when somebody hits, where you allow your shadow to fall in relation to the person hitting, when you speak, even what you speak about. You don't, for example, constantly criticize or give unsolicited advice about your opponent's game. So it's wonderful when you play a game of golf with somebody who knows the etiquette too.

However, for a few bucks, anybody can play on a public course. So often etiquette is out the window. Once, playing Indian Island, a public course in Riverhead, the starter had us join with two people who barely knew which end of the club to hit the ball with. And one of them was incessantly badgering the other about his game. At one point, the receiver of this badgering was just about to hit when it started up again. I was quietly standing next to him at the time.

"Maybe, if I beat the shit out of him he'll shut up," he whispered. He was shaking when he said this. Then he hit the ball about three feet making a huge divot in the fairway. "Shit!" he said. "Goddamn Mother Fucker."

Actually, now that I think about it, there was one time I had been on the golf course of the forbidden Maidstone Club. It had been about twenty years earlier, in the middle of the night just after a winter snowstorm. I was with a girl I had met at a bar at the time, and as I drove by the Maidstone, all sparkling white in the moonlight with nary a footprint on it, she got inspired.

Oh, stop the car, she whispered excitedly. When I did, she jumped out, took off her mink coat and threw it in the snow, then quickly took off all the rest of her clothes and began running around naked. She did that for about five minutes. After that, she grabbed everything she had thrown off, scurried back to the car, got in the back seat and dressed again. "Nice!" she said. I continued on.

In late July, we got three invitations, none of which were from the Big Three, but all of which were from lesser known private clubs. They were Westhampton, Amagansett, and Gardiner's Bay on Shelter Island.

We played at Westhampton—I think John had arranged it because he bartended at Magic's Pub in that town at night—and it was a nice course, rather flat, on what had at one time been farmland. And we tried to play at Amagansett, but it turned out that the phone call from a member there might have been a hoax. When I called back the number left on my office phone answering machine and spoke to the person who answered the phone, he said he didn't know what I was talking about. And then, in the last week of July, we did play Gardiner's Bay, one of the two golf courses on Shelter Islander.

What a surprise this golf course was. I hadn't even known it existed. Hosting us at this private club were Giorgiana Ketcham and her husband Jack, wonderful people who owned a real estate firm on the island. We enjoyed their company.

And we fell in love with the course. It is gentle, with rolling hills and great trees, broad fairways and magnificent views of the bay. Giorgiana told me it is kept up without the use of pesticides.

Then one day, I got a call from a member of one of the three major exclusive clubs, the Maidstone. Alfred Devendorf was inviting me (but not John) to attend a cocktail party at the club in honor of a favorite charity of his, Children's House.

"I think this is a big chance for us," I told John, waving the invitation at him. "I don't know this man or what he's about, but I'm going to slip our hope to play golf there into the conversation."

At the party in a patio dining room, I was trying to find a proper time to sneak the question into the conversation when he simply beat me to it. He waved at the beautiful fairways outside and asked me if I'd consider playing a round of golf with him sometime. My reply would be impolite, but I had to take the chance.

"I wonder if I could bring a friend of mine, John Darden, to play too."

"I've heard about him."

"You have?"

"Yes. That ad of yours is quite a hoot."

We played on a Tuesday, the day after Labor Day weekend. Things slow down in the Hamptons after Labor Day. So I wasn't sure if he wanted the two of us to play with him because after Labor Day nobody would care or because it was fine with him if they did. Maybe both.

Before that round, however, I got another call to play at the Maidstone. It doesn't rain but it pours. It came from another member, Jay Eastman, who said he had read the ads and would be delighted to have us.

"Well," I said, "We already have an invitation from Al Devendorf to play, so maybe another time," I told him. Why I turned him down I don't know, but I rather enjoyed doing so.

The Maidstone course is stunning to play, and very ingenious. It's a bit long but not that difficult. Instead, it is full of surprises. You come around a dogleg turn and are confronted with an elevated green that seems to float in the air. There is a hole where you tee off through an almost peek-a-boo opening in some woods only to find yourself on an enormous wide, flat fairway. One hole, the fourteenth I think it is, runs along the back of a sand dune parallel to the ocean. You climb a flight of wooden stairs to the tee box atop the dune, set your ball down and look out to a fairway extending 450 yards along the low hollow in the back of the dunes. The green is at the end. From up on that tee box, you can also see, off to your right, however, the beach itself. Hit a slice to the right and your ball flies over the dunes and out among people in bathing suits lying on beach towels in the sand.

Coming up the eighteenth fairway, both John and I agreed it was the most beautiful course we had ever played. And I played the best game I'd played in ten years. Hit the ball a mile. I'd have beaten Winnie Hatch if she had played here with the same score she had played Bridgehampton.

When the round was over, we sat on the slate patio out front of the magnificent clubhouse—it looks like the country home of a Scottish lord—had drinks and watched the sun set.

And Al invited us to play with him again. At the end of that round, in the locker room, he turned to John to ask him a question.

"Would you consider becoming a member of this club?" he asked.

Town Pond and The Bonackers

〰〰〰〰〰〰〰〰〰〰〰〰〰〰〰〰〰〰〰〰〰〰〰〰〰〰〰

Sometimes, when an issue in one of the towns would come up that I couldn't quite figure out, I would make an appointment with an appropriate mayor to get a better understanding of it. And so it was that on a sunny day in July of 1994, I went to the office not of the mayor, but of the Village Administrator in East Hampton who the mayor had recently hired to assist him.

Larry Cantwell worked out of what had at one time been the second of two bedrooms on the second floor of a former private home on Main Street in that town at the end of a row of stores. The other bedroom was now the office of Paul Rickenbach, the official mayor, who wasn't in that day. He was off playing golf. Reaching the top of the stairs, I once again looked through the mayor's open door and once again thought that was the reason he had Larry.

East Hampton Village was in the throes of big changes during those years. All you had to do was look out that second-story window. Where once there had been a long row of mom-and-pop stores—Marley's Stationary, East Hampton

BONACKERS IN THE POND
(Courtesy of the author)

Five and Ten, Valerie's Tennis Shop—there were now, among
them, many stores with very expensive merchandise and very
familiar names: Tiffany, Cartier, Polo, Mark Fore, and Strike.

The value of real estate had skyrocketed with the influx of
the rich and famous. The moms and pops couldn't afford the
rents anymore. Indeed, the main street where Cantwell and
I were now standing in his office, looking out the window
together, was a testament to that fact. Not long before, Village
Hall had been in one of those storefronts. But then, forced to
move because of skyrocketing rents, the Village had bought
and fixed up this run-down historic nineteenth-century home
and made it the Village offices. We looked down at the cute-

sie little picket fence the Village had installed, at the modest sign on the lawn that announced it as the Village Hall, at the flower arrangements and town park benches up and down the street leading out to the treasured old English windmill. Life had improved greatly since the Hamptons had been "discovered."

"I remember the first high-end store in town," I said. "Do you?"

"You got me there," he said.

"It was Dean & DeLuca," I said. I pointed to what had been originally the scruffy town post office on Newtown Lane. "I went in with my sales pack under my arm to sell them an ad. The manager was waiting on a customer. I thought it was just a sort of fancy deli. So I looked around. I will never forget this, Larry. I picked up a little jar of jam. It was priced at $28. I was so startled I almost dropped it on the floor and broke it."

"If you break it, it's yours," Larry grinned.

"So I hung on tight. It was a jar of jam made in the mountains of Bulgaria or somewhere."

"But you haven't come here to talk about a jam made in Bulgaria," Larry said.

"I'm sure you know why I am here," I said.

"I'm sure I do." We both turned and walked over to look out the opposite window in this office, the one that faced all the way down Main Street to the town green and, upon it, Town Pond.

There was an enormous, twenty-foot-high pile of muck and mud sitting in the grass alongside the pond.

"Why, Larry?" I asked. "Everybody is up in arms. The environmentalists. The nature people. The wealthy."

Larry sat down at his desk and sighed. I sat down facing him.

We both knew the history of the pond. It was one of the reasons why so many rich and famous had come to settle in town. They'd drive out here, perhaps to visit a friend, and they'd make the turn from Wood's Lane onto Main Street and there it would be, a beautiful pond with two enormous mute swans in it, with ducks and geese, with children playing with their toy sailboats in the summer and in the winter skating on the pond. The rich would fall in love with our pond; and would buy a house for a million dollars near it.

And yet, there had originally not been a pond there. From the seventeenth century when the white men first settled here until the 1930s, it was just a big old ratty swamp. Cleaning out this swamp and turning it into a pond was a giant Depression-era reclamation project. WPA workers had come into town. They'd built the wooden borders of the pond, dug a pit, put in a huge drainage pipe so that the water, when it collected in the pond, would go down the pipe and into an underground stream and into the ocean. It was so gorgeous, it had made the town beautiful.

"It was the damn algae," Larry said, motioning at the mound. "All that nitrate rich fertilizer people use these days, leeching into the pond, turning it brown."

"The brown tide. So you dredged it?"

"We had to."

"With heavy equipment?"

"We had to get it out of there. And so we dredged it. Brought in a guy with a backhoe. We are off the record here?"

"We are off the record."

"Three days ago, around four, the big Highway Department trucks came to take the first load over to the waste area. But then something broke. Something on the backhoe. A bolt or something. They couldn't load the trucks. And then they couldn't finish the job. Not even half the pond was dredged."

The following morning, the townspeople, and especially the wealthy people living nearby, soon realized they had in their midst a steaming hot pile of muck next to their precious Town Pond. And they went nuts. The backhoe had come back the next morning to continue the job. But the people wouldn't let it on to the sacred ground. They called the police. Now, two days later, the muck was still there. The backhoe had been banned. And nothing had been done.

"What are you going to do?" I asked.

"I don't know."

We sat in silence.

"But when I do, you will be the first to know."

Two nights later, around two o'clock in the morning, we finished laying out that week's newspaper in our office in Bridgehampton and the staff and I began our respective drives home. For me, that meant heading east toward my house in East Hampton up on Three Mile Harbor Road, nine miles away. About halfway along this journey, I passed under the great archway of elm trees that line both sides of Wood's Lane as you enter downtown East Hampton, came to the stop light, and then turned left to head down past Town

Pond onto Main Street. The mound was gone. You could see the tire tracks. But then I also saw, barely, in the darkness of that hour, a group of grown men in rubber overalls and work shirts, wading around armpit-deep in the pond itself.

I pulled off the road. Whatever this was, I had to know. In fact, after getting out of my car, I got back into it, picked up my camera and went back out. What the hell was going on? On the shore, there was a boom-box radio with its aerial sticking up playing country-western music. In the water, the men were poking around with wooden poles and nets, tarpaulins and rakes. Then I recognized them. The Bonackers. The men who were the descendants of the very earliest settlers of this town, the hardworking laborers, fishermen, clammers, and oystermen who now were being squeezed out of their community by the ever-encroaching owners of the giant McMansions. I'd even lived among the Bonackers in one of those small houses on Three Mile Harbor Road for twenty years.

They stopped working briefly when I arrived. I talked to Stuart Vorpahl. "When did they get to the muck?" I asked him, waving an arm at where the big pile had once been.

"Earlier in the night. Big truck and backhoe."

"I guess they had to do it at night or they'd have never got it done."

"Yes, yes."

"What's with the sweatbands?" I asked him.

All of these men, five of them, were wearing, besides overalls and cotton shirts and waders, these Lycra tennis sweatbands around their heads.

TOWN POND BONACKER BOAT
(Courtesy of the author)

"Only way we can keep the sweat out of our eyes," Stuart said. "It's hard work. And we're covered with muck. We go like this."

He demonstrated by lifting an arm and, with just his forearm, slid his sweatband down to his eyebrows and then back up.

"This is not about tennis."

"No. But it's sort of a badge."

"Hey, Dan, if you're going to write about this, don't use my name," one of the other men said.

Two other men began laughing. "You're being ridiculous," one of them said. Then, after this brief encounter, they all went back to work. They pulled their rakes along the bottom as if they were clamming, and then with great effort pull up heavy, thick black muck and dump it into wicker baskets set inside inflated car tire inner tubes floating on the pond, then drag the baskets to shore with ropes to dump into the back of pickup trucks. Sometime it would splatter. I tried to keep clear.

"You sell this stuff?" I grinned.

"The Japanese buy the muck by the barrelful," Tiernan Crowley told me. "They wrap sushi around it. Tastes great."

Off in the center of the pond, I recognized Captain Jack O'Day wading around, pushing the green algae toward the shore in a large rubber tub and tube. The water was up to his chest.

"We found a bicycle," Vorpahl said. "Dug it up from the bottom."

"Yeah. It's from the 1950s," Crowley said. "An antique."

"Aren't you guys just dredging like the big backhoe was?" I taunted. "Isn't that against the law?"

"Ask Larry," one of them said. "He hired us."

"We're just cleaning up," Vorpahl said.

Turned out they had been hired to do this three nights a month. There was a contract. It was for a year. At other times they were out making a living clamming or long-lining in the bay.

"Do the swans go after you?" I asked.

"Nah. They're gone. Saw us comin'. There's a big frog in here, though."

"Two big snapping turtles, too," Vorpahl said.

I asked if I could take some pictures of them, and they said sure, go right ahead. So I did, the automatic flash lighting up the scene and causing the Bonackers to bring their hands to their eyes. Then I said my goodbyes, wished them luck and headed off in my car to home. All the summer people would ever know was that the muck was gone and the pond was sparkling clear. And the Bonackers had a few extra bucks for their effort.

WQXR

~~~~~~

I can still recite it today.

"Hello, this is Dan Rattiner, high above the Hamptons in the *Dan's Papers* helicopter with the weekend report for WQXR."

For many years, I broadcast occasional shows on local radio or TV stations. But what I really lusted for was a show, an ongoing show if possible, on the nation's greatest classical radio station, WQXR, which, with offices in Manhattan, was "the radio station of the *New York Times.*"

It took me many years to get such a show. It's a bit of a story, but it does have a shocker for an ending.

In the late 1980s, this country was agog with wonder at what could be accomplished by a high school student genius in his garage with the right computer equipment. Many movies were made with this as the premise. *War Games* was one of them. *Real Genius* another. In these movies, the experts would be dumbfounded by some serious problem, such as the possibility of nuclear war. A kid would be brought in

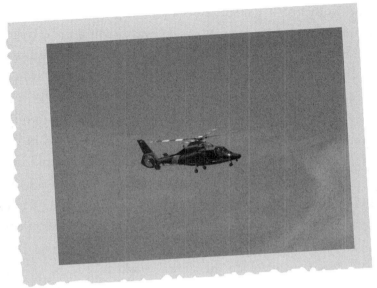

THE DAN'S PAPERS HELICOPTER, HIGH ABOVE THE HAMPTONS

eating a slice of pizza and drinking a Coca-Cola, and in two minutes he would press some buttons and everything would be okay. It was amazing.

In real life, there were kids who got treated to this god-like stature just by saying they had developed a new Website that could make millions of dollars. Investors would line up at their door. Of course, by about 1999, there was a big dotcom crash in Silicon Valley, a sort of sober re-thinking of this situation.

In any case, around 1989, I met a man having a party to celebrate the purchase of his new mansion in Amagansett, who wondered if I might consider having a show on a new national Internet radio network he was heading up. I forget the name of this. It was not XM or Sirius. It was a precursor to them. And it came and went in about six months with a great thundering loss of cash to all concerned.

"We'd pay you $200 a week to do a Friday morning broadcast about the upcoming events for the weekend in the Hamptons. You'd talk for about three minutes," he told me.

Three minutes is a long time for a radio show. But I did know there were things to do and places to go, and I could surely pick them out from our coming events columns, write a script and speak it into a microphone.

"Where would I do the show?" I asked.

"We have new studios in midtown Manhattan we're now just completing."

"Could I do it from the Hamptons?"

"I think you could phone it in, if we had a good connection and the call were clear."

"I have an idea," I said. "Let me give it a try."

My idea was to use a bad telephone connection as part of my broadcast. Regular radio stations in big cities sometimes had broadcasts from helicopters looking down and reporting on highway traffic. I'd report on upcoming events in the Hamptons from a noisy helicopter flying over the Hamptons.

It would be easy to get a "helicopter." I actually wouldn't get one. I'd go down to the beach in my car, park there, and, while sitting in the passenger seat with the motor running and the waves crashing outside, call the station on one of the boxy cell phones we had at the time and pretend I was up in the air.

"Well, that's all we have time for," I'd say at the end, "This is Dan Rattiner, high above the Hamptons in the *Dan's Papers* helicopter, signing off until next week."

I did this broadcast for all ten weeks of the summer, and everybody at the station told me it sounded fine, though nobody I knew ever listened to it and I, lacking a subscription, couldn't listen to it either. Then, after ten weeks, it was Labor Day and the season was over and that was the end of it. In the spring, after the company didn't call me to set this up again, I called them. Their phone was disconnected. And so that was that.

The next spring, we got advertising in from a New York City classical music station called WNCN, which was a competitor of WQXR. I knew what I had to do. And I got it done. By the second week of June, I was back in business and up in my flying helicopter, once again giving my reports. This time lots of people heard it.

I was to continue doing this every summer for WNCN for three years and, among other things, I still have the souvenir WNCN coffee cup that the station sent me to prove it. I also got $50 for each broadcast, and that had not been my original idea. My original idea was that I'd do it for free. I liked the idea of having it and didn't need the money. It was just a way for the newspaper and advertiser to help each other. But the WNCN people insisted they had to pay me something, so I said, okay, $50 a broadcast. After that, I found I needed to be a member of a broadcaster's union called AFTA to get my pay. I applied, and was given a membership card. I think the membership cost me $100. But I didn't care. I was now a performance artist.

I also found that WNCN would prefer that I do my broadcasts from an actual broadcasting studio in the Hamptons, recording it on a cassette tape and overnighting the tape to them. For this purpose, I went to a radio station on Main Street in Amagansett, in those years next to a gym and down the lawn from the Amagansett Library. This was WBEA, and once a week I strode in with my typewritten script and was set up with earphones and all the other paraphernalia to make the tape. I'd send it in just with the voice. WNCN dubbed the sound of an actual helicopter, BRACKA BRACKA BRACKA over my voice. I could listen to it. It sounded great. I would also, on the way out, be allowed to reach into a bin and take any number of CDs that had been sent in unsolicited from music promoters that the station was not interested in. WBEA never charged for either the studio time or the CDs.

In the fourth year, however, after some struggles, WNCN went out of business too. Actually, they sold the license and it became a country-western station. A woman with a southern accent from that station told me very politely over the phone that they had no further need of my services. "Sorry," she said. "But I have a helicopter," I said. "Sorry," she said again. "We're just not into the Hamptons."

Thus it was, that with all this under my belt, I felt emboldened enough to call WQXR and pitch my flying helicopter broadcast to them. I had a cassette tape of it that had been given to me by WNCN, with the full symphony orchestra helicopter engine accompaniment.

"We'd be interested in doing it," an executive there told me after receiving and listening to my cassette tape.

Having dinner a few nights later with John and Chris Lyons, my two friends also in the radio broadcasting business, I told them what had happened.

"How much are you going to charge them?" Chris asked.

"Well, WRCN paid me $50."

"$50?"

"Honestly, I'd do it for nothing."

"Did you tell WQXR that?"

"No."

"You tell them you need $300," Chris told me.

"I can't do that," I said.

But I did do that, and they said okay. And so, once again, this time in the big leagues and for real, "The Hamptons Report" was once again on the air.

I did "The Hamptons Report" with WQXR for five years. At one point, I think it was after the third year, I thought it might be nice to put a face on all the people at that radio station I was dealing with, and so called them and asked if I could come into New York City to meet them, and they said sure. So I did.

Their offices were on the tenth floor of a midtown office building. I expected a modern place and lots of greetings from my engineer and marketing guys and maybe get introduced to some guys in suits who would show me around and introduce me to everybody. But that's not what happened. When I got there, everybody just went about doing what they were doing. Yes, I was free to walk around if I wanted to. They looked at one another. Why was he here?

It felt awkward, but I had a look around. The offices were decorated in a warm and friendly way, with mahogany on some of the walls and counters, thick glass-paneled interior windows, and thick rugs everywhere.

"Hi, I'm Dan Rattiner, who does 'The Hamptons Report,'" I told people as I walked around. I offered my hand and people did shake it, but then they had to go to what they were doing. They were people with things to do. I left. Not exactly with a broken heart, but not even with a cup of coffee offered, either.

In the spring of the sixth year, this was in 1998, I once again called my contact at WQXR to set up things for the summer. During the winter leading up to this, I had been reading that WQXR was not doing well financially. The *New York Times* was even considering selling the station. But hey, that would never happen. WQXR is an institution. It was an arm of the *New York Times*. People don't cut off arms. They might fix them a bit. Surely there would be no problem with my show though. What was $300 a week, anyway, for ten weeks? Not much.

Anyhow, I called and was told my contact was not with the company anymore and I would be put through to some woman who was there from the *New York Times*. In a few moments I was talking to this woman and had the following conversation:

"Hi," I said. "This is Dan Rattiner, who gives WQXR 'The Hamptons Report' show. I just called to set things up again for the summer. They told me you are who I am supposed to talk to now."

"You're who?"

"Dan Rattiner. In the flying helicopter, giving 'The Hamptons Report' for WQXR."

"When is this on?"

Uh-oh.

"It's on Friday evening at 5:05 p.m. Then they repeat it on Saturday morning at 10:05 a.m."

"And what do they pay you for this?"

"Three hundred dollars a week. No charge for the re-broadcast."

"That is ridiculous. How long is the show?"

"Well, it was originally three minutes, but they knocked it down to a minute and 30 seconds after they got an advertiser for it. It's sponsored by Mercedes-Benz."

"The idea that we would pay you $300 for a minute and a half show is ridiculous. Do you know somebody here at WQXR? What are you, somebody's brother or something?"

"It is sponsored."

"You won't be doing this anymore. And I've got other things to do. Sorry. Goodbye."

"But . . ."

But she was gone.

I felt terrible for the rest of the day. I thought briefly about calling Christine Lyons to tell her what had happened, and ask her if there was anything I could do to save this situation. But then I thought of what she would say, which was "Don't budge about the price," so I called this woman back.

"How about $50 a week?" I asked her.

"No."

"How about I do it for nothing?"

"No."

And so it was, bereft and with tears in my eyes, I took my hands off the controls of the helicopter just for a moment and down it went to crash in flames.

After that, I felt ashamed of myself. I had groveled for my job before a mean woman who didn't deserve the time of day. What had I come to? No proper TV or radio personality does this sort of thing.

I recovered my dignity.

I swore at that time to never tell anybody I had made that callback.

Wilbur Ross

~~~~~~

The first time I drove onto the property of the South-ampton Bath and Tennis Club I was surprised. For one thing, there was no sign out front of the tall hedgerows on Gin Lane to tell you it was there, and so, for the thirty years I had lived on the east end, I had never known about it.

The second surprise was to see how beautiful it was. It sat on a seven-acre piece of lawn that extended from Gin Lane to the beach. The part closest to the Lane, about three acres, was mowed and landscaped with flowers. The part closest to the beach had six tennis courts, a swimming pool behind some hedgerows, and a magnificent, three-story nineteenth-century Victorian house, with cedar shingles, wrap-around porches and various turrets and peaks above. And there was this odd thing about the house. Here in the summertime, many of the doors and windows of this grand house were open to let in the salt sea air. As a result, in many places, you could look right through the house and out the other side into the ocean. What a beautiful place.

WILBUR ROSS ON A HORSE
(Courtesy of the author)

Why had I never seen this place before? I had thought, when I first saw it, that there were only four exclusive private clubs in Southampton that, as a Jewish person, I would not be welcome to join. This meant there were five. And the fifth one was more beautiful by far than the other four. How many more were there? Well, anyway, I was there as the guest of a member. Actually, not just a member, but the president of the club, Wilbur Ross. I parked my car on the big mowed lawn under a trellis of roses between the parking lawn and the main part of the club. Nearby, a young woman sat at a table with a phone on it.

"Wilbur Ross," I said. "I'm having lunch with him." She made a phone call. Then she smiled and politely announced that I might pass.

Wilbur was waiting for me at a table in the breezy dining room. There were ceiling fans to further stir the air, a redundancy on that day.

We talked for a while about business and politics. Then we talked about women. Both of us, at that time, were heading into divorce situations and so we had a lot to talk about.

"I will be moving out of the Dakota," Wilbur said, referring to that famous apartment building on Central Park West. "My wife and kids will keep the apartment."

"Where will you go?"

"I have no idea. Maybe rent an apartment somewhere, I guess."

Wilbur Ross was, at that time, the Managing Director of the American office of the big French investment firm known as Rothschild's. He often dealt with distressed companies, working out arrangements through which they could either avoid or enter bankruptcy. He often represented the stockholders against the owners, and, sometimes, he worked out the financing for new owners to come in and, with new investments, take over the remnants of the bankruptcy. He was a legend in New York in this field. When the Aladdin in Atlantic City spun toward bankruptcy during its construction, he negotiated with Donald Trump successfully so the shareholders got a bigger piece of it.

On two occasions, just to see him in action, I had gone to lectures he gave in hotel banquet halls to young men new to this field of distressed properties. Once, I spent time with him in his office, watching him on the telephone, walking back and forth while he rolled out a new public offering for the Greyhound Bus Company.

In any case, here we were at his club in Southampton. Besides being president of this club, he was also president of the Parrish Art Museum in town at that time.

At that lunch, I asked him how this club had come about. Obviously, it had originally been built as a grand turn-of-the-centruy oceanfront private home. It had not been built as a club as the other four had. And was it really an exclusive club like the others?

"This club was created in the late 1940s by people who could not get into the other four exclusive clubs," he said. "Mostly, they were, at that time, wealthy merchants who wanted a beach club of their own and were not eligible to apply to the older clubs. These days, wealthy New Yorkers with 'New Money' have memberships here. If you look at the membership names, you'll see there are a lot of Italians and Irish and Jewish people here. The club does not adhere to any restrictive laws."

I thought, well, I'm a successful publisher now. Maybe, this would be a good place for me to be a member.

"Is membership expensive?"

"Not at all," he said. He quoted me a ridiculously small number.

"Well, I was thinking maybe I would apply here. But I do live fourteen miles away in East Hampton. It really is a stretch. I wouldn't be able to use it much."

"Well, let me know if you want to apply," he said. "In any case, you'll always be a welcome guest as long as I am here."

Wilbur and I had become close friends. I don't know quite what the attraction was. Maybe it had to do with women. But he was, unlike many businessmen I knew, such a mild-mannered and down-to-earth fellow. And he was very funny. He also seemed very happy all the time and very happy to have a friendship with me.

In 1997, Wilbur Ross made a big move. He left Rothschild's, and he founded his own firm, called Wilbur Ross LLC with offices in midtown Manhattan. Now, instead of ushering others as they took over distressed firms, he'd be the main principal himself.

Over another lunch, at his office in New York, he told me about a bank he had bought in Japan. He was now doing a lot of business in Japan and he was going back and forth a lot. And that wasn't easy. This is an eighteen-hour flight.

"I've learned of a wonderful way to avoid jet lag," he said. "There's this new device you wrap around your ankles on the plane that shines a light on the back of your knees when you sleep. I don't know exactly how it works. It has something to do with fooling your body into thinking the sun is shining when it's not. But I can tell you it sure works."

He told me about the bank. It was not a big bank, it only had five or six branches. And it was based in a small town outside of Osaka. But he needed a Japanese bank to handle his affairs.

"I've always wondered how you do business in Japan," I said. "I know about bowing. And I'm told there's lots of rituals."

"Let me tell you how we had the closing. It was a great ceremony. It took place in a courtyard. Both the owners of the bank, all men, together with their wives, were in traditional costumes. There was a kabuki drummer and other musicians playing. There was also a religious leader. And when the time came, there was a teenage girl in costume who brought the deed over to me on a small pillow. Then there was celebrating."

Wilbur also told me about how you could not say anything bad directly to anybody in the Japanese culture.

"For example, I might get a message from one of the vice presidents of a company saying that the weather in Tokyo was very bad this past week. That would be the whole message. That meant my offer had not been accepted."

"Next time you go," I said, "take me with you. I'd like to be a fly on the wall watching you do these things."

I enjoyed having lunch with Wilbur at this club and he invited me often. One day, in 1998, a member came over to Wilbur, not just to say hello, but to talk to him about a very serious problem. Denise Rich, a wealthy Southamptonite who was not a member of the club, was about to buy the place from its longtime owner, Southampton developer George Semerjian. And Mrs. Rich was saying she intended to convert the club into her private home. So the club would be no more. They would have to move everything out, she said. What were they to do?

"I'll look into it," Ross said, very calmly.

This man looked at me. "Now don't you go putting this in your newspaper," he said. I shrugged.

"Of course not," I said. But I meant at least not until I saw the story in other local papers. Soon the man walked away.

"Could that happen?" I asked Wilbur.

"It could."

I tried to visualize this wonderful club now just once again a private home. We ate much of the rest of our meal in silence.

I soon learned that George Semerjian, this dapper older Southampton developer who owned the club, had gotten into deep trouble with his personal finances. He was, in addition to owning the club, the owner of several condominium projects and retail buildings in town. But he had overextended himself. To make ends meet, he had taken a second mortgage on the club, which was for more than the club was worth. The club was now valued at $2 million. He also owed a Dutch Bank $3.5 million and was now unable to make payments on that mortgage.

In addition to this, he was also mourning the untimely death of his beautiful wife. Altogether, it was a terrible year for Mr. Semerjian.

Denise Rich, the prospective buyer, was a well-known Manhattan songwriter with a number of hits to her credit who had many years earlier married a man named Mark Rich. Mr. Rich, in 1989, had been convicted of fraud, and, inasmuch as he was out on bail, afterwards simply vanished. Months later, he surfaced in Basel, Switzerland, where he had bought a home and was now beyond the clutches of the American authorities.

In any case, Denise Rich was now making Semerjian an offer that was hard to refuse. She would pay $4 million for the Southampton Bath and Tennis club—half a million to Semerjian and the remaining $3.5 million to the Dutch Bank. Semerjian would be free and clear.

Oddly, the membership of the club was angry at Semerjian. I think it was because he had re-mortgaged the club to cover his losses elsewhere. Why put a private club in jeopardy like that?

And there was another thing. Semerjian not only owned the property where the club was—it was thought he paid about $50,000 for it in 1955—but he had also set himself up as the manager of it which meant that he could be paid to be there, a member of it, and on the premises taking care of it all at the same time. He was a nice man and it must have given him great pleasure to hobnob with everybody as the King of his domain. But now, one way or another, that was coming to an end.

In any case, when the news of this possible purchase finally appeared in other papers in town, I felt free to write about it in *Dan's Papers*. "This club is a revered private institution," I wrote. Considering that, and the fact there were so many other big oceanfront estates for sale in town, why buy and close the only non-exclusive club in town? It would make a lot of families very unhappy.

At one point, by phone in my office, I learned that a lawyer named Tom Golub was representing Denise Rich.

So I called him. Usually lawyers are very happy to talk to you. It's billable time by the hour to their clients. And the press needs to be informed, right?

"Mr. Golub?" I asked, when I got him on the line. I explained who I was and what I was about.

"You keep your snotty nose out of this," he said. "This is not your f—king business. Screw you." And he hung up on me.

In the end, Wilbur Ross met with Golub and Rich. Then he had a big meeting with the Board of Directors of the club. Then he had a few more meetings. Golub, who it now turned out was an equal partner with Rich in this business, was holding out. And now he was saying there was no amount of money that would make Mrs. Rich give the place up. She loved the building. She loved the swimming pool and tennis courts, etc., etc. Soon, continuing with my occasional lunches with Wilbur and now other members, people began to talk darky about Denise Rich's "henchman."

And then, quite suddenly, there was a deal. I do not know the amount that would make Rich and Golub part with Mrs. Rich's new home, but it was significant. Both would walk away, just by pushing papers around, with several million in profit. And all that money would have to be coughed up by the membership, which meant that the dues would go up tenfold and there would be a one-time assessment of about $50,000 per member.

I don't know if anybody left because of that. Being a member of that club, it had seemed to me, had been the biggest bargain in town up until that point, members paying a small sum each year while the property values climbed up into the millions.

"She flipped it," Wilbur told me at a lunch when this was all over. "Maybe she intended to do it in the first place," he said. "Probably she did."

"Just a sweet couple of million dollars," I marveled.

"More. And for both of them."

Until that moment, I had thought a flip was something you did in gym.

After this bit of financial education, though, over the years I began to see things being flipped all over the place. As long as it only involved private ownership, I thought, it would be okay. But then three men formed a partnership to buy the Poxabogue Golf Course cheap. This was a major privately owned recreational facility in town that had a driving range and a nine-hole course. I figured, at first, that these three men were correct in reassuring everybody that all they wanted to do was continue to run it as it was. But a part of me wasn't all that sure.

The three men had learned that a woman had owned the club for the last forty years and was now elderly and approaching the end of her life. What should she do with her golf course? The trio told her this forty-two-acre nine-hole public course in Sagaponack was worth $1 million. And she sold it to them for that price. Soon, however, the three men said what they really wanted was to shut the place down and replace it with a thirty-two-house residential development. Everybody got all upset about this, including me. I thought it was just awful to be working a flip with a public recreational facility, and I wrote about that fact loudly in articles in the paper.

In the end, the town of East Hampton and the Town of Southampton got together and each ponied up $3 million. (The club is quite near the property line separating the two towns so it's equally important to both.)

So, in six months, $1 million became $6 million divided by three, and you get the picture.

Interestingly, at further lunches with Wilbur, I began to see Denise Rich walking around the club, smiling and shaking hands with her many fans and friends there. The first time I saw her, I pointed it out to Wilbur.

"Why is she here?" I asked.

"Part of the deal," Wilbur said. "She has a lifetime membership at the club. So that is that."

From then on, I frequently saw her getting her lifetime of congratulations from different club members, who apparently saw what she did as a great accomplishment—flipping the flippers. It might have cost us all a pretty penny, they'd say to her. But that is what it's all about, isn't it? Sure wish it had been me that did it.

Dr. Oz

~~~~~~

In 1995, Linda Shapiro, an advertiser and longtime friend who owned an exercise studio in the Hamptons, came up to my office in a state of crisis. She was very upset and almost in tears.

"I want to ask your advice," she said. "I need help."

"What's going on?" I asked her.

"My life is falling apart. My husband and I are getting divorced."

This was a real shock to me. She and I and our two spouses often did things together.

"How can I help?"

"Maybe you can give me a job."

"What about your exercise studio?"

"I don't want to do that anymore. Dan, this is a major crisis for me. I want to change my life."

"I don't think working for me is the answer for you," I said. "You're too independent. You wouldn't like a job."

"I need something to do."

DR. MEHMET OZ

"Linda, you should stay in business or find a new business. You need to do something you love. Everybody does. And I know what you love. You love running things, organizing things. You're on two telephone calls at the same time, all the time. You should be an event coordinator. You'd love it."

"There's a need for this?"

"In the old days there wasn't. There were three charity events a year. Now there's three charity events every weekend. Every one of them needs somebody like you to run them."

"I can't."

"Yes you can. You are already doing it. And I can prove it."

I told Linda something she already knew, which was that for fifteen years I had been producing an annual 10K running race in the summertime along the farm roads that border the potato fields in Bridgehampton. I handled the permits, the program, the map showing the route, the advertising, the timer, the police and ambulance, the charity we'd give the profits to, even the getting of the guy who fired the starting gun.

"For years you've been part of this. You lead exercises before the race. You've brought your leaflets and fliers, sold products, gotten others to give away their products. You know what? You do it."

She stared at me, her eyes wide.

"Do the whole thing. As a test. There's no money in it. I don't make any. What's left over is about $2,000, and we give it to the hospital. And so I can't pay you. But run it this summer. You'll see this is what you should be doing. And then after that, go into business running charity events."

"Okay," she said.

And so it was later that summer that I just showed up at the race without having much to do. The truth was, Linda ran it better than I ever had. She had people there that could measure your fat percentage, give weight-loss advice, lead yoga, give out free samples of suntan lotion, sell exercise jackets, do massage. There were even, that year, people in potato T-shirts running in the race—she had made it an optional costume contest, and one couple came as two french-fried potatoes. The event even had a lead sponsor, a Manhattan exercise clothing company that suspended a huge banner across Main Street. In that first year with her running it, we gave $4,000 to the hospital. It was wonderful. All I had to do was smile, wave, get in the convertible and lead the biggest crowd of runners we ever had, 800 of them, down the road. Her new career thrived. That very next year she was handling four big charity events and loving her new business. I had been right.

In 2003 she ran a huge gala, for several thousand people under a great white tent, for heart research. It had the usual stuff—an M.C., a band, a buffet, dancing, mingling, drinking. Her medical honoree that year—usually you'd have two, one a doctor and the other a rich person—was Dr. Mehmet Oz, a little-known surgeon who ran a heart research division at Columbia University Hospital.

I went to the gala—I went to many of Linda's galas—and she introduced me to Dr. Oz. He was not some old specialist unaccustomed to public speaking. He was a very handsome young man with a winning smile who had written a new book entitled *Healing from the Heart*. He gave a wonderful speech there.

"One of the things I do," he said at the gala, "is to teach women about their hearts. It is the leading cause of death in women, and the reason is that women do hear what they should do to take care of their hearts, but they don't translate that knowledge into action. That is because women are the caregivers of the world, and they place their own health second. I tell them that the first thing the heart does is pump blood into itself to keep being able to continue to work. It takes care of itself. I tell women if you want to help others, you have to help yourself first."

Linda asked me what I thought of Dr. Oz, and I told her I thought him quite remarkable. She then told me that the following year, she'd like to have his charity be the recipient of the money we raised at the race. But I told her I had already made another commitment to the hospital for next year.

Dr. Oz gave a speech in the gym at the Ross School the following week, where he demonstrated some new meditation and exercise techniques. And the week after that he was honored again at a dinner at the home of Ahmet Ertegun, the head of Atlantic Records, in Southampton.

At this point, I was getting to know Dr. Oz a bit. He invited me to come for breakfast one morning where he was staying at a friend's house in Water Mill.

We sat at a picnic table in the yard, near the breakfast buffet set up by the pool. I asked him how he became a doctor, a question I often ask doctors.

He told me his father had been a doctor.

"My dad took me to get an ice cream at a local soda fountain one day when I was eight years old," he told me. This was in Wilmington, Delaware. There was a young soda jerk there and dad asked him what he wanted to do with himself when he grew up, and he said he didn't know. After we left the store, he turned to me and said, 'There are some things you have to know, and what you are going to do is one of them. You can change what that is, but you always have to know the answer to that question.' I thought about the fact that I loved to play with animals and I liked biology and I liked that doctors helped people. I decided I would be a doctor. And that was that."

Dr. Oz was basically raised in Delaware. His father, a native of Turkey, had been trained to be a physician at Emory College in Atlanta, but then had returned to his homeland to practice medicine in Istanbul when he was in his early twenties.

"My father belonged to a family of people who worked as tax collectors for the Ottoman Empire. But that empire collapsed in 1912, and so after that it was a struggle to put food on the table. But then he met this woman from a very rich family and they fell in love and got married. Her family owned chemical plants and pharmaceutical companies. Still does."

When his mother became pregnant, the couple decided to emigrate to America. They wanted their firstborn, and any others after that, to grow up in America.

"My dad had become a cardiologist by this time and had two offers to run surgical programs in America, one in Wilmington, North Carolina, and the other at Wilmington, Delaware. He chose Delaware because it was closer to New York."

Mehmet was the firstborn. And he and his father and mother embarked on a very unusual lifestyle. They would spend nine months a year in Delaware—Mehmet went to the Tower Hill School—and then three months a year in Istanbul, where for the most part, they stayed with their mother's family.

Soon, two daughters followed. Now they were a family of five.

"And I will tell you something really interesting," Oz said. "Among all my uncles and aunts on both sides of the families, I remained, for a long time, the only boy. I have thirty-five cousins. All girls."

"Women's heart health." I beamed. "It explains everything."

On other occasions, Mehmet Oz told me other wonderful stories about his family life, such as how he met his wife. He had, by this time, gotten bachelor degrees in biology and joint studies at Harvard, an MD at the University of Pennsylvania Medical School, and an MBA at the Wharton business school.

"It was at a French restaurant in Philadelphia called Le Bec-Fin. My dad had invited me. And we were joined by a medical colleague of his, who came with his daughter. I started dating Lisa. But I didn't want my father to know because I thought it might embarrass him. Then one day, my father, noting that I didn't seem to be going out with different girls much, said he thought I might want to date his colleague's daughter. I told him we were already thinking about getting engaged. He was silent for a while."

"Do you have kids?" I asked.

"Yes, three. Two girls and . . ."

And we both began to laugh.

The next year, the year Oz had hoped to be the charity recipient of the 10K, the race developed a critical problem at the very last minute. Linda, quite upset, told me about it. The route for the race had been the same for all these years. It passed the Bridgehampton windmill, the Sagg Two Room School, the Sagg General Store. It crossed this little stream tributary of Sagg Pond over the one-lane Sagg Bridge, built originally in colonial times and rebuilt in the 1930s during the Depression. Then it passed a horse farm, went by several churches, and came back to a finish line on Main Street in Bridgehampton.

The problem was the bridge. Indeed, I did know there was a problem with the bridge, but I couldn't imagine how it could affect the race. It needed to be rebuilt. It was a narrow wooden bridge. It needed to be rebuilt about every fifty years. But this time, the local government, to save money, had asked the federal government to take it over and fix it. Federal money would handle it. Local taxes wouldn't be involved at all. But then, when the plans to rebuild the little, historic wooden bridge were presented, people went nuts. It would now be four lanes wide, almost a superhighway. It needed to be that big because federal law said any bridges they took over had to be wide enough and strong enough to allow tanks to pass across them in wartime. It would be steel reinforced concrete.

SAGG BRIDGE PSYCHIATRIST ON RACE DAY
(Courtesy of the author)

"Save Sagg Bridge" became the cry. A banner saying that was put up on the bridge. Painter Bob Dash made an oil painting of the old bridge and put it up for sale for $10,000 to pay for the fight. There were lots of other painters who had painted Sagg Bridge. An exhibition of these works was mounted in a local art gallery. And so, the federal plan was withdrawn.

At this point, though, the bridge was in big trouble because engineers had determined it too weak to handle cars and trucks. It was now closed to vehicular traffic. A barrier was put up. You could walk across the bridge, though. That was okay. So you could run across it, right? It was three days before the race.

"The Town Police won't let us have 800 runners racing across the bridge," Linda told me. "They want us to change the route."

I told Linda we could not change the route at the last minute. The race course needed to be exactly 10K. The runners had personal best times they wanted to beat every year. They needed the race to be accurate to the nearest inch, or millimeter.

"Eight hundred runners aren't going to cross the bridge at the same time," I said to Linda. "The bridge doesn't appear until halfway through the race. All the runners are spaced out for a mile or more by then. So it's just like walking across the bridge, which is legal. Just quicker."

"They won't change their minds," Linda said. "They are afraid of lockstep. If everybody runs in lockstep, the bridge collapses."

"Let me call the Town," I told Linda.

In the end, I worked out this wild compromise. The honchos from Stony Brook University Hospital, which has an alliance with Southampton Hospital, sent a psychiatrist to monitor the runners at the bridge. He would, as a volunteer for this good Southampton Hospital cause, stand at the foot of the bridge where the runners would start to cross and make sure that no runners crossed in lockstep. Thus, the police agreed to let the race be run.

I actually spent time standing with this doctor, taking time off from his $300-an-hour day job to do this, hollering at the people if they came along in clumps to break it up, break it up.

The following summer, the race was held again, this time with the proceeds benefitting Dr. Oz's charity. He had just published his runaway best-seller *YOU: The Owner's Manual.* And he was negotiating to have a TV show. I did hope everything would be fine with the bridge. In the fall, the county began their much less elaborate construction of it. They hoped to create an exact reproduction of what had been there before.

Fortunately, the workmen finished and the bridge reopened to traffic the week before the race, and so, an hour before the race started, I was able to take Dr. Oz out in my car for ten minutes to drive him around the course and show him how it passed various points of interest.

On Sagg Main Street, we passed the old farm building that contains the Sagg General Store and Post Office, which, a hundred years earlier, had been completely turned around 180 degrees so the old front faced the back and the refurbished back became the front. Then I drove him to where the road rises a bit at the entrance of the one-lane Sagg Bridge. I pulled off the road. In the center of the bridge, several men were fishing at the railing. We looked out at them, and I told him the story of the Sagg Bridge and the Stony Brook doctor who oversaw the bridge foot traffic the year before.

"I was hoping I wouldn't have to ask you to stand down here this year hollering at people. Lucky you. It's been fixed just in time."

And then we drove on.

The Great Ecuadorian Eel

No matter how successful the Hamptons were to become as a world-class summer resort—and by 1999 it had become one of the greatest resorts in the world—there was still the grimness of winter for those of us who lived here year-round.

DAN'S PAPERS EMPLOYEES HOLD UP THE GREAT ECUADORIAN EEL
(Courtesy of Tom Radcliffe)

The clouds closed low over the landscape in December, the sun set at the impossible hour of 3:30 in the afternoon, and so no matter what time it was, we knew dark was coming soon. And it was cold. The air was salty and wet. The wind howled. And sometimes, on particularly bitter days, the rain or snow would come down sideways.

Besides all that, not much went on in the wintertime. The town board met. They'd discuss patching a road. Or they'd discuss a new zoning law or a new sign proposal. It was pretty discouraging having to write a newspaper every week when nothing was going on and then put it out there on all the stands.

And so on one winter afternoon, I sat down and wrote about the giant eel that was scaring the bejeezus out of the

Hamptons. In fact, he had eaten someone. Here's what I wrote about it.

———

MAN ATTACKED BY
THE GREAT ECUADORIAN EEL

Peconic County Public Safety Commissioner Thomas Brody held a press conference in Riverhead today to talk about the man who was dragged below the ice and killed in Water Mill last Sunday and Monday. People need to know what countermeasures the authorities are taking.

"If you are at a pond walking across the ice, ice skating or playing ice hockey stay away from holes in the ice, from thin ice and from places where the ice drops off quickly into water. And definitely do not chip a hole in the ice."

The general public should be reassured, he said, by the appearance of policemen armed with spear guns who have now been assigned to every skating pond on the east end after dark. They are trained marksmen and they will be on duty beginning at 5 pm and remain at the ponds until midnight when, as Brody said grimly, the ponds will be "officially closed."

The death took place last Sunday on Big Mill Pond in Water Mill north of the railroad tracks. At first, the authorities failed to comprehend what had happened.

"Two men from Bay Shore drove out to the edge of the pond at eleven p,m.," Brody said, "walked out on the ice with a hammer and chisel and cut a hole to catch eels. Then they dropped a line in. According to the testimony of Anthony deCarlo, his friend Joe Anderson of Cutler Road in Bay Shore felt a tug on his line, said 'I got one' and then began to pull. Then something leaped through the hole, wrapped itself around Anderson's lower leg and pulled him down through. Anderson died under the ice."

"It was initially reported as an accident," a reporter said. "Comment?"

"We were wrong. We know better now. DeCarlo raced to the nearest house, and babbling hysterically, reported what he had seen was florescent green and made a hissing sound. The environmentalists tell me this is some kind of monster eel. I'll let Dr. Witkiss here tell us about it."

Dr. Edgar Witkiss, the official County Environmental officer, got up to the microphone.

"We got the police report Monday morning. And we knew right away what it was. The hissing sound, the fluorescent green color. There could only be one explanation. This had to be a Great Ecuadorian eel, an adolescent male, migrating north, looking for colder water. We've had this cold snap which has frozen the ponds. This is a very exciting find."

If anyone has further information about this eel please call 631-727-0400.

After the paper came out we received a flurry of phone calls, including one from Peconic Bay Motors in Riverhead, during which a secretary told us they had logged thirty-two calls asking about the eel. I spoke to the manager, who I know, and who I had recently bought a car from, and said that I would change the number in next week's issue. I had just picked that number out of the air. I guess it had been in my mind from my recent purchase.

"Some people believed this story," he told me. "We appreciated the calls. We'd turn things around and try to sell them cars."

All of this did not stop the eel, however. Three days later, he struck again. First it was a police officer. Then, a dog. Here's the part about the dog.

～

Around two a.m, Tuesday morning, the same night the police officer was eaten, a large black Laborador retriever was swallowed up while walking across Little Mill Pond. Little Mill Pond is across the Upper Seven Ponds Road and the railroad tracks from Big Mill Pond and is considerably smaller. A stream connects them. The lab had been let out for a run, according to its owner Bill Van, who lives on Upper Seven Ponds Road, and since the lab is sometimes ornery and won't come right back, Van was out at the back door overlooking the pond calling to him. The dog was walking back when Van witnessed the attack.

"Van had no idea about any of the earlier attacks," Police Chief Brody reported at the press conference. "But when he lost his lab he said that something florescent green and as thick as a tree trunk had wrapped itself around his dog and pulled him under. He yapped once. And there was a hissing sound."

"Here's something to think about," County Environmental Officer Dr. Witkiss said, interrupting. "adult males will make not only hissing sounds, but they also roar and snarl. And in Missouri, Dr. Wreckson has gotten adult males to snort and wheeze, even purr and giggle. It's amazing what he has done."

～

As you see, a plot was beginning to form this second week. But before I could proceed further, winter came to an end, and the eel had swum back to its mountain stream and waterfall in Ecuador for the summer season. So that was that in 1999.

The following winter, there was more mayhem. The eel had gotten his coils around a hunter from Lake Ronkonkoma who had been walking across the ice of Trout Pond in Noyac. We dutifully interviewed him in his hospital bed, where he was recovering.

～

"At first I didn't know what hit me," he said. "Then I was in these coils and looking at this beast right in his eyes. He had green eyes. I wanted to get my gun, but it was nowhere near by."

The hunter suffered several broken ribs from being squeezed, third degree electric shocks to his scalp and feet and some sort of rash on his chest and stomach from some slime. The eel also bit him in the nose. A truck driver in a van, delivering 16 store mannequins to a store in Riverhead, parked by the side of Trout Pond, witnessed this encounter.

"There was this huge thing under the ice, it must have been twenty feet long, and it seemed to be shadowing the guy with the gun. He'd walk along and this thing would glide at the same speed, under him and just behind him so he couldn't see. But then the hunter stopped. He sees him. And this thing just kept going forward a few feet and then leaped up with a terrific bang, battered its head I guess under the ice and the ice just crashed upwards like it was an egg shell. Then the thing was hissing and spitting and it just wrapped itself around the guy, counterclockwise, like in a spiral. The guy's gun went flying. I couldn't have that. I got out of the car and started onto the ice, and then I thought of the mannequins. I ran back to the back of the van, opened it, and pulled one out—it was a female—and I ran out with it and threw it in the direction of this thing and yelled 'HERE!' and it just leaped from the man to the mannequin in just nothing flat and dragged it under. Just like that."

———

This was the first time the Great Ecuadorian Eel had attacked and someone had lived to tell about it. It was a watershed moment. And so ended the winter of 2000.

By this time, many people were telling me they were looking forward to eel stories during the winter of 2001. I gave it my best. I wrote how the eel was captured during the winter of 2001. The reason was not because of the chaos he was inflicting, but because Dr. Witkiss was anxious to get the Great Ecuadorian off on a flatbed truck to the University of Missouri Department of Amphibian Affairs, where the afore-mentioned Dr. Wreckson was doing great things in teaching eels to communicate with humans.

———

Before the flatbed truck left, however, members of the Sagaponack Volunteer Fire Department who were to drive the truck learned that there was a law forbidding the transportation of eels in excess of 15 feet through the City of New York. It was included in a new law on the books preventing the transport of toxic waste. They were going to have to sneak the eel across the city secretly strapped to the flatbed with a canvas tarp over it.

The flatbed went along the Montauk Highway until it became the Sunrise Highway, then up Manorville Road to the Long Island Express-way, and then west toward New York. The plan was to take the last exit before the Midtown Tunnel, and then go across the Queensboro Bridge into Manhattan. Then they would cross Manhattan, take the Lincoln Tunnel and head out along the New Jersey Turnpike toward Missouri.

"But we missed the last turn," fireman Burns said. "How anyone could give a direction that said to take the last exit of anything I do not know. Some of these firemen had never been out of Sagaponack in their lives. And so we went past that exit and then we were at the tollbooth at the entrance to the Midtown Tunnel."

The scene at the tollbooth is one that Burns, driving a chase car behind the flatbed truck, said he will never forget. Apparently, nobody in the flatbed truck had the three dollars to pay the toll.

"They had the money for the Lincoln Tunnel," Burns said. "And they knew they couldn't spend that. And so, they panicked."

There was nobody at the toll booth station at that hour except the tollbooth taker, the flatbed truck, and the car following. They had come to a halt at the toll booth window. Now the driver of the truck made a decision. He floored it. And the truck picked up speed and headed out of the toll station.

"Hey!" the toll taker, a black woman in her forties, shouted after them.

From the car following, Burns recoiled in horror as he approached the toll booth and, watching out the front windshield, saw about ten feet of the eel leap out and eat her.

"He did it like a snake might," Burns said, shuddering at the thought. "He just leaped out, there was this scream and crunching sound, and then he leaped back under the tarpaulin. I can still see the top of the tarpaulin jumping up and down."

Apparently, those in the cab of the flatbed truck did not see what had happened. They simply drove on, down the ramp and into the tunnel. Burns followed.

"The Inside of the tunnel, particularly at night, is very well lit," Burns continued. "The tarpaulin continued to jump up and down. Then it stopped. We tried to pull out to pass the flatbed, but, you know, there is a double white line in the tunnel and you are not supposed to cross. Also, the eel stuck his head back out, licked his mouth with this forked tongue he has, and gave us this evil grin. I fell back."

———~~~———

Eventually, of course, a phalanx of police cars following the caravan caught up with them for not paying the toll, found out what was under that tarpaulin and, after giving them a ticket, required them to turn their illegal cargo around and take it back to the Hamptons, at which point, once again, as it always does, winter ended.

I tried a different approach in 2002. I tried an *entirely* different approach in 2002.

———~~~———

Call them Mister and Misses. On Saturday afternoon, after three days of trying, the Hamptons at long last rid itself of the giant 37 foot long eel that had terrorized this area for much of the past few winters. Accompanied by military helicopters, five police boats, forty pleasure craft and three tug boats from the Port of New York spraying jets of water from fire hoses, this blue killer eel from Ecuador, accompanied by an even longer pink female Ecuadorian eel, sailed off side by side through Peconic Bay to the open waters of the Atlantic.

The operation began, appropriately enough, on Thursday morning, St. Valentines's day, with the arrival in Sag Harbor of a huge tractor trailer truck bearing a pink female eel strapped on the back. It had been a long ride from Kennedy Airport, where this female eel, called Edna, had resided briefly after flying in from Ecuador. A veterinarian, Xanuwheel Gul from Quito, Ecuador, accompanied Edna on the trip and, arriving in Sag Harbor, seemed anxious about her condition by waving off the crowd of reporters in front of the American Hotel there. He spoke no English, but made his intentions clear by making that universal sign of sleep, raising his hands to his cheek, cocking his head against them, smiling and closing his eyes, to indicate that was what Edna needed. Certainly, she was breathing rapidly and shallowly at that time, making little wheezing noises, her eyes with the long lashes closed and her tongue hanging out. Her body, which was supposed to be pink, was grey.

"I believe Edna will sleep through the night," Chief Pasta said, pushing back the reporters. "That's what the people in Quito, Ecuador said would happen in the fax they sent."

That evening, a grand buffet feast was held in Mr. Gul's honor at the American Hotel, about fifty people attending. At that time, it was learned that Mr. Gul spoke not only no English but no language that anybody knew. A long distance call was placed to Quito to our contacts there and Mr. Gul was urged to speak into the phone, which he did, but in Quito they said they didn't understand it either. Chief Pasta took the cell phone back and talked awhile.

"Apparently," he said, "there are people in the mountains of Ecuador who speak languages that have never been translated."

After dinner, Mr. Gul was taken down to the Sag Harbor Inn for the night where, apparently, he slept outdoors on the lawn.

And so, the next morning, the Great Ecuadorian Eel was introduced to Edna, cavorted around with her in Trout Pond for a bit, and was soon, with his bride, gone. Or was he? Here is the first of several stories that were published the following winter, in January of 2003. The dateline is New York City.

Last Monday night, two burglars backed a moving van up to Pier 17 on the Hudson River in Manhattan, and, in the darkness, after picking the lock on the warehouse door there, began to load their van with merchandise. What had just come in were more than 5,000 new DVD television sets from Taiwan, fresh off the boat.

"This is quite a haul," chuckled one of the burglars as he maneuvered a fork lift toward the boxes of merchandise.

"Like stealin' candy from a baby," laughed the other one.

Suddenly, in the night sky, a searchlight beam, coming from somewhere in midtown, came to rest on the surface of a cloud. The beam was a perfect circle, and inside it there was, in silhouette, the outline of a Great Ecuadorian Eel. The searchlight beam wavered for a moment. Then it was gone.

"Hey, what was that," one of the burglars said.

"Ah, it was nothing," said the other.

<hr />

Had the Great Ecuadorian Eel left his mate? Apparently, he had now gone off to be the heroic crime fighter for Mayor Rudy Guiliani in his successful effort to clean up the City of New York.

By this time, it was 2004 and I was running out of ideas. That winter, all was quiet on the Great Ecuadorian Eel front. But then the following fall, the vice president of a subsidiary of Shell Oil, John Hritcko, called my office. There was a project he wanted to tell me about. I told him to come on over.

The project was a huge $2 billion regasification factory, longer than a cruise ship, which his company wanted to build in Long Island Sound, 8 miles from Riverhead. He told me the benefits of this plant. Gas was the future. It would power America. But there was not enough of it being produced in this country, so America, particularly along the east coast, would have to import huge tanks of liquid gas from Europe and elsewhere. There were jobs to be created. $2 billion in construction costs alone.

He showed me a color rendering of the floating factory. Giant freighters, a thousand feet long, would tie up to it in the middle of Long Island Sound. Great hoses from these ships would offload their cargo, liquid gas, into the hold of the degasification plant where it would be held until furnaces could raise the temperature of it to the boiling point to become gas. If nothing further was done, the gas would take up a huge amount of space. So instead, it would be offloaded from the plant through underwater pipelines to all the states in the Northeast—Maine, New Hampshire, Vermont, Massachusetts, Connecticut, New York, and New Jersey. It would solve our energy problems far into the future.

"Is there some other place you could build it other than at the entrance to Long Island Sound?" I asked.

"No. This is our first choice. And it will be a great economic boon to the area."

"Terrorists blew up the Twin Towers just four years ago," I told him. "I'm not sure I am in favor of building a floating factory like this so close to the Hamptons."

"This plant will be perfectly safe," Mr. Hritcko said.

"Well, I'll think about it," I said.

"That's all we ask," he said. And then he was gone.

In the months that followed, the entire community on the east end debated the merits and drawbacks of what was to be called "Broadwater." The general consensus was a resounding "no." But could we prevent it? I knew someone who could. And now, it was winter again.

———⁓———

J. Worthington Greeley arrived in a black helicopter to the facility at exactly 2:45 pm, and with great fanfare strode down the quarter mile length of the ship under the main degasification pipes to the bow where folding chairs had been set up for members of the press and visiting dignitaries. At the last minute, it had been decided that it was warm enough to hold the press conference outdoors, in the fifty degree weather, on deck in the sunshine.

Greeley spoke over a microphone, in order to be heard above the din of the hissing of the pipes, the grinding of various motors and lifting machines below decks and the cries of the sea gulls that had come over to look and were now circling around overhead.

"You are and we are—all of us—on board a vessel that represents the twenty first century," Greeley said. "The New York Metropolitan area consumes about three and a half billion feet of gas every day. And that thirst is growing. It will soon surpass the ability of all the existing pipelines to bring it to New York from other parts of the country. Natural gas will have to be imported.

"How much gas can this facility process? One billion cubic feet a day. About one third the entire demand. Broadwater will be the single largest supplier of natural gas for the New York area, but our true concerns are for you, our customers. You have nothing to fear.

"The plant is perfectly safe. We have all the latest fire extinguishers on board. And plenty of other safeguards. There will also be patrol boats with trained men aboard to keep pleasure craft from getting within a mile and a quarter of this plant—they are doing their job as we speak—so there will be no terrorist attacks. Now you will notice that off to the east over there, you can see that huge freighter coming toward us. This freighter is from North Korea, carries nearly two billion square feet of natural gas, and will dock here momentarily. Shortly, you will see how this plant works."

People shifted in their chairs.

"Do you have any questions?"

A man with a sombrero got up.

"I just want to warn you," he said. "I am Dr. Jose Garcia Alvarez from Ecuador. There is a very dangerous eel from our country that was seen last week swimming toward these waters. It has come to eastern Long Island before. Many times. It is electrified. And it is enormous. It could be a danger to this operation if it heads this way today . . ."

Greeley looked from side to side. "Who IS this hombre?" he asked. "Get him out of here."

Armed security people moved swiftly through the folding chairs, and took him under both arms and removed him, kicking and shouting in some sort of South American Indian dialect that nobody could understand.

"Any other questions?" Greeley asked.

———

And so it was that in a great explosion of gas, steel, marketing officials, dignitaries and pieces of eel, that the Great Ecuadorian Eel made the supreme sacrifice to save eastern Long Island from the evil clutches of an offshore regasification factory.

After publishing this fantasy, I wondered what John Hritcko thought of my response to his plea.

Of course, this was long before fracking, which, when it came into general use, would have made Broadwater, had it ever been built, which it was not, irrelevant.

Well, we did not know that at the time.

The Ira Rennerts

~~~~~~

In 2008, a friend who had Googled my name told me that I was a footnote on the Wikipedia page of Ira Rennert, the billionaire industrialist who lives in the Hamptons in the second-largest private residence in America. I thought, when I heard about this, now why is that? So I looked it up. It was there because the year before, in 2007, I had written an article in *Dan's Papers* about him and his palace, and he must have liked it. It was the only footnote on his Wikipedia page.

Rennert's oceanfront mansion, "Fairfield," was built on sixty-eight oceanfront acres of the miles and miles of farmland in Sagaponack. This was, until he built there, a part of the Hamptons where you could see forever. The land was flat and treeless, and from Daniel's Lane south across a mile of potato and corn fields, you could see to the back of the dunes and the sea. On rough days, when the ocean roared, the mist from the surf would billow over the dunes into the fields and the smell of salt would fill the air. To the north of Daniel's Lane, there were more vast stretches of flat farmland. It was only

INGEBORG RENNERT
(Courtesy of Barry Gordin)

in the late summer, when certain fields of corn grew high, that this wonderful vista was to a certain degree obstructed.

I had had an experience with this particular sixty-eight acres when it was a high cornfield. One evening, many years earlier, I took a girlfriend out in an old Volkswagen camper bus down a tractor path into that privately owned cornfield, hoping that the danger and romance of that situation would result in us sparking up a relationship. We spent the night in the bus in that cornfield. We talked. We slept. Nothing much else happened. In the morning, I took her back to her house in Sag Harbor, we shook hands, and that was that.

In any case, in 2000 the property was sold to this wealthy industrialist named Ira Rennert, a man nobody in the Hamptons had ever heard of, who then announced he was going to build a private home on this vast acreage. People figured it would be a big house. But they had no idea how big he had in mind.

The plans showed six huge buildings in the Italian Romanesque style totaling 110,000 square feet. It was of such enormous size that after a building inspector approved it (saying that from the plans it certainly did look like a private residence, although a very large one), and after Ira Rennert's construction crews began to build it, the Town went to the trouble of passing a law making it illegal in the future to build any private home larger than even one-fifth that size. One horse may be out of the barn, but there would be no more future horses out of the barn.

The article in the footnote to Ira Rennert's entry in Wikipedia got there because it was the last of seven different articles I wrote over the five years about the house and the $100 million it took to build it. It was an apology. I wrote that my prior articles, in which I condemned what he was doing, railing against the excessive cost of his project when so many others were poor and starving, decrying the fact that this would change the look of this farming community forever, even commenting on the way he had made his money—which was by buying and selling mining operations that were among the worst industrial polluters on the planet—all these articles were wrong.

Of course, I had not been alone in writing these condemning articles. Many in the media were writing them. Writers scoffed at the belief that this would be a "private home." They didn't believe it. The project would have twenty-nine bedrooms and parking for a hundred cars, thirty-five of them in garages. It would include a pool house, a guard house, a play house, a beach house, and a four-hole golf course. In a world of excess, it was excess unbounded. And it was all for just Ira Rennert, his wife, their three children and, on occasion, some guests.

Early on, as the media fired these shots at Rennert while the house was in the planning stage, it seemed that the project might be halted before it would even begin. This was not a private residence. It must be a resort hotel, or a religious retreat. Rennert was and is very active in the Jewish community. There was a two-story chapel noted on the plans. What else could this be?

Some of the most famous writers in America lived in this beautiful farm community. Kurt Vonnegut lived here. So had Truman Capote, Irwin Shaw, and James Jones, the author of *From Here to Eternity*.

The outcry continued on for years because it was taking years for this mansion to be built. Physically, this project would divide Sagaponack in two. There would be some potato fields on one side, some on the other. The vistas would be gone forever. How could this happen?

The building inspector who'd approved it was damned to hell. Kurt Vonnegut publicly stated that if this project went ahead, he would sell his home and leave the Hamptons.

But after four years of this, with the project moving slowly toward its conclusion, the protesting died down. It was there. There was nothing to be done about it. In fact, there were now many people curious to see what this place, now named "Fairfield" looked like. People asked others if they had been there. None had.

And Vonnegut, contrary to what he said he would do, didn't move.

And so, one year later, I offered this final piece in the paper as a kind of capstone for what had happened. I wrote that, in the end, the vast landscaped forest that Rennert had planted on his property—some trees came delivered forty feet high—completely masked what had been done in there. There were the gates to get in. Then there was just the woods. And inside that, well, it was Rennert's private palace, apparently. You really couldn't see it.

"A lot of the opposition was over the construction itself, of the dirt, the noise and the building materials and workmen," I wrote. "Now that it was all covered up, it looks like nothing so much as a great forest. It is fine."

Also, I wrote, Ira Rennert, at the very beginning of this controversy, explained it all himself in a single, dignified statement that he sent as a letter to the Southampton Press newspaper.

"This house is being built for myself and my family, so that when my children and grandchildren want to come visit me they can."

And that is exactly what he had done, I concluded.

IRA RENNERT
(Courtesy of Barry Gordin)

But then, after this conclusion, a devilish thought came over me. I wrote one more sentence.

"Can I get invited over now?" I asked.

This sentence, which changed the entire tone of this article, does not appear in the full article referred to in the footnote on the Wikipedia page when you click on it. The Rennerts, or someone in their employ had taken it out.

Then, one day, an invitation came in the mail.

"A playdate has been made for Mr. Dan Rattiner," the invitation began, "for FAMILY FUN DAY on Sunday, September 6, 2009. Playtime at 11 am. BBQ at 12:15 pm. Fairfield. Daniel's Lane, Sagaponack, New York."

There was a large donation involved to come to this party. It was a benefit for a charity in Israel. But below that information there was written, in pen, that "Mr. Rattiner is to be Mrs. Rennert's personal guest."

Had this been because of that last article in the paper? It had to be that.

The next day, I got an email from Mrs. Rennert's assistant asking that I confirm that I was going. Mrs. Rennert wanted to know if I would be bringing my wife or perhaps some guests, too. All would be all right with her. Let her know.

And so, at the appointed time, I and my wife, my son David, who was working at the paper, and Bill Collage, a screenwriter who lives out here, were waved through the gate on Daniel's Lane, and went down a long, narrow winding road through the newly planted woods to still another manned gatehouse. Here, there were actually two gate buildings, one on each side of the large gate that spanned the road, and in front of this, there was a circular asphalt area bordered by hedgerows, where it was possible to simply turn around and drive back the way you had come if you were being turned away. A woman with a clipboard approached my car.

"Mr. Rattiner, Mrs. Rennert is so glad you have come," she said. "The apology you wrote meant so much to her. She simply *had* to have you come here. Look for her when you arrive in the entryway courtyard, where the valet will take your car. She so much wants to meet you. She is a very fine lady."

And with that, the grand iron gate between the gatehouses swung open and we proceeded. The road made a graceful curving arc between rows of newly planted trees, and we passed rows of iron lanterns just above the lawns, past signs reading "Children At Play 15 MPH," until finally, after perhaps a quarter of a mile, we arrived at a palace that rivals in proportions almost any palace you might find in Europe. It embraces you on three sides, with a Roman portico on the right at the top of some marble steps fronting a grand two-story palazzo, a series of Romanesque arched breezeways in the center flanking several larger residential buildings, and, on the left, a two-story arched rococo entryway separating two other buildings through which it was possible to see, beyond its lacy fretwork, a great lawn. On this day, the lawn was filled with youngsters, parents, and servants of the Rennerts, flying kites and creating soap bubbles that emitted from shiny plastic toy pistols they pointed skyward.

We circled around the glorious fountain that serves as a centerpiece to this scene, and came to a halt in front of the rococo entry with the arches, alongside three brand-new shiny Hummers lined up in a row—Rennert had bought the Hummer Company, then sold it to General Motors, but kept these three.

Two valets in white jackets helped my wife out of one side and me out of the other side of our car, after which we were immediately approached by Mrs. Rennert herself coming down the marble steps. She was a beautiful blond woman with a friendly demeanor.

She offered me her hand.

"I am so glad to finally meet you," she said. She spoke with a heavy European accent. "That was such a nice thing you wrote about us. So heartfelt. So true. We are most appreciative that you did that."

A few other people were getting out of their cars just after us—there was a line of approaching cars—and she gathered up a few people along with us and asked us to follow her on a tour through the house, beginning, she said, with the prayer room.

She was so enthusiastic about this tour. We went.

The synagogue, for that is what it is, is a masterpiece. It is all marble and stained-glass hallways and prayer rooms, all gold and mahogany and oil paintings and vases. It is directly attached to the lacy two-story portico but is, in fact, a separate building with half a dozen rooms and lobbies surrounding an interior sanctuary that, if she had said had been transported from the palace grounds of the King of France, I would have believed her. It rivals any sanctuary I have ever been in, anywhere in the world. Indeed, the whole residence, all the rooms everywhere in this palace, rival in opulence anything in the world.

"I feel as if I have gone on vacation," I said to Mrs. Rennert as she walked us around the synagogue. "I don't know where I am. The Winter Palace in St. Petersberg? The Blue Mosque in Istanbul? Where the hell are we? This is magnificent."

"Wait until you see what is out here," Mrs. Rennert said, approaching some elaborately carved bronze doors. She swung the doors open and the light from the outside flooded in. We were looking out at a garden, with a lily pond in the middle and a white statue of a man on a base at the far end.

"That statue is an exact replica of Leonardo da Vinci's Moses," she said proudly.

I commented, as we left the synagogue, that the way the prayer room was arranged, with the rabbi's space in the center with the parishioners all around and upstairs on a balcony a place for the women, all reminded me of a particular synagogue out here.

"The Hampton Synagogue in Westhampton Beach is similar," I said.

A shadow passed over Mrs. Rennert's face.

"We don't talk about that place," she said.

I wasn't about to disagree with her. "They do a lot of P.R. there," I said, which was absolutely true. "A lot of press releases and programs."

"We really don't need that," she said.

She showed us more. There was a cobblestone outdoor courtyard café with tables and chairs in an arrangement surrounding a reflection pool. There was a bowling alley and bar. There was a swimming pool with cabanas and a pool house that had an elaborate iron fence around it that Mrs. Rennert unlocked to walk us through. All of these would not have been out of place in Caesar's Rome. Guards were stationed at the corners of the swimming pool.

"We are keeping the gates closed for the party, what with all the children running around," she said. "For safety reasons."

She took us up the steps of the porticoed temple with the Romanesque columns, and we went into a vast anteroom with magnificent bronze friezes on the walls. There were eight of them. They were from a church in Italy.

"We found one in Rome," she said. "Then, later, we found the other seven in Bulgaria. We had to have them."

The friezes, by a Renaissance sculptor, each portrayed events in the Bible. One was of Adam and Eve leaving the garden, another was Abraham about to sacrifice Isaac.

We moved on to another courtyard, which faced out onto still another vast hedgerow bordered lawn. And there the tour ended.

Now, she said, she was going to look for her husband. "I know he's here," she said.

"Why don't you call him?" I asked.

"Cell phone service is almost nonexistent here," she said.

"So he's *home*," Bill Collage said, and we all laughed. Then she was off, at least for a while.

Alone, the four of us walked down the lawn to a circular beach house with still another Renaissance-style dome. The Atlantic Ocean lay beyond it over a dune, but because of the dune, you could not see it. It was a strange thing, being in the Hamptons but not being aware of the sea.

Most of the day we spent on the children's side of the main mansion. We stood on the lawn, watching the servants and a dozen or so children and parents flying their kites in the strong wind. One kite got caught in a fruit tree and a child fretted. A servant came over to help get it down.

There were sack races on one lawn, a playground with climbing things and swings that any park would be proud of, a basketball court with an adjustable-height basket, and a soccer field. There was a movie theatre and an indoor swimming pool. There was an outdoor café set up with a barbecue that went from burgers and fries to Thai wraps and steak tartare. Children were running around. A drumming group called "Samba Boom," all in white, snaked through the various courtyards and buildings, banging on drums and playing cymbals and dancing along.

Later, when we met up with Mrs. Rennert again, she asked if we had seen the merry-go-round and I said we had not, so she took us to it. It was at the end of a playground and was a sort of pièce de résistance to the children's area. I asked where it had come from.

"We had it made," she said.

"This is like a whole little world in here," I said. "Leaving it is like going to the Hamptons."

"Really, I have everything I need right here," she said. "I never have to go out."

Bill Collage asked her how much time they spend here at Fairfield.

"We spend all summer here," she said, "except for the high holy days, which we spend in Israel. The rest of the year we are either in Manhattan or Palm Beach."

At one point, as we walked along across a grassy field, I told Mrs. Rennert the story of me, the girl, the potato field and the camper bus. I tried to stop myself from telling it, because I didn't really know her at all. But she took it well.

"I think we were parked about *there*," I said.

We still hadn't seen Ira Rennert. There were a few times that my wife thought that a particular older man was him. But I had seen his pictures, and it wasn't him. He was not there, at least not where we were, but he must have been somewhere. He was home.

The next day, I got a personal phone call from the woman who had arranged the invitation and had greeted me at the gatehouse. She told me again how much Mrs. Rennert had enjoyed my company. I told her that I had enjoyed hers, which I did.

My wife walked by. I asked her if she might be interested in becoming friends with the Rennerts. From the welcome I got from Mrs. Rennert, it certainly seemed possible I could arrange it.

"We could invite them out to a restaurant," I said. "Or to *here*." I motioned to our regular-sized house.

"I wonder how Ira Rennert feels about all this," she said. "We never even met him, after all."

It occurred to me that maybe it was *he* who had ordered my last sentence removed. Perhaps his wife didn't even know he had done that.

As it happened, the following year, we *did* come to meet Ira Rennert. We were invited—again the invitation came from Mrs. Rennert—to a fundraising dinner for another Jewish charity at their home. And there was Ira Rennert, with his wife, at the cocktail party in one of the Italianesque courtyards on the property. There were about forty people there, mostly men in suits and ties but also some well-dressed women in cocktail dresses. But we didn't know anyone. Mrs. Rennert

RENNERT HOUSE UNDER CONSTRUCTION
(Courtesy of the author)

was stunning as usual. Ira Rennert was dressed in a white linen suit that was tailor-made for him. He had, as I had seen from pictures, this great shock of white hair. It went perfectly with the suit below.

As it happened at this pre-dinner cocktail party, I never found an occasion to speak with him. But I did think I might get the opportunity to speak to him at the sit-down dinner that followed in the great ornate formal dining room. The uniformed waiters came in and out with course after course. The string quartet played. During the dinner, Rennert sat at a table in the center of the room with his back to me. We had been seated—there were name cards—with two other couples, both of whom were in the construction business. Now, I again thought, I would never get to talk to him.

Under the circumstances, during the pause between the last main course and dessert, I decided to go over to him. When he saw me standing alongside his chair, he turned, smiled, stood up to face me and extended his hand. Up close, I could see he was sort of dazzling. Manicured, coiffed, magnificently set out. I took his hand and introduced myself.

"I know who you are," he said. "That was a wonderful thing you did, writing what you did. You should be proud of yourself."

"Thank you," I said. And with that, it seemed a good time to walk away.

Later, I thought, it wasn't that *he* was proud of me. It was that I should be proud of myself. I couldn't quite figure out what to make of that.

And then I decided to re-read that article I had written in the paper. I have all the back issues in black volumes. I found the appropriate one, opened to where I had written it, and re-read it. The snide little last sentence about inviting me to the house, the one that completely changed the tone of the article, was not there. It was I who must have ordered it removed at the last minute. Apparently I had second thoughts. The story would proceed without it.

And then I had forgotten completely that I had done that.

Morris Welte

~~~~~~

In 2004, I went to a yard sale in Amagansett and bought a wonderful mantle clock. Actually, there were two of them to choose from. They seemed identical, but one was fifty and the other sixty dollars.

"Why is one more expensive than the other?" I asked.

"The one at sixty chimes the hour," the seller said.

"But they both work?"

"Oh yes, perfectly."

I sprang for the sixty dollar one. And I soon realized that it was one of the most wonderful things I had ever come to own. For one thing, on the face it had a lightning bolt and the word "Electric." When they built it, which must have been in the 1920s, having a clock that was electric was a big deal. So they were treating it as a special feature. No winding and winding this baby. Just plug it in. The electricity does the rest.

The second thing was that it had this most wonderfully clear carillon of chimes, announcing not only the hour and half hour in very stately fashion, but even every quarter hour. And it had a flaw. It would play its little tune on the quarter

MORRIS WELTE
(Courtesy of Mrs. Morris Welte)

hour, you know the one, and then it would bong. And the bongs would be wrong. It would bong four times at two o'clock, then eleven times at three o'clock and, if it felt like it, it would bong six times at a quarter past four.

I came to really like it though. People would hear it and then look puzzled. Or they'd look at their wrist. Was it really . . . couldn't be. And of course the clock face itself with the big hand and little hand telling the correct time confirmed that it couldn't be.

I thought there was something very philosophical about this. If you looked at it, you got the right time. If you listened to it, you didn't. The clock was off somewhere else. This was fine with me. I wrote about it in the paper. Published its picture.

But then, as the years went by and the time continued on, the clock mechanism began to deteriorate. About once every month, it would begin making a grinding noise with all the wheels turning inside suddenly in trouble. And it would fall behind in telling the time. You could open the back and push a little metal wheel in there spinning around to speed it up and the grinding would stop and it would return to a normal pace again. But then you'd have to reset the hands of the clock again.

Soon, though, this grinding noise would interfere with things once a week and I'd open the back and give the wheel a push and reset it. But then, it got even worse. It was happening every day. And then it was happening two or three times a day. And then, one day, it just began bonging and grinding endlessly and there was nothing I could do but pull out its plug to make it stop. At that point I knew the end was near.

But it broke my heart to put this clock aside. So I took it to a clock repair shop in Hampton Bays where I was told they could look at it for $85 and probably fix it for $265 but maybe it would be more. From what they could see by opening the back, they didn't even think it was the original workings back there. "Things get replaced all the time with these old clocks," the owner of the shop said. "So we might not even be able to get the right part. Or even know the right part."

Since it would cost more to "look at" the clock than I had paid for it, I retreated and came home with it. Tearfully, I put the clock up on the top of a bookcase. I could look at it from time to time and remember all the laughs we used to have. But I knew it was always just two thirty six up there and that would never change. I decided to write about my affection for the clock in the paper. Sort of an obituary and reminisence. I did that.

About three months later, I got a call from a man who said his name was Morris Welte and he and his wife lived in Southampton.

"I read your latest story about the mantle clock," he said. "And I have not been able to put it out of my mind. I am a clockmaker and I think I can fix it. Or at least I'd like to try. Could you bring it by?"

I told him I had already visited a clockmaker and there was no point in it, but he persisted. I asked what he would charge to look at it. I told him I had only paid sixty dollars for the clock.

"I know all that from when you wrote about it," he said. "I wouldn't charge you at all. I've been reading your paper for years. You have given me considerable enjoyment. I would like to repair it for you at no charge." He told me how to get to his house. I should bring the clock.

And so, in February of that year, I went to meet this older couple, Morris and Alice Welte at their home on Willis Lane in Southampton. They were polite and gracious to me. I was offered tea and cookies. And Morris gave me his card. "Tick Tock Clock Repair," it said. He told me that this is what he was doing in his retirement. And he had been retired for twenty-five years.

"Just leave it with me," he said. "I should know in a few weeks."

In mid-March, I got a progress report from Morris Welte by telephone. He told me the clock had improved, but was still in intensive care.

"I'll get back to you in another week or two," he said. "The prognosis is good."

Two weeks later, at his request, I went to his house to pick up my clock.

"All done," he said, patting it on the top of its head. The wood was all shined up. The face had been cleaned. He had it on his dining room table, all plugged in. It was humming along happily.

"I saw you sitting out in the car for a minute or two before you came to the front door," he said. "So you missed it bonging the hour. It was just a few minutes ago."

The clock said three minutes after eleven. That must have been something.

We both stood there staring at it silently, contemplating the fact that it would be twelve more minutes before it would fire up again. Ten seconds passed.

"Would you like to see my little repair shop?" Morris asked.

He led me through the kitchen to a flight of stairs that went down to his basement. There was a workbench there, right near the furnace. All the different tools were sitting there on it, all oiled and lined up in a row. There was a grandfather clock against one wall. The place was very neat.

"That one is going through testing," he said, pointing to the grandfather clock. "I promised I'd get it fixed in a week. Here on the bench you can see where I have built a metal rack. I take all the parts out of a clock and attach them in appropriate relationships one to another on this rack and then I can walk around and work on them front and back unobstructed."

I was curious to know how he had come to be repairing clocks. Had that been his career?

"Oh no," he said. "I worked being a radio man aboard ships at sea. I grew up in upstate New York and I learned Morse code in school. When I graduated, I worked for a private company that trained radio men and then assigned them to ships.

"In the thirties I traveled all over the world. Egypt. Japan. France. Athens. When you are a radio man like that, you can get assigned to a freighter or a government ship or a passenger liner. I was fortunate to always get passenger liners. I had a wonderful time."

I imagined him as the radio operator on the Titanic. But that would have been a generation earlier. And anyway, the radio guy on the Titanic didn't make it. Yet here was Morris Welte. So it wasn't him.

Then I suddenly realized something. If Morris Welte was traveling the world in the 1930s, he must be nearing a hundred years old. This was extraordinary. He looked no more than seventy. And he was fine.

"During the Second World War," he said, "I became a radio operator aboard airplanes. I worked for Pan Am. They were making bombers during the war. And they'd fly them down to Miami, six at a time, brand new, and I'd be aboard one of these planes as we delivered them to England or the South Pacific or somewhere. We delivered B-25s and B-26s."

Welte's career took a strange turn after the war.

"I got a job offer from Mackie Radio on Long Island," he said. "They had a contract to monitor all the ships at sea from a tower they had built in the woods of Southampton. So I moved here."

Welte told me a fascinating story about how Mackie got started in the business.

"Around 1910, a German firm built a Morse code radio tower and office in Sayville, Long Island to monitor all ships at sea. You didn't need a government license in those days. You just built a tower and the government would, if they needed you on the grid, hire you to keep track of everything. So the Germans ran it and linked it to Berlin without telling anybody. By 1914, when Germany attacked France to start World War I, they could tell immediately which of the American ships were at sea because of what they built in Sayville. Finally, around 1918 just about when the war was winding down, the Americans realized this and shut it down. After the war, a man named Clarence Mackie bought it from the government, disassembled it, and brought it out and reassembled it on a tall hill here in Southampton. He's who hired me."

Welte worked for Mackie for thirty years. He not only worked the Morse code but also learned how to fix the equipment when it was in disrepair. He retired from the firm in 1975 and three years later, Mackie went out of business. Morse code wasn't needed anymore.

"Today, it's a hill with lots of expensive mansions on it. No trace of Mackie. Just north of County Road 39 off Major's Path."

In retirement, Welte learned residential clock repair at BOCES in Riverhead and, at the little house he and his wife now lived in, opened Tick Tock Clock Repair. He'd been fixing clocks ever since.

"I think it's time to go upstairs and listen to eleven fifteen," he said.

And so we did.

Welte had completely fixed my clock. It played its tune once on the quarter hour, and as the tea and cookies and conversation proceeded on, twice on the half hour, three times on the three quarter hour, and then four times at the top of the hour, followed by the exact number of bongs to correspond with the hour.

I said my goodbyes after the triumphant sounding of the hour, and Welte ushered me to the front door carrying my baby.

"Be careful of the step," he said as he accompanied me out to my car.

As I got in behind the steering wheel, he spoke through the open window. "It was the chime wheel that was gunked up," he said. "The rest was fine. It's just as it was, brand new. These are its original workings. The motor was fine. But I think I'd keep the little wooden door in the back just a little ajar all the time. It does generate some heat when it spins around. And it's always spinning around. Leaving the door open a little will allow the air to circulate through and help keep it healthy."

I took the clock home and set it back where it had been for all those years—on my mantelpiece over the fireplace. It continued bonging the correct hour far into the evening. I thought, well you know what? I kind of miss it being ten o'clock but the clock bonging whatever the hell it wanted to.

But then again, I didn't miss it that much. It's nice that I didn't throw it out when it died, but had the chance several months later, thanks to Morris, to have this beautiful clock brought back to the robust fullness of its life.

Thank you, Morris Welte.

Tahoe Trouble

~~~~~~

On a late, near freezing afternoon in March, 2008, my wife and I, together with our Wheaton terrier Moo, got into my Tahoe and drove the two miles into downtown East Hampton to run some errands. First on our list was Gruen Optica on Main Street to pick up my new pair of glasses. Finishing there, and with the new glasses in hand, we walked out to the car, which was parked in a spot directly in front of the Citarella market about a hundred yards down Main Street from Gruen Optica. It was a lucky thing for us to find such a space on a busy Saturday afternoon in town.

From here, it was our intention to next go to the North Main Street Dry Cleaner and pick up some clothes, then walk over to Crossways Music a few doors down to get some musical equipment we had ordered, then, after dropping off the dog at home up the street, go to a restaurant for dinner. We had a reservation at seven.

None of that happened.

A police officer was out by my car, looking at it. Was something wrong? I had parked properly. I knew the stickers on the windshield were up to date. What was it? The officer,

DAN'S PAPERS, April 4, 2008 Page 15 www.danshamptons.com

Tahoe To Go

FRONT PAGE OF AN ARTICLE IN *DAN'S PAPERS*
ABOUT MY CAR ON A FLATBED TRUCK, 2008

who I did not know, saw me coming and said something very odd as he walked out into the center of the street.

"Mr. Rattiner, I need you to wait for me here, please. Outside your car."

"You are lucky I caught you before you drove off, we're only going to impound your car. You won't be arrested."

Our dog Moo was now looking at the shiny, ramrod straight police officer through the passenger window.

IN THE HAMPTONS 4EVER

I thought—is there a bomb in the car? I said "Is there a problem?"

"Oh yes," he said. "There was a lapse in your insurance. We have these new radar sensors on the roofs of our police cars. And we can check the license plates of every car on the road just by driving by. When we went by yours, an alarm went off. Your registration was suspended. An insurance payment was missed or something. The plates have to be taken off and sent up to motor vehicle. And the car goes to the police impound."

"All my paperwork is right up to date. This is a mistake. I'll drive it home if you like and I won't drive it at all after that. Whatever it is, I'll get it straightened out first thing Monday."

"I can't do that," Bartelmy said. "The car stays here. It cannot be moved. Except by us."

"It'll get a ticket. It's in a one hour zone."

"We'll watch it."

"You can't let me just drive it home?"

"No. We'll arrest you if you try."

"So we're just dumped out here on the street?"

This went on for about ten minutes, this back-and-forth. The officer was very clear about what he had to do. There would be no variation from it.

My wife, meanwhile, asked if it would be okay for her to go into Citarella for a few minutes. She'd buy us something for dinner. We actually had no food to prepare at home, because we were planning to go out. He said go ahead.

"What about my dog?" I asked. I was trying veiled sarcasm. A bad idea. "Are you going to impound him too?" He was not amused.

"We can call the taxi cab company to come get you to take you home if you like," he said. "We'd offer to drive you, but all three cars are off on calls." All three were right there, within the sound of his voice.

"Is this really happening?" I asked.

"You can get things out of your car if you want. You can do it now. Hard to believe nobody picked this up before."

I took the registration out of my wallet and showed it to him. It was good until November 30, 2008. There was nothing saying it was suspended and there had been no notice to me that it had been suspended. This was impossible.

At this point he held out his hand, and in it I placed my car keys.

So that was it. Chris returned with a bag of groceries from Citarella, which she set on the grass by the side of the Tahoe. I told her how it had all turned out. Then we opened the car doors and I took out a portable car charger, some cash on the dashboard, my wristwatch in the change well, a folding chair, and a blanket from the back—I have no idea why I did that—and my dog Moo, who looked at me. "What fun place is next?" he wanted to know.

At that moment, the wrecker with flashing lights appeared to haul off my car. It was Jigger from Balcun's Gas Station on North Main Street a block away. We know each other. We waved. He seemed a happy camper in all this.

As his cable lifted up the front end of my car, The officer wandered over to tell me what I'd have to do on Monday coming up. Go to Riverhead Motor Vehicles. Pay the $8 a day for the time it was uninsured. Get your plates back. Go to the impound lot and bail out the car for $150. And that was it. "You'll be done before the end of the day," the officer said.

"Could we have the car towed just to the house?" I asked.

"Oh sure."

"Can I tell Jigger?"

"Oh no. It has to go the impound lot first. So you'd have to pay to have it towed twice," he said cheerfully. "Once to the impound, and then to the house."

"How long have you been doing this?" I asked.

"Being a police officer?"

"No. Today."

"Just twenty minutes. We've already got two cars. Yours and another one, right there."

"At the rate you're going, you'll have the traffic problem in downtown East Hampton solved in no time." I thought that tone was about right.

My hands were cold. I was wearing a thin jacket. But at that moment, friends we know, Fred and Robin Seegal, came out of the Citarella parking lot in their car, pulled up to see what was happening and they wound up driving us home.

At the house, we had wine, crackers, and cheese and watched sunset overlooking Three Mile Harbor. Fred said this must have been a cured lapse. He couldn't understand why, if it was not a current lapse, they could do what they did.

I said I had no notification of any lapse. Nothing. I had no idea there had even been a lapse.

"If it's two days, it will be $16. If it's two hundred days it will be $1,600," I said. "I guess I will find out when I call."

We also talked about the time, three years earlier, when the Village contracted with a company to put metal boots on the tires of cars that overstay their time in Village parking lots. An attendant would wait nearby, sitting in a car with the key. He'd see a woman hauling shopping bags and maybe a kid in a stroller walk back to her booted car and say he'd use the key to unlock it but not until the fine of $375 in cash was paid.

People would get very angry. There was a woman with an elderly mother in tow who had to be taken somewhere. She didn't have $375 in cash with her. She'd drop her mother off, go home and get it and come back. No, she was told. No cash, no car.

Andrew Baker, who owned the Sag Harbor Music Store, broke his big toe trying to kick the metal boot off his wheel in front of this guy. George Plimpton, the author, *did* kick and break the boot with one solid shot. It broke into two pieces, which fell to the ground with a clang, causing both the attendant and George to gape at them in wonder.

Just keep the car, George told the attendant. And he walked off. It was, he later told me, a very old car not worth $375.

Here in our living room, with the sun now set, I made a decision.

"This is a terrible thing for our town," I said. "I'm going to call the Mayor."

And so right then and there, I did. I found him at home. "You should junk these computer radar devices," I told him. "Throw them in the trash. They are Orwellian devices that we should not be allowed to possess."

He said they had brought a lot of money to the village in a very short amount of time, catching scofflaws and people who had arrest warrants against them. "But I do understand," he continued. "And I really appreciate that you called."

And so, after the Seegals left, we had a small dinner at home. And off to bed, but not before checking Moo's collar. Rabies good. Dog license good. Good dog.

For the next thirteen days, my Tahoe sat in the East Hampton impound area waiting while my insurance people tried to sort out what turned out to be mixed up paperwork from a year and a half ago. The Tahoe had not been the problem. The seizure was because of a 13-day lapse that occurred in my insurance coverage on a 2005 Land Rover that I owned *before* I bought the Tahoe. It was a paperwork screw-up in the transfer to it.

Turns out, an insurance lapse follows the plates. If I had said, when I bought the Tahoe new, that I wanted new plates and not the old plates taken off the Land Rover and transferred to the Tahoe, a decision that saved $35, this never would have happened.

I also wrote in the paper about what was now happening. Perhaps it might have had some effect on the authorities. Not a bit.

A friend drove me to the Riverhead Motor Vehicle at 3 p.m. on Friday with the appropriate documents thirteen days after the seizure. Three dollars and about half an hour later, I walked out with a new registration and a new sticker for the windshield.

Thirty miles later, I was dropped off by my friend at the East Hampton Village police station, which is part of the emergency services building on Cedar Street.

The lobby there is not a citizen friendly place. There is no place to sit down. You enter a narrow, shiny-walled room with a twelve-foot ceiling, where high up on one wall there is what appears to be a sliding glass mirror.

"Hello?" you shout. The voice echoes.

The glass mirror, which you now realize is a one-way glass, slides open. And a woman officer peers down. She's up there. You're down here.

"Yes?"

I stated my case. And after a while, the officer who had been there when they towed my car, came out a door below the window to where I was. He would drive me to the impound area to get my car.

I would need to show him, he said, my driver's license, my new registration and the green form showing I had paid my fine in Riverhead.

"And then there is the impound fee," he said. "It's also one hundred and fifty dollars, and with tax, it's exactly one hundred and sixty two dollars and fifty cents. And it has to be in cash and you have to have the exact change."

I told him I had been told all this in Riverhead and had the money, and I checked my wallet and told him I had lots of twenties and a ten and a five. I also had everything else except the receipt for the towing. And I had also not been given any green form in Riverhead, just the new registration.

"You need the green form that shows how much fine you paid."

"There was no fine. The lapse was rescinded."

"Then I need a green form showing that."

We stared at each other for a while. I repeated there was no form and there was no fine. And he decided to give way. But he had another card to play.

"I can't do anything without the towing receipt showing you paid," the officer said. "You have to have that."

I suggested that since to get to the impound area from the police station you have to pass Balcun's, that we proceed as if we had it and we stop off there and I'd run in, pay it, and get the receipt. I also told him I had been dropped off and was on foot.

He told me to walk there.

And so I did. Round trip is about half a mile. As a half mile walk might take twenty minutes, I decided to pick up the pace and do it in ten. I also took the heavy shoulder bag with all my stuff in it that I cart around. I thought it might be a good thing for me to do this brisk walk with the heavy bag. Also, I thought I really didn't want to leave the bag in the station because it might get stolen.

On the way there and back, I had some adventures. First of all, walking along hefting this bag, it occurred to me that I had just made a decision not to leave a shoulder bag in a police station. It's the *police* station. I am so ridiculous.

At the light where Cedar meets North Main, I was hailed by a friend in a car stopped at the light.

"Hey, Dan!" he shouted.

I waved, smiled and marched on.

This is a terrible corner to have to negotiate on foot, even with the traffic light in your favor because of the turning lanes. In the crosswalk heading by the turning lane, a Prius menaced me. "Move, buddy, we're comin' through," it said. I stopped and glared at the driver and pointed to the white crosshatch I was standing in. And he decided not to run me over. So I stared at him further and made various victorious postures at him.

I wondered why I had challenged him like that. I decided that it was because I was so pissed I would have felt a great sense of satisfaction if I had been run over. That's the mood I was in.

Balcun's Gas Station was an interesting experience. They are usually very nice. This time I walked into the cluttered office there to find three people I didn't know motionlessly staring at a TV set directly over the door where you come in. They continued looking up there. There was no nod, no hello. Apparently it was the interesting part. I told them I was there to pay the $150 towing fee.

One of the three people was a woman sitting on an old upholstered chair with a cat on her lap. She patted the cat. And she spoke very slowly.

"It's one hundred and sixty two dollars and fifty cents," she said, pronouncing every word very carefully. "How do you want to pay it? And what kind of car was it?"

I told her cash and a Tahoe. She motioned to a young man who had also been looking up at the TV to get the file for her and then handle the transaction. The interesting part was still going on when we had finished. I walked back, the receipt for the towing fee in my hand.

The officer took my money and went over the receipts, told me another officer in a police car would be coming around front and, when I saw him, to get in and he'd take me to the impound.

This only took a minute or two. The car pulled up. There was a big black leather bag on the passenger seat, so I got in the back where the prisoners go. A cage separated the back from the front. And I noticed the door locks had been removed. Most interesting was that there was no upholstered rear seat at all, just a molded plastic bench for a rear seat. Also, there was a panel under the bottom of the front seat so you couldn't put your shoes under the front seat.

This officer was Steve Shades who also asked to be remembered to my son David because he went to school with him.

"I'm really not a danger of going wild back here," I told him.

"It's something new we're trying. Some people, when we're taking them in, they shove things into the upholstery of the seat back there. So we have to search every time. With this we don't have to."

I was sitting sideways and banging around with every bump. I told him I didn't think this would catch on with cars for the general public.

He was very polite. When we got to the impound area—and I could see my beautiful Tahoe still in there!—he walked around the car to let me out.

I hugged my car. You're such a good car. I'm just so happy now. And I slowly drove home, the officer following me for a bit as I went on my way, apparently wanting to see that I got home safely.

On the Next Page: *Every summer, it seemed, traffic in our downtowns was becoming worse and worse. Parking was becoming a terrible problem. I thought there ought to be another way to get around the Hamptons. Here was the lead story in* Dan's Papers *on July 10, 2006 in which I said that help was at hand. The authorities had unwittingly discovered a long lost Hampton Subway system—built underground by a friend of a well-known real estate developer of the 1920s named Carl Fisher.*

SUBWAY SYSTEM BUILT IN 1920S
FOUND UNDERGROUND IN THE HAMPTONS

As most people know, the single most spectacular real estate development ever attempted on the east end was that of Carl G. Fisher. In the mid-1920s, he bought the entire peninsula of Montauk, 12,000 acres in all, and during the years between 1925 and 1929 began to build a great city in that community. The centerpiece of it, built on the downtown plaza he created in a field, was the seven-story building that continues to dominate this community to this day.

But he also built a polo field, a race track, a yacht club, a gambling casino, a boardwalk and swim club, a 250-room hotel high on a hill—it still stands as the Montauk Manor—the entire network of roads in downtown Montauk, including pink sidewalks that survive in many areas, half a dozen downtown commercial buildings, two churches and an automobile racetrack. He also imported sheep and built a section for the help, known as Shepherd's Neck.

His intention from the get-go was to build a big beach resort city, similar to the one he had built in the early 1920s in Miami Beach. Among other things, he had recently been married for the third time, to a 16-year-old named Jane. These were heady times for millionaire Carl Fisher.

What has never been known until now is that while Carl Fisher and some of his wealthy friends were building the resort of Montauk, (it failed in the Crash of '29), there was a lesser known and very shady figure by the name of Ivan Kratz, a wealthy builder, who had designs on creating a transportation monopoly for the Fisher project.

Ivan Kratz, between 1900 and 1925, had made millions by building the New York City Subway System. His work was good, but the way he went about securing contracts was crooked. In 1900, offering up a whole slew of bribes to New York City officials, he had bid high but got the contract to build the New York City Subway System. By paying notoriously low salaries to his workmen, he made huge amounts of money at both ends.

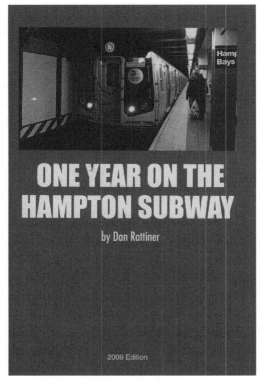

ONE YEAR ON THE
HAMPTON SUBWAY
by Dan Rattiner

2009 Edition

FRONT COVER OF A BOOK ABOUT HAMPTON SUBWAY,
BY THE AUTHOR

By 1924, however, he was under investigation as part of the Teapot Dome scandal. Amazingly, in 1928, when it came time for investigators to look for the money Kratz had made—he was by this time the owner of a vast oceanfront mansion in East Hampton—it all came up empty. Where had the money gone?

Last month, auctioneers selling the contents of the Kratz mansion—only recently put up for sale by his heirs—came upon an extraordinary document. Copies of it were turned over to the Town of Southampton and the Town of East Hampton. And representatives of the New York State Department of Transportation had become involved.

Kratz, between 1925 and 1929, had secretly constructed an enormous underground subway system that he called the Hampton Subway.

It has its main terminus right under the open plaza in downtown Montauk. And it is connected up to underground "stations" in Napeague, Amagansett, East Hampton, Bridgehampton, Southampton, Quogue and Westhampton Beach. There is a spur that goes up to Sag Harbor and North Haven, and another that goes up Three Mile Harbor Road in East Hampton and then splits off to end at Maidstone Park in Three Mile Harbor and Gerard Park at Accabonac Harbor.

"At first," said Tom Larson of the NY State Department of Transportation, "we thought that the subway map that had turned up at the auction was some kind of joke."

But then Town bulldozers from the two highway departments were brought in, and the first of the holes was dug—the first just under the large and unused gas ball in Sag Harbor just behind the Post Office. In just four days of digging, the workmen uncovered twin platforms, two sets of rails (including a third rail that went down into some dark tunnels), a ticket booth, some turnstiles and a flight of stairs that went up to a steel bilco door that had been covered up by grass. It was the Sag Harbor station for the G Train.

"It's all in place," Larson said at a press conference. His eyes welled up with tears. "The whole thing. We've been through it from end to end. And it's all there. It has the same white ceramic tiles on the walls that they have in the New York Subway. The names of all the station in blue tiles. There are nine stations. And all we have to do to make this whole thing operational is bring in a modern air exchange system to the tunnels, build some escalators to get down to the platforms to bring this up to code—there were no escalators in use in subways until the 1940s although they surely had them—and bring in some subway cars.

"The track gauge is also from the New York Subway. In fact, we believe that all these materials were FROM the New York Subway system. Stuff supposedly 'stolen' by Kratz and brought out here. It's all amazing. And it is an answer to our prayers. The transportation nightmare in the Hamptons is over."

Someone asked the locations of all the underground subway stations, and Larson told them. There is one under the parking lot at the Montauk Lighthouse, there is one under the crossroads of Flamingo Road and Westlake Drive at the fishing village there, there is one on Ditch Plains Road where it makes the 90-degree turn to the left, there is one under the Kirk Park Beach parking lot in downtown Montauk named "Montauk Beach," which is what Carl Fisher called the place, there is one just under the Montauk Railroad Station, another behind the restaurant called LUNCH on the Napeague Strip, one at the corner of Montauk Highway and Napeague Lane in Beach Hampton, and one in the Amagansett parking lot by the Amagansett railroad station.

Other locations heading further west include under the intersection of Further Lane and Egypt Lane in East Hampton, under the Main Beach parking lot in East Hampton, under the parking lot at South Ferry in North Haven, under the old Alison By the Beach restaurant on Route 27 and Town Line Road, under the Bridgehampton Railroad Station, under Fedi's Market on Noyac Road, under the field in back of Corrigan's Service Station at Hayground Road and the Montauk Highway in Water Mill, under the village green in Water Mill, under the back parking lot of the Princess Diner at Hampton Road and County Road 39 in Southampton, under a lot adjacent to the Sandpiper Motel in Shinnecock, under the street in front of the Blue Moon Café in East Quogue, at the corner of Lewis Road and the Old Montauk Highway in Quogue and under Jessup Neck and Main Street in Westhampton Beach.

"We don't know why a station was not built in Hampton Bays," Larsen said. "Members of the Kratz family say that their grandfather once complained about a yacht he bought in Hampton Bays from a marina owner that sprang a leak and sank. That we think might be as good a reason as any. Anyway, if we get all this together, we think we will probably put in a Hampton Bays stop."

A reporter asked Larsen who will be in charge of restoring the system.

"I am pleased to announce today that Governor Pataki has created a Hamptons Transportation Authority, with a base funding of $10 million. We will go from there."

A reporter asked if Peter Kalikow, who heads the Port Authority in New York and has a home in Montauk, might be interested in the job.

"It's possible," Larsen said.

Another reporter asked if Carl Fisher himself, who had an excellent and above board reputation, was involved in this.

"We have dug deep in the Fisher archives," Larsen said. "Apparently he thought it was some kind of drainage subcontractor. He seems to have been aware of it, but didn't know anything about it. He was a big-picture sort of guy."

"Any idea when the Hampton Subway will become operational?"

"We're looking at the summer of 2008."

Barack Obama and Tim Bishop

~~~~~~

As the year 2010 approached, a year that would mark the fiftieth anniversary of *Dan's Papers*, my thoughts turned to Barack Obama. He was my President. I had voted for him two years earlier. Surely he would do what presidents before him had done when faced with an anniversary for my newspaper ending in a zero, and acknowledge the success of *Dan's Papers* on that occasion with a congratulatory letter.

There is, it turns out, a way to get the President of the United States to do this. I learned about it when Jerry Finkelstein, my partner at the newspaper, decided in 1990 to go all out on our 30th anniversary. He arranged for the Montauk Yacht Club to have a big party for the newspaper. There was a buffet, an ice sculpture with the number 30 on it, feathered dancing girls from Las Vegas, lobster, steak, and caviar on the menu for dinner, and humorist George Plimpton on hand to act as master of ceremonies for a roast onstage, where people Jerry had assembled said naughty things about me. It was a wonderful event.

DAN AND TIM BISHOP

The biggest surprise of the evening was a framed certificate from the President of the United States at the time, George H. W. Bush, congratulating me on thirty successful years, on the number of people I employed, about the number of pages in every issue, and about certain causes I had championed. At the bottom of it was the President's signature, signed by someone in the President's office who was very good at forging the President's name. It was presented to me by our congressman from this district, George Hochbrueckner, who was at the party among many other dignitaries.

"However did you get this?" I asked the congressman late in the evening.

"There's an office set up in the White House for this sort of thing. Jerry gave me all the information about you. I'm really glad you liked it."

I really did like it. Who wouldn't? A week later, Jerry confessed that not only the letter, but the entire event, had cost him almost nothing. A friend of his had bought the Montauk Yacht Club, was in the process of upgrading it and re-opening it to a breathlessly waiting world as a magnificent replica of a 1920s speakeasy and showplace, and was happy to provide the hall, the food, and the entertainment in exchange for several full-page ads and an article I could write about it in the paper the following week, which I did.

When my 40th anniversary came, the congratulatory letter came from President Bill Clinton. And then it came time for my fiftieth anniversary.

In the first week of February 2010, I called my congressman, Tim Bishop, about getting this letter from the President's office. I anticipated there would be no problem.

Tim Bishop, for many years, was the Dean of Southampton College. He was a prominent member of a family that went all the way back to the first settlement of the town in 1640.

I was only an acquaintance of Tim Bishop's, but frankly, after this, I was surprised to find that after he took office, he simply disappeared down a rabbit hole into the void of Washington, DC. That was unusual. Often, at my newspaper, we would be in touch with our various representatives on different matters, and they were, for the most part, very responsive. With Tim Bishop, however, we'd call him and he'd have a member of his staff call back to take care of whatever it was. There was no sense that he was involved. Indeed, in the two terms he was in office before 2010, I cannot recall a single time I had spoken with him directly. It was eerie.

On the other hand, how hard could this be, getting a letter from President Obama's office?

"Hello? This is Tim Bishop's office."

"Is Tim there?"

"May I ask what you're calling about?"

I told this person what I wanted, and was then referred to someone else in the office, who referred me to still another person, who said his name was Dave. Dave sounded very young. I told Dave what I hoped he could do. I told him about why I started the paper, about the number of pages we published every week, the number of people we employed, and the causes we backed, all useful information he would need drafting a letter of commendation, and I told him we needed it for July 1, which was the date of the anniversary party. It was January, there was plenty of time.

"I'll take care of it," Dave said.

When a month went by without my getting a call back from Dave, I called him again. He said he'd been busy but he'd get around to it. A month later—this was now March—he said he had sent in the request, so now it was up to Obama's office. I asked if it would be helpful for me to call Obama's office to follow up and he said no, he was taking care of it.

In April, I called again. "I said I was taking care of it," he said. He seemed a little cross. "We have lots of things we have to do around here," is how he ended the conversation.

Around the first of May, when I had received no further information, I decided I'd better do something about it. The date was right around the corner. We had rented a hall, arranged the band, it was going to be a big deal. Perhaps Tim Bishop himself could take a call from me.

But then I thought, what the heck am I doing? What kind of person am I that I would think I'm entitled to a letter from the President? I thought about it for about a minute. Then I dismissed that thought.

"I'd like to speak to Tim Bishop," I asked whoever answered the phone.

Once again, I explained things, and mentioned time was growing short. And once again I was passed along to another person. It was not Dave.

"Can I speak to Tim Bishop?"

"He's in Washington today. But I'm the person who takes the calls from people who want to speak to Tim Bishop. Can you give me your information?"

So I did again.

Sixty days later, we had a wonderful party to celebrate the 50th anniversary of *Dan's Papers*, without any warm wishes from the President. Frankly, I had put the matter of his good wishes aside. This was a half a century. I had done my paper for half a century, whether he appreciated it or not.

"To another half-century!" somebody toasted.

As it happened, the summer of 2010 corresponded with the beginning of Tim Bishop's campaign to win another term.

I had not received a call-back about the Obama matter. But now I did receive calls from Bishop's people about the re-election matter. Would I endorse him? Write something nice about him? It was going to be a very close election. He was running against a much younger man in the western end of the district with a wife and two children, who had made millions of dollars running a business that outsourced jobs overseas.

In the end I did and Tim Bishop won the election by 56 votes, out of 30,000 cast. It was one of the closest elections ever, and I might be forgiven for thinking that my endorsement of him got him those few winning votes. Indeed, the election had been so close that nearly two weeks after it was over, while they were still counting, his opponent, seeing what he thought was a little daylight with the write-in votes, took a trip down to Washington to meet his upcoming colleagues and see his new offices. And then he learned that he had lost.

One month after that, the letter of congratulation from Barack Obama arrived in our offices. It consisted of a large overnight envelope that had come from the office of Tim Bishop. Inside the overnight envelope, there was a smaller envelope with the Presidential Seal on it, and inside that was the commendation. I thought, "This is GREAT!" But then I read it.

Dear Friend:

I am pleased to send my congratulations to you on your anniversary. As you celebrate this important milestone, I hope you will look back on what you have accomplished

with joy and pride. I wish you all the best for continued
success and happiness in the future.

Barack Obama.

I turned it over. Perhaps there was something else written on the back, like, for example, my name. There wasn't.
The President of the United States was congratulating me for
whatever it was I had done, and was urging me to not fail
to look back upon it, whatever it was, with joy and pride.

I thought about this for a while, and then I thought, this
was perfect. *Everybody* should get a letter like this.

And so, I took it downstairs to the front desk and made
100 copies of it. I put these 100 copies in a nice stack on
the front counter and put a note on it that read "Take One,
It's For You." I also wrote an article for the paper about the
letter that had come from President Obama, and invited
readers who felt good about something they had done to
come in and pick one up. I then waited a week to see how
many got picked up.

According to Lisa at the front desk, not one person had
ever come in and done that. Oh well.

On the Next Page: *In the fall of 2013, the local towns in the Hamptons made an arrangement with the Federal Farm Bureau to have sharpshooters come to our community in February of 2014 and, working at night with laser sights and high-powered rifles, kill as many as 3,000 of what are believed to be a herd of 30,000 in this community. The community became polarized about whether this ought to be done or not. As it wrestled with itself to decide how to proceed, I published this hoax on December 27, 2013. It went viral and received more than one million hits.*

LIONS WILL KILL ALL DEER IN THE HAMPTONS

A solution to the deer problem in the Hamptons will take place next week, courtesy of a wealthy South African industrialist who has recently bought a home here. It will be at no charge to the taxpayers, and it will pre-empt the need for Federal sharpshooters here in the Hamptons. They had been scheduled to arrive here, and also in the other east end towns in February to cull the herd on the East End.

The problem, as everyone knows, is that there are too many deer roaming through the woods of the East End and the deer eat everyone's shrubbery, get hit by cars, and leap over the fences that everybody builds to keep them off of private property. A survey done from the air recently estimated that there are 30,000 deer on the East End, 8,000 of which are in the Hamptons.

Local realtors were very pleased last year when Hans Van der Klerk bought the old oceanfront Kallen estate. It had been on the market for more than a year, but few wanted to put in bids. Since it is twenty eight acres, including a main house, guest cottage and private dock, the asking price was quite high.

Van der Klerk, of Capetown, has parlayed several small silver and bauxite mines in the outback of South Africa into a conglomerate of more than twenty factories around the world, mining everything from boric acid to asphalt to gold to sand and gravel. Recently, in response to protests by environmentalists, he closed an asbestos mine in Tanzania, in spite of the fact it was quite profitable. He is retooling that mine to be able to separate out cobalt, which is in considerable abundance on the site and which is in great demand by the nuclear power industry. Fortune Magazine has estimated der Klerk's net worth at one billion two.

Der Klerk bought his Bridgehampton property sight unseen. Upon arrival here, he expressed astonishment at the crowds of deer that had broken through the hedgerows to feast on his gardens and lawns. He was even more astonished to learn that the five eastern towns, including those in the Hamptons, had agreed to have Federal sharpshooters out here, free to roam on private property with high powered rifles in February to kill as many deer as they could. The shoot is expected to last 40 days.

"I will not allow anyone I don't know on my property," he said. "I can't speak for the other east end towns, but I am sure that there are others in the Hamptons that feel the same way as I do."

Der Klerk's solution has been to bring twenty six male African lions from South Africa to Bridgehampton. He plans to release them into the woods here in the Hamptons on Monday.

"They are the natural predators of deer in South Africa," he told this reporter at a meeting at his house on Friday. "I have done the math. Based on the rate that these carnivores eat meat, the deer herd should be gone in ten days. This is mother nature at work."

Der Klerk also had his attorneys do some research. There is an ordinance in the Hamptons prohibiting the harboring of "wild animals," but in the list of such animals, there is mention of coyotes and American Mountain Lions, but not the South African Lion.

"It may have been an oversight," de Klerk grinned. "But I have a problem here and I am someone who solves problems."

The lions, each 800 to 1000 pounds, were caught in the Kalahari Section of South Africa using blow guns with darts that have been dipped in a sleeping potion. The lions were caged while asleep, flown to Kennedy Airport, and then taken by boat to der Klerk's private dock on Wednesday. Currently they are being housed in the der Klerk garage, built by Mr. Kallen for his seventeen antique car collection. I could hear them roaring there in his library, several hundred yards from the garage.

"Why have you only brought male lions?" I asked.

"We wanted them to only have one thing on their minds."

"What happens after ten days?"

"The lions will be caught, they should be well fed and lazy by that time, and returned to South Africa."

Der Klerk is delaying the releasing of the lions until Monday so he can get the word out—Dan's is not the only newspaper he has contacted.

After leaving der Klerks, I spoke to Emmett Greengrocer, the President of the East End Environmental Group (EEEG) based in Sag Harbor, who has often spoken out against desecrating the land and the wanton shooting of the wildlife by the local hunters.

"It sounds like this has been thought through," Greengrocer said. "Prey and predator. Survival of the fittest. Lions are beautiful creatures. This is the stuff we have been talking about for a long, long time. Somebody has finally heard us."

A spokesman for the Hamptons spoke on condition of anonymity and said that Hampton officials were in a great quandary because of these developments.

"Der Klerk is right. We checked the law. Local residents are not prohibited from harboring South African lions. South African lions are also not mentioned in the list of animals specifically prohibited from running wild either. We have attorneys working on this 24 hours a day. But it seems the only thing we can do is stand aside while Der Klerk's lions eat, and then not let the sharpshooters in in February, and get our money refunded."

A spokesman for Brookhaven Town, which borders the Hamptons at Westhampton Beach, said they had heard about the plan when the lions were flown in on Wednesday. But they were ready.

"African lions may be not be prohibited in the Hampton ordinances, but we have an ordinance 26 section 7, which specifically prohibits South African lions in Brookhaven. We have plans to have police cars at the border with the Hamptons beginning on Monday morning at 1 am and they will be armed with high powered rifles and will shoot lions on sight."

Half of the force was trained in the use of high powered rifles on Thursday and Friday, he said. The last group will be trained over the weekend.

A spokesman for the Town of Southold said he doubted that any lions would sneak into his town because to get there they'd have to take the ferry. Nevertheless, he said that if any lions did do that and were leftover in February when the federal sharpshooters arrived, the sharpshooters would shoot them."

"We've paid them to shoot deer. Surely they can shoot lions."

A spokesperson for the Village of Greenport lamented Mr. de Klerk's actions.

"He could have gotten more lions, some we could use in our towns too, but he didn't," he said. "And now it's a no win situation. The Towns in the Hamptons, having paid for the federal sharpshooters, will now get refunds. So the rich just get richer and the poor get poorer. But not us. Also, the Hamptons can breathe easier in February because they won't have to put up with sharpshooters for forty days in February. And March too. Isn't that's the way it is with the snooty folks in the Hamptons. So we get the short end. It's a quadruple whammy."

In any case, residents of the Hamptons are urged to stay indoors from December 29 to January 8 while the lions are loose.

ACKNOWLEDGMENTS

There are many people, places and institutions I would like to thank: my agent Scott Miller of Trident for his guidance and advocacy, my wife Chris Wasserstein for her patience and understanding and suggestions, James Peltz, the co-director of SUNY Press, Diane Ganeles at SUNY Press for her editorial work, Editor at Large Sharon Green for her suggestions and editorial work, the Montauk Library, the East Hampton Village Library, the Bridgehampton Library, Mayor Rickenbach of East Hampton Village, the people of Montauk, to Adelaide de Menil for her fact-checking help and remembrance for her chapter, John Keeshan, my compatriot in Montauk out at the Point, to many of the subjects of this book that I remember so fondly, to Dick Brass, Nick Vasilli, Dick White Jr., my longtime friend in Montauk, the New York Society Library for their workspace, the Metropolitan Museum of Art for their cafes where I sometimes work and also for the Sustained Membership Room, Martin and Judy Shepherd, publishers and editors; Editor Eric Feil of *Dan's Papers* for his editorial advice, book reviewer Joan Baum for her advice, the beautiful elm trees and windmills of eastern Long Island, Bonacker Stuart Vorpahl, Emeritus English Professor Richard Gollin from the University of Rochester, the late English teacher Harry Friedlander from Millburn (N.J.) High School who got me going on this career, to the late Jean Shepard who taught me about personal radio shows, Constantia Constantinou of Stony Brook University, to realtor Tina Fredericks for her longtime friendship, to WQXR and Pia Lindstrom at Sirius XM radio, to Geoff Lynch of the Hampton Jitney where I sometimes find time to write going back and forth to New York City, to beaches at Napeague, East Hampton, Sagaponack and Sag Harbor where I sometimes find time to write, to the Maidstone Arms where I sometimes write, to Michelle Cannon and Paul Jeffers of the Bridgehampton Child Care Center, to Gary Vegliante of the Village of West Hampton Dunes, editor Julie Pastore for her ideas to do what became this four book set of memories for Random House and SUNY Press, to Bob Caro, to Barbara L. Goldsmith, the fine writer and philanthropist who wrote the foreword to this book, to Walter Isaacson, Alec Baldwin and Edward Albee who wrote forewords to the earlier books in this series and for my granddaughter Solange Baker, who I think may be the next generation writer in our family, to the Maidstone Arms in East Hampton where I sometimes, with my dog, write these stories, to Richard Burns who is a great inspiration to me, to the late Jerry Finkelstein, one of New York City's great characters, to my late mom and dad, Jen and Al Rattiner who taught me to care about things, to my four children Maya, Adam, David and Gabriel for all their encouragement, to the Harvard Graduate School of Design where, in three years, I learned so much, to my childhood friend Mark Larner and his wife Sherry, to Scoop and Ben and Pam Wasserstein, my stepchildren, and to my step-grandchildren Owen, Abraham and Eli and especially to my remarkable young grandson Rhone Baker who may be the next whiz in the Silicon Valley.